THE ECONOMICS AND PSYCHOLOGY OF HAPPINESS

This book applies the analytical framework used by economists to investigate how one can make the most out of one's life, thus achieving happiness and fulfilment.

Building upon the author's earlier work, this book blends the classic theories and empirical evidence of positive psychology with economic concepts of choice, capital, information costs, and household production. Its topics include happiness at work, corporate culture, and sustainable development, which are at the forefront of this interdisciplinary field. Every chapter is accompanied by a summary of key points, as well as reflective questions for students.

This book will interest researchers and students in happiness economics and positive psychology, and anyone keen to learn more about living fuller, happier lives.

Lok Sang Ho, a past President of The Hong Kong Economic Association, was Director of the Pan Sutong Shanghai-HK Economic Policy Research Institute and Head of the Economics Department, Lingnan University, Hong Kong. Presently an Adjunct Professor of the Academy for Applied Policy Studies and Education Futures of the Education University of Hong Kong, his research spans many areas, from housing to education to psychology to international finance. He has authored several books including *Psychology and Economics of Happiness*, *Public Policy and the Public Interest*, and *Health Policy and the Public Interest*.

THE ECONOMICS AND PSYCHOLOGY OF HAPPINESS

The LIFE Framework and Sustainable Development

Lok Sang Ho

Routledge
Taylor & Francis Group
LONDON AND NEW YORK

First published 2026
by Routledge
4 Park Square, Milton Park, Abingdon, Oxon, OX14 4RN

and by Routledge
605 Third Avenue, New York, NY 10158

Routledge is an imprint of the Taylor & Francis Group, an informa business

British Library Cataloguing-in-Publication Data
A catalogue record for this book is available from the British Library

Library of Congress Cataloging-in-Publication Data
Names: Ho, Lok-sang author
Title: The economics and psychology of happiness :
the LIFE framework and sustainable development / Lok Sang Ho.
Description: Abingdon, Oxon ; New York, NY : Routledge, 2026. |
Includes bibliographical references and index.
Identifiers: LCCN 2025012784 (print) | LCCN 2025012785 (ebook) |
ISBN 9781032829579 hardback | ISBN 9781032829562 paperback |
ISBN 9781003507093 ebook
Subjects: LCSH: Happiness | Positive psychology | Self-actualization (Psychology)
Classification: LCC BF575.H27 H62 2026 (print) | LCC BF575.H27 (ebook) |
DDC 158–dc23/eng/20250605
LC record available at https://lccn.loc.gov/2025012784
LC ebook record available at https://lccn.loc.gov/2025012785

ISBN: 9781032829579 (hbk)
ISBN: 9781032829562 (pbk)
ISBN: 9781003507093 (ebk)

DOI: 10.4324/9781003507093

Typeset in Galliard
by Newgen Publishing UK

To Paul T.P. Wong

CONTENTS

ACKNOWLEDGEMENTS

I thank Professor Claude-Hélène Mayer, Professor in Industrial and Organisational Psychology, the University of Johannesburg, for writing the Foreword to this revised and expanded version of the earlier book *Psychology and Economics of Happiness: Love, Life, and Positive Living*. I am also grateful to Dr. Richard Cookerly and Professor Yew-Kwang Ng for contributing the earlier Forewords. I am also grateful to Centaline Property Agency Ltd., ING Inc., the Early Childhood Development Research Foundation, Hong Kong Productivity Council, as well as Lingnan University for funding various studies that provided very important inputs to the current book. Professor Simon Lam and his team contributed a new chapter on psychometric testing of the LIFE framework. Professor Lam also helped improve Chapter 6 significantly so he is listed as a coauthor for that chapter.

FOREWORD

The pursuit of happiness has fascinated humanity since ancient times. Many people have been wandering on this universal quest, asking questions like what happiness is and how it can be achieved—the journey to explore happiness is shared across cultures, generations, and various subgroups within our societies. Accordingly, the responses on how to find or even create happiness are multifold. In a rapidly changing world, which is shaped by shifting socio-cultural norms, economic challenges, and psychological discoveries, the question of how to achieve and sustain happiness remains as relevant and compelling as ever. That is precisely why this second edition of *Psychology and Economics of Happiness: Love, Life, and Positive Living* is both timely and essential. Expanding the first edition and to underscore the economic approach in examining the choices one makes in life and the value of this approach to sustainable development, the new edition has taken a new title: *Economics and Psychology of Happiness: the LIFE Framework and Sustainable Development.*

When the first edition of this book was published, over ten years ago, it resonated deeply with readers internationally for offering a new and original perspective on the interplay between our internal psychological states and the external economic and social forces that shape our lives. The author of the book, Professor Lok Sang Ho, an ardent researcher on happiness, describes complex ideas with clarity and compassion, bridging the void between research and the real experiences he had gone through across his own life. He has crystallized his reflections about the human striving for happiness in a simple, easy to remember formula: Love, Insight, Fortitude, and Engagement. Accumulating Love and Insight (Wisdom) and living out Love and Wisdom day by day (Engagement), one builds Fortitude and accumulates even more Love and Wisdom through thick and thin. The Conquest of Happiness (*à la* Bertrand

Russell) is achieved by facing and transcending suffering and obsessions into "mature happiness" (*à la* Paul T.P. Wong) (Wong, Paul T.P. 2023; Wong, Paul T.P. et al.2023). This updated and expanded new edition builds upon the previous foundation, expanding its insights and incorporating the latest developments in the fields of psychology, behavioral economics, and positive living to cover happiness at work and sustainable development. This book offers a fresh perspective to positive psychology and an immense contribution to the research and practice body.

What sets this book apart from others is its ability to blend empirical evidence with profound humanistic perspectives. It recognizes that the pursuit of happiness is a learning process and a journey of self-discovery that varies from person to person. Notwithstanding diverse ethnic and cultural backgrounds, however, to Professor Ho, identifying Love as the purpose of life is essential. Love is treasuring life as a scarce and an immensely valuable resource and a strong yearning to realize what life can offer. This dynamic and multifaceted journey varies from individual to individual, and yet the need for a spirit of transcendence is the same. By exploring topics such as love and relationships, the influence of culture, human weaknesses, and personal growth, the book invites readers to reflect on their own lives and empowers them with tools to create positive change.

As a reader, you will find that this edition is more than an update; it is a deepening of the conversation and it presents the learnings of the author and his personal discovery over the years. The second edition addresses emerging challenges—from the mental health implications of a globally connected digital age to the growing importance of sustainability in our lifestyle choices—while maintaining its core focus on what makes life fulfilling across cultural and ethnic backgrounds. This edition further articulates the LIFE framework and focuses on sustainability even more than the first edition. It provides reflections of our times and the trendy topics in economics and psychology.

The author's dedication to the topic and to this work is evident in each and every chapter. This book is not merely an academic treatise; it is a guide informed by both scholarly rigor and lived experience. It speaks to the thoughts and the feeling, encouraging readers to think systemically and critically, while inspiring them to transform, live authentically, and contribute to a sustainable world.

In reading this book, the reader will discover practical insights grounded in science, thoughtful reflections drawn from philosophy, and an overarching message of hope: that happiness is attainable, not through fleeting pleasures but through engaged living, meaningful connections, and a balanced understanding of the world around us.

Whether you are returning to this book after exploring its first edition or discovering it for the first time, you are in for an enlightening journey. I encourage you to approach its pages with curiosity and an open mind. Let the author`s thoughts and wisdom challenge you, uplift you, and guide you toward a life with greater joy and purpose.

It is a privilege to introduce this work to you. I am confident that it will leave a lasting impact on your perspective and your life journey. As you turn these pages, may you find not only knowledge but also inspiration to craft your own unique narrative of happiness.

Claude-Hélène Mayer
Professor in Industrial and Organisational Psychology
University of Johannesburg, Johannesburg, South Africa

PREFACE

I am thankful for this opportunity to improve the early version of this book, which was originally titled *Psychology and Economics of Happiness: Love, Life, and Positive Living*. That book was written for a course "Understanding Life and Happiness" that I developed at Lingnan University. I was tremendously encouraged when a book review by Grant J. Rich in APA's *PsycCritiques* highly commended it as an example of "humanistic economics." I was truly humbled when he wrote that it "recalls books such as Seligman's (2002) *Authentic Happiness* and Csikszentmihalyi's (1990) *Flow*." I have all along been a student of life, and I am still learning every day. But I do hope that what I have learnt over the years can be widely shared, and that this much revised version will benefit more people and help build a more peaceful and sustainable world.

I was motivated to write the first edition of this book by the surge of interest among economists in the subject of happiness, as indicated by the works of Angus Deaton, Richard Easterlin, Bruno Frey, James Heckman, John Helliwell, Alan Krueger, Lord Richard Layard, Yew-kwang Ng, and Andrew Oswald, among others. Many of their works have appeared in the psychological and science journals. Oswald and Wu (2010) reported, in *Science*, one of the top journals in science, objective confirmation of subjective measures of well-being. In a sample of one million Americans across 50 states, they found a close match between people's subjective life satisfaction scores and objectively estimated quality of life. Reflecting on the validity of such subjective measures, many contributions of psychologists on life satisfaction or happiness have found their way into the mainstream economics journals. Indeed, Daniel Kahneman, a psychologist, has won the Nobel Prize in Economic Science for his contribution to illuminating human behavior. Unfortunately, however, I had yet to see an economics textbook that takes life as a hugely scarce resource and that, as rational decision-makers, we need to maximize utility by achieving what we value, subject to the various constraints that we face. Constrained maximization is called "the economic problem": human beings face various constraints and need to make wise decisions in order to achieve a fulfilling life. Sadly, in practice, most people fail to make the most out of the opportunities that they have. Many people do not realize that a change in attitude and an increase in understanding can make a huge difference. Positive psychology is not unrealistic optimism based on faith that somehow things will work out. Positive psychology is about the will—the determination, and the way—the wisdom, to make the best out of every situation. Conceptually, this is no different from "constrained maximization," the key concept that economists talk about!

In a typical introduction to an economics course, students are told that (micro) economics deals with *what* to produce, *how* to produce, and *for whom* to produce. This book is also about what to produce, how to produce, and for whom to produce. However, the focus here is on the often-overlooked *mental goods*, which we MUST recognize to be as important as physical goods. "Mental goods" are qualities perceived in our minds which are important to our well-being, but which do not fill any physical needs. Examples of mental goods are peace of mind, freedom from anxiety, honor, self-esteem, a sense of being accepted by others, a sense of success, achieving what we set out to do, self-actualization, and love. Indeed, we know that, across time and space and throughout the human existence, people have been killing others and themselves when they feel that they are deprived of an essential mental good. The truly horrific "honor killing" of tens of thousands of people each year is a case in point. "Disgrace to the family" is a "mental bad"—sufficient to cost lives! Even where honor killings are seldom heard of, people may kill or commit suicide when insulted. A wife's extramarital affair may shame the husband so much that he kills the wife or the wife's lover. Suicides due to bullying at school have now acquired the term "bullycide."[1] The victims may not be physically bullied at all, but they cannot stand the insults and being ostracized by their peers. Abhijit Banerjee and Esther Duflo (2012), in their highly acclaimed book, *Poor Economics*, documented how the very poor may prefer to suffer hunger and even go into debt in order to pay for an honorable wedding, dowries, and funerals.

Thus, parents who love their children must not merely procure their physical needs, but also their emotional or mental needs. So, we must help produce and procure mental goods for those whom we love! But mental goods are quite unlike physical goods, which we can readily buy with money. Mental goods need to be produced by the person who enjoys those mental goods, often but not always with physical goods acting as a medium. The economics of love is about helping our loved ones acquire the mental goods that they need, and not only procuring the physical goods required for their physical needs.

An understanding of the importance of mental goods throws light on a number of strange phenomena that are widely considered as irrational (Ariely, 2008). Why are people not happy when they are given a sum of money when they know others get much more than they do? In a "dictator game," which allows one of the players ("the dictator") to get as big a share as he likes while leaving what is left to the other player, provided that this other player agrees, it is often found that the other player often prefers to reject an unfair division, ending up with nothing for both players. Under the mental goods framework this can be easily explained and is entirely rational. The utility from getting more money is more than offset by the disutility of the mental bad of swallowing an unfair division.

To produce the mental goods that we need, we need to have "mental capital." Production of mental goods is not unlike that of physical goods, since both require "capital" as an input. Formally, capital is a produced means of production. I first introduced the concept of "mental capital" in my 2001 book *Principles of Public Policy Practice* (Kluwer). Since that time, Rifka Weehuizen wrote a doctoral thesis on mental capital in 2008.[2] The UK government, through its Department for Business, Innovation and Skills and Government Office for Science, produced a report on "Mental Capital and Well Being", later published in a volume edited by Cary Cooper et al. (2009). Cultivating and accumulating mental capital, and clearing away negative mental capital, are two things we need to do ourselves and for our loved ones in order to live a happy, fulfilling life. They are both an act of investment and an act of love.

One interesting and often-overlooked aspect about the differences between mental goods and physical goods is that, while the latter is subject to "the law of diminishing marginal utility", and so "satiation" is possible, the "law" does not seem to apply to the former. This distinction offers an insight into the paradoxical effect noted by some psychologists, namely that extrinsic rewards sometimes do not work and that they can be counterproductive in motivating people in specific tasks. One classical experiment (Deci, 1975) separated college students into two groups. For one, a monetary reward is paid for solving a puzzle. For the other, no monetary reward is paid, but the students are asked to solve the puzzle in their free time. It turns out that, in repeated experiments, the group that is not paid typically outperforms the group that is paid. They seem to be more interested in the task and to find more satisfaction in solving the puzzle. This result should be seen in the context of the fact that the students taking part in the experiment generally enjoy a degree of relative material abundance. The material reward does not provide that much incentive and indeed may detract from the mental reward of overcoming the challenge of solving the puzzle.

Imagine that a similar experiment were conducted in another context, this time involving two groups of starving students who live in dire poverty. Because the extrinsic reward becomes much more important, in the sense that marginal utility of the extrinsic reward is in the high rather than the diminished range, we can expect that the group offered the extrinsic reward will work very hard to solve the puzzle. On the other hand, in relatively well-off communities where the monetary reward is no longer as important, the extrinsic reward does not motivate nearly as much and indeed may signal to players that solving the puzzle is worth no more than the money paid.

Although I seem to have been the first to propose the term "mental goods," the concept has been in literature for a long time. Abraham Maslow (1954) clearly indicated that there are non-material needs that need to be satisfied. More recently, in the literature on motivation, it has been shown that when an employer demonstrates trust or confidence in an employee, the employee often becomes strongly motivated and will perform better. The knowledge that one is trusted is a mental good that can be quite powerful in motivating people. Thus, quite apart from a pay and benefit package, "people are motivated by interesting work, challenge, and increasing responsibility—intrinsic factors. People have a deep-seated need for growth and achievement."[3]

By now there is more and more evidence that happiness is associated with Love, Insight, Fortitude, and Engagement, or LIFE for short—four qualities that reflect the mental capital of a person. Some of this evidence will be reviewed in this book. To be happy, we need to build a capacity to love (Love), a habit of self-reflecting and learning, a realization that the greatest success in life is making the most out of our own lives, and a sense of proportion (wisdom or Insight), nurturing the strength within ourselves so that we and our loved ones can face adversity without losing heart (Fortitude), and we need to lead an active life with a clear purpose (Engagement). These qualities offer us self-efficacy, optimism, resilience, and hope—the aspects of mental well-being that psychologists have come to call "psychological capital" (Page and Donohue, 2004).

It is sad to see that many within our community need to consume so much of our increasingly scarce resources in order to bolster their wavering and feeble self-esteem and sense of self-dignity. We know that a culture of conspicuous consumption and competition with each other threatens the survival of our own and other species and is not sustainable. Conspicuous consumption constitutes the single most inefficient (household) production that threatens our very survival, because each time one gains self-dignity by out-consuming others, one's gains are at the same time destroying others' sense of dignity.

I thank the Editor and three reviewers who endorsed my proposal for expanding and revising the contents of the earlier book. The new title, *Economics and Psychology and Happiness: the LIFE framework and Sustainable Development*, is their suggestion. I have added several new chapters to this book, restructured the chapters for better coherence, corrected some careless mistakes, and added an abstract on the central message of each chapter in the beginning, and "key points to note" as well as "some questions to ponder" at the end. These changes will consolidate students' and readers' learning and provoke them to think about some of the challenges that face the world today with the new perspectives offered in each chapter.

Several totally new chapters have been added. They include a chapter on "Human nature: human needs, character strengths, and weaknesses ," another on "Corporate LIFE and Happiness at Work," still another chapter on "Psychometric Properties of LIFE Mental Capital Scale across Different Populations," and a much-expanded last chapter "Epilogue" that draws upon findings in my recent paper in *Singapore Economic Review.*

I took the suggestion of Grant J. Rich to heart. He suggested that I discuss the similarities of LIFE to Seligman's (2011) PERMA model of well-being, where PERMA stands for Positive emotion, Engagement, Relationships, Meaning, and Accomplishment. I also referred to the 24 character-strengths and Values in Action, both of which I believe are great tips for personal growth. LIFE, which stands for Love, Insight, Fortitude, and Engagement, is really no different from Peterson and Seligman's recommendations. Its main advantages are that it is easy to remember and that it reminds us of Albert Schweitzer's Reverence for Life philosophy. Schweitzer is my hero because he lived what he preached.

I hope that this book will contribute a little towards building a happier, more sustainable world.

Lok Sang Ho
Lingnan University
Hong Kong

Notes

1 For statistics, visit: www.bullyingstatistics.org/content/bullying-and-suicide.html
2 Downloadable from: www.merit.unu.edu/training/theses/Thesis_Weehuizen_final.pdf
3 See Williams R (2012) "Wired for success. How to motivate employees: what managers need to know." *Psychology Today*. Downloadable from: www.psychologytoday.com/blog/wired-success/201210/how-motivate-employees

Reference

Grant J. Rich, "Humanistic Economics: the Human Lifespan as Valued Resource: a review of *Psychology & Economics of Happiness* by Lok Sang Ho" PsycCRITIQUES (American Psychological Association), August 4, 2014, Vol. 59, No.31, Article 3.

1

INTRODUCTION TO THE ECONOMICS OF LIFE

The "Economic Problem" can be summarized by the term "Constrained Maximization." Our lifespan is limited and is therefore a truly scarce resource. The economics of life is the study of how to put our life into the most productive, most fruitful, and most fulfilling use. Economics is a decision science. Life consists of a series of different kinds of decisions. How we spend our day, our youth, our adulthood, and our senior years requires wise choices.

Introduction: the economics of life is about making the most out of life

Economics is about making choices amid many dilemmas and scarce resources. But life is certainly the most precious and certainly the scarcest resource for all of us. It is therefore very strange that there is hardly any genuine study of the economics of life in the sense of treating our limited lifespan as a scarce resource and offering a systematic approach to making the most out of our lives.

One reader of an early version of this book objected to this observation, and offered several titles as counterexamples:

- *Freakonomics* and *Superfreakonomics* (Levitt and Dubner, 2005, 2009)
- *The Undercover Economist* (Harford, 2005)/*The Logic of Life* (Harford, 2009)/*The Undercover Economist/Dear Undercover Economist*
- *The Armchair Economist: Economics and Everyday Life* (Landsburg, 2012)
- *The Economic Naturalist: Why Economics Explains Almost Everything* (Frank, 2008)
- Works by Dan Ariely, Robert Cialdini, Richard Thaler and Cass Sunstein.

DOI: 10.4324/9781003507093-1

I had really enjoyed reading *Freakonomics* and had taken delight in reading Tim Harford's Dear Economist column in the *Financial Times*. However, I see these and most of the others on the list are more in the category of *the economics of everyday life* than in the category of *the economics of life*. The former tries to explain human behavior in terms of incentives, and to apply some economic principles to unique situations that we may come across in life. The latter, on the other hand, is about viewing life in its entirety as a scarce resource, and confronting human nature as it is, again in its entirety, and finding insight into how we may live a happier, more fulfilling life. Works by Ariely, Cialdini, and Thaler and Sustein are altogether another category. Ariely teaches us about the flaws of human perception; Cialdini tells us how we may be persuaded or motivated; Thaler and Sustein offer advice to policy makers taking human nature as a constraint, trying to justify their brand of "soft paternalism." This present volume takes human nature as a constraint and recognizes the flaws of human perception and offers suggestions as to how we can become better masters of ourselves.

A number of articles by Gary Becker have been collected in a book with the title *The Economics of Life: From Baseball to Affirmative Action to Immigration, How Real World Issues Affect our Everyday Life* (Becker, 1998) but, again, it is not really about making choices over how we should best spend the limited number of years of our lives. To his credit, however, I certainly agree that his "A Theory of the Allocation of Time", published in 1965, is indeed a pioneering study on the economics of life. In that article, he sees various alternative uses of time as competing for the scarce time that individuals have under their command, as they try to optimize given the time constraint.

Typically the life of a person in developed countries today is limited to about 80 years or fewer. According to the World Population Prospects 2024 of the United Nations the world is home to an estimated 722,000 centenarians, implying a merely 0.0009% globally are living beyond 100. In the United States, male life expectancy at birth is only 75.8 years and that of females is only 81.1 years (2023 estimate, National Center for Statistics).[1] Out of the 78.4 years average for the population as a whole, if we subtract 20 years from infancy to adolescence, there are only about 58.4 years of adult life at our disposal. For this short space of less than 60 years, when we can make decisions about our own lives, each day gone is gone forever, and each decision made is *totally irreversible*, in the sense that you can never go back to the time of the decision and make a different one. So, looking back we may say there is no "if." What is done is done. We have no choice but to take all past decisions as made and given, and to accept whatever consequences come out of those earlier decisions. For good or for ill, we have to live with them.

Economics is about making the most out of the limited resources that we have—notwithstanding the difficulties that we may face and the misfortunes that could hit us. This book is about how we can make the most of our lives.

Optimizing

Too many people struggle with making the best decision over something that does not really matter much in the long run!

Optimizing in economics usually means maximizing "utility," subject to the constraints of limited resources, technology and know-how, laws and regulations. "Utility" is a generic term referring to what the decision-maker values and seeks. "Making the most of our lives" is "maximizing" the fulfilment of achieving what we want. Paradoxically, without seeing the big picture and thus without a sense of proportion, trying to "optimize" could turn out to be counterproductive.

Most people will not lose sleep over which menu they would choose for a dinner, but some would for a banquet for important guests. Many students will have a hard time deciding what program they will take in university. For the more able ones who face many choices the decision is even harder, as they struggle over whether to study medicine or law or finance (or the like).

These program often open up different career paths, and they certainly would make a lot of difference to one's life. But, unless you go into something that really goes against your personality, so that you feel you do not belong there, people can build equally happy lives through totally different careers. It is, of course, natural for people to think about career opportunities and ponder over the possible incomes that these different career paths would bring. However, psychologists and economists now tell us that making more money beyond some threshold does not matter that much to happiness. On the other hand, if you accumulate a good amount of mental capital you may be able to enjoy life regardless of which path you take and regardless of where you live. (Mental capital is an important subject that deserves more in-depth discussion; see Chapter 5).

In order to optimize, we need to understand that there are different kinds of choices in life, and we also need to understand the nature of constraints and to realize that there are real and imagined constraints.

Especially early in life, the most important choices are choices about investment. In general, choices about consumption are much less important. In this context, investment is about investing in LIFE: the mental capitals that enable us to reap the fruits of positive living. For young parents in particular, nurturing LIFE mental capitals in their children will certainly be a wise investment. "Mental capital" refers to the mental habits that we develop, and LIFE mental capitals refer to Love, Insight (Wisdom), Fortitude (Resilience), and Engagement. We will elaborate throughout this book, but it suffices to note here that our habits become our "second nature". Our lives are intimately conditioned by our habits, to the extent that we become different kinds of persons depending on what mental habits we have formed in the early stage of our lives.

Love mental capital makes us into a loving person, who is connected to others rather than alienated from others, who genuinely cares for his/her[2] own and others' well-being.

Insight, or wisdom, is the art of love, i.e., knowing how to care for oneself and for others effectively.

Fortitude is stamina and the strong will that will enable us to confront difficulties.

Engagement is acting with a clear purpose in life so one's love and wisdom shine on a day-to-day basis.

When LIFE becomes our "second nature" we do not merely know of and understand love, wisdom, fortitude and resilience as concepts. When LIFE habits have formed, we naturally love; we naturally love with wisdom; we naturally are courageous and strong; and we naturally engage ourselves every day in various activities that contribute to a richer and more fulfilling life.

Thus, the most important decisions that determine if our lives will be fulfilling or otherwise are those related to building up or not building up LIFE mental capitals and other life skills. If we have the requisite mindset and life skills, many good things follow, because we will then be able to take advantage of opportunities that knock and to weather the storms that may come. If we do not have these skills, we will miss many opportunities and waste the most valuable and scarce resource at our command.

Building up LIFE mental capitals and life skills is the best investment and the most important choice that one can make.

Is happiness a choice?

Happiness is not always a choice. When people face violence, abuse, hunger, discrimination, and are on the edge of survival day in, day out, happiness becomes almost impossible, even for the most strong-willed. According to The State of Food Security and Nutrition in the World report 2023, about 735 million people faced hunger in 2022. According to the United Nations High Commissioner for Refugees, more than 114 million people worldwide had been forced to flee their homes by the end of September 2023, due to conflict, persecution and human rights violations. According to the United Nations, and the following is copied from its website:

- 2.2 billion people lack access to safely managed drinking water services. (WHO/UNICEF, 2019)
- Almost 2 billion people depend on health care facilities without basic water services (WHO/UNICEF, 2020)
- Over half of the global population or 4.2 billion people lack safely managed sanitation services. (WHO/UNICEF, 2019)

- 297,000 children under five die every year from diarrheal diseases due to poor sanitation, poor hygiene, or unsafe drinking water. (WHO/UNICEF, 2019)
- 2 billion people live in countries experiencing high water stress. (UN, 2019)

The harsh reality is that many people do not have much choice. Many people die young because of hunger, war, lack of medical care and other unnatural causes.

For those of us who live in a relatively peaceful country and are blessed with having access to relatively good amenities and clean water, education and healthcare, happiness is indeed possible for most. But some still may not have the choice. An example is children who suffer from child abuse, and whose parents may suffer from drug addiction or alcoholism, and who die young with little knowledge about what they could do. For those who have a choice, the key question is whether they invest in LIFE mental capital or instead form habits that undermine the possibilities of life. A natural question that follows is why anyone would not choose happiness if happiness is possible.

Seeing the big picture

One reason is that humans suffer from their innate weaknesses. We will discuss this subject further in Chapter 2. At this point, we would just mention the weakness of shortsightedness. Humans tend to be shortsighted, and they also tend to have hangups over some matters like disappointments and are excessively concerned with gains and losses. Being too calculating and overly concerned over marginal comparisons makes us lose sight of *the big picture* (Figure 1.1).

Marginal comparisons could take you up a local hill, but you could be losing big in terms of missing the much higher mountain that yet awaits to

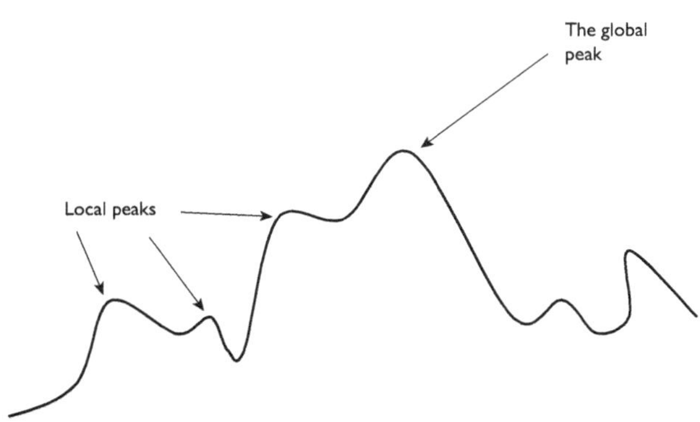

FIGURE 1.1 Seeing the big picture to truly optimize.

be climbed. Even worse, because we do not have perfect information and have difficulty meeting the exact optimality conditions, worry over failing to maximize leads to a loss in well-being.

Technically we can say there may be many local maxima, but only one of the maxima is the global maximum. In life especially, there are so many targets that appear appealing at any given moment. There is always the temptation to achieve each desirable target as it appears. There are two problems with excessive concern over maximizing these short-term targets. First, you could lose sight of an even more attractive target. Second, if, for some reason, the attempt to achieve a short-term target fails, you could be disheartened and lose the spirit to take on other challenges in life. You could dwell upon the failure for too long, and unwittingly give up precious time, which is part of your limited life.

In maximizing profit, economists advise that, as long as marginal revenue is larger than marginal cost—i.e. as long as producing an additional unit of a good costs less than the additional revenue it brings in—we should produce more. At profit maximization, marginal revenue would be equal to marginal cost. Similarly, the total benefit of a project is maximized by equating the marginal benefit with the marginal cost of every quantity that is a decision variable. So, one would need to make marginal comparisons in various dimensions in order to maximize. Suppose we run a train service. We have to consider the marginal benefit of extending the hours of service against the marginal cost; the marginal benefit of increasing the frequency of the service at different hours of the day against the marginal cost; and the marginal benefit of extending the distance covered by the train service and that of adding an additional stop. Similarly, there are various decisions in various dimensions that we have to make over different time horizons.

Yet excessive focus on marginal calculations is counterproductive. Being too calculating makes us miss greater opportunities in life. The key to successful living lies in being able to tell which decisions are important and which are not. While many grow anxious wondering which choice will make them marginally better off, the wise ones see the big picture and quickly learn to acquire useful tools and accumulate capital that they can use along the life journey later. Unfortunately, most people take up a lot of junk that would make the life journey that much more difficult later on. *The paradoxical truth is that, while people all want to optimize, without knowing it some accumulate positive mental capital whereas others accumulate negative mental capital.* This leads to totally different qualities of lives.

Real and imagined constraints

Constraints define the boundaries of possibilities. Within the boundaries of possibilities we want to make the most out of our lives. But what are these boundaries? Unfortunately, the constraints that define the boundaries of possibilities are not as clear as "budget constraints." There is a famous prayer in Christianity, known as the "Serenity Prayer," that is attributed to Reinhold Niebuhr, a Lutheran theologian (1892–1971), that reads:

> God, grant me the serenity to accept the things I cannot change,
> the courage to change the things I can,
> and the wisdom to know the difference.

Because we do not really know the constraints, the life journey is truly a journey of self-discovery. We all need to find out the potential that life has given us. To self-discover, or to learn what life has in store for us, we need to be open-minded and be ready to test our potential through exposure to different things. We must not overestimate or underestimate our abilities. We owe ourselves a genuine effort so we know if we can or cannot master a particular skill or if a dream project can fly. Surprisingly, many "handicapped people" have achieved much more than "normal people." How do they do it? The explanation lies in LIFE. They love and treasure their lives. They have the support of the family and people who love and care for them. They wisely focus on what they can do instead of complaining or ruminating over what they cannot. They make a genuine effort consistently and persistently. And they spend each day with focus and a sharp sense of purpose.

Another aspect about constraints is that they are not static. At a point in time, some constraints are indeed binding. But with effort, a constraint that was binding at one time may become not binding any more. Some constraints take generations to overcome. Not too long ago, humans could not fly or travel very fast. Today humans routinely fly, and there are cars, trains, ocean liners and submarines. Humans have even landed on the moon. Human history is a history of humans overcoming many barriers and constraints.

Cost–benefit analysis

There are four principles in the cost–benefit analysis that pertain to personal decisions in life. First is the need for discounting future costs and benefits appropriately. Second is that all costs and benefits relevant to decision-making need to be forward-looking, i.e. they should be the results of the decisions under consideration. Past benefits and costs do not count. Third is that we should take into account all the benefits and costs that matter to us, and that includes the benefits and costs that relate to other people whose welfare we care about. Finally, we need to recognize that there is always uncertainty in life, so any cost–benefit analysis that we do may be wrong in the end! This is not, however, a reason for not making an *ex ante* cost-benefit comparison of our decisions. Once the decision is made, for good or ill, the decision is made, and we need to accept the consequences instead of looking back and blaming ourselves for having made a possibly wrong choice. While learning from past mistakes will make us wiser, excessive regrets may make it difficult to look forward so we can take advantage of new opportunities that come our way.

There are strong economic reasons behind each of these principles. First, future benefits need to be discounted, not so much because of a pure time preference as such, but because future benefits are subject to uncertainty: we might not even survive, and, if we survive, our bodies might not be fit enough to enjoy the contingent benefits. If, say, there is a 5% chance that we might not survive, then the expected benefit should be the possible realizable benefit multiplied by 0.95. Since, further into the future, our survival probability declines, benefits further down the road need to be discounted more than benefits that are less far off. But then all discounted future benefits need to be added up into a present value of future contingent benefits.

To be forward-looking in counting the benefits and costs associated with a decision means that we should ignore completely the costs or benefits of things that have already happened or cannot be changed no matter what we do today. We only need to care for the benefits and costs arising from a decision to be made now. Since past benefits and costs are already past, they cannot be counted as a benefit or cost from a decision or choice at hand. Economists call costs that have been incurred and cannot be reversed sunk costs.

The third principle says that our decisions could affect others. If we care for or love these other people we should certainly take into consideration the benefits and costs that they derive or incur from our decisions.

The fourth principle says that while we should make the best decision *ex ante,* we can never be certain and should not look back once a decision has been made, except to learn from the experience if there is something to learn or to cherish the memory if there is a memory to cherish. Looking back but not intending to learn from the experience or to cherish the memory is entirely a waste of time. If we learn from the experience, we gain mental capital. If we cherish the memory, we enjoy a "mental good." If we blame ourselves for having made a wrong decision, we only end up losing more. We would be inflicting a "mental bad" on ourselves and losing the chance to build up more mental capital for the future.

While future benefits and costs need to be "discounted" to obtain a "present value" we should note that the choice of the discount rate would make a huge difference and would affect the ranking of different options open to us. Those whose discount rate is very high would tend to ignore investing for future benefits, since future benefits do not count as much as present benefits. They are more likely to smoke, for example, even though they know that smoking may lead to poor health in the future. In general, in countries where the life expectancy is low, such as countries where there is much violence or a civil war, the chances of surviving into old age are low, and future benefits will be discounted heavily. But the implied behaviour when one adopts a high discount rate would lead to a lower life expectancy. Although their lifestyle, such as, for example, smoking or practicing unsafe sex, may not have any obvious immediate effect on "functional health"—their ability to carry out day-to-day functions is not yet impaired—it may hurt their "health stock" and reduce their life expectancy (Ho, 2012). Thus life expectancy is "endogenously determined" rather than given exogenously. In general, people who treasure their lives and look forward to living a long life will adopt a low discount rate for future benefits, and they will actively pursue a lifestyle that will help bring about a long life.

Household production, physical goods and mental goods

Economists generally assume that consumers maximize utility. Over the last half-century, the term "household" is increasingly used in place of the word consumer, and the concept of household production is fast replacing the concept of consumption, at least in microeconomic theory. Gary Becker's truly seminal paper, "A Theory of the Allocation of Time" (1965) can be said to be the first and one of the very few papers on the economics of life. He argues that utility, instead of being directly dependent on goods and services purchased in the marketplace, depends on "basic commodities" (his terminology) or "end goods" that must be produced by the household, often with various market goods or services as some of the inputs, in combination with time inputs through various household activities (**Figure 1.2**). Moreover, households are seen to supply labour, and they can potentially work more to increase their income. For those who can work more to earn more, then, income is not given. There is thus no "fixed budget" constraint as such. On the other hand, time is a real constraint: the more one works, the less time one has after work.

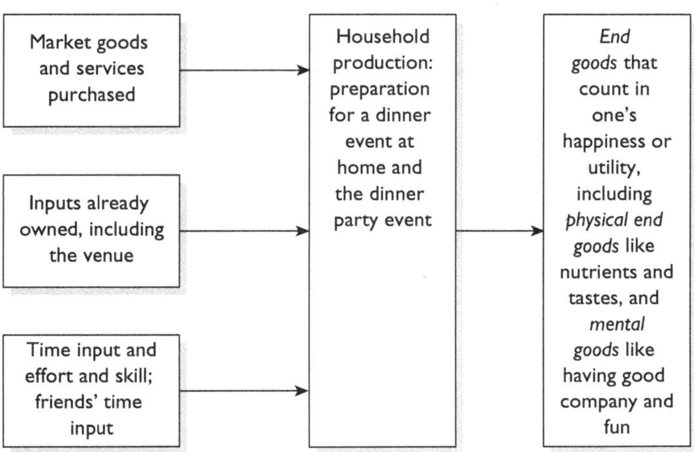

FIGURE 1.2 Household production.

Under the time constraint, the more one works, the more income one enjoys, but the time worked translates into less time available for household activities. Becker highlighted the trade-off between work and leisure, as people give up earnings in favor of more leisure or free time, which they need in order to procure the "end goods" that they need to enjoy life. This pertains to the important subject of work–life balance, now a hot subject in psychology. While using Becker's concept of household production, this book stresses that *end goods* that affect people's well-being comprise *mental goods* as well as *physical (end) goods.*

Mental goods include a long list of things that we value, including a sense of autonomy, freedom from anxiety, being respected and self-actualization. Much of this was discussed by Abraham Maslow (1954) in the context of the human hierarchy of wants. Maslow proposed that physical needs are more basic, which seems obvious as people will die of starvation but do not die because of a lack of self-esteem. But we also know that people could kill themselves or others if they are shamed. We know that in some countries and among some people the horrific practice of "honor killing" is considered legitimate. In the United States we heard of a very sad story of a student at Rutgers University killing himself in 2010 when his sexual activity in the dorm was secretly video-recorded by his roommate and broadcast on the internet. Which are more basic—physical or mental needs—is thus really not as obvious as may be thought. Just as a failure to procure a minimum of physical goods kills, so does a failure to procure a minimum of mental goods. Mental goods are just as important as physical goods to human existence.

Among the mental goods, loving and being loved are two of the most important things that enrich people's lives significantly and make living meaningful.[3] Although a lack of financial resources may lead to many mental bads like anxiety and insecurity, some of the mental goods cannot be acquired simply by expending more, and loving and being loved are two of the things that money cannot buy. This explains why some rich people, who can get all the physical goods and services—including caring services—that they want, are still unhappy. A nurse hired to care for you, even when the care is meticulous and well executed, is no substitute for loving care from one's family.

Mental goods are also related to "prospective happiness" and "retrospective happiness". When someone is very much looking forward to something that is expected to happen, one may be full of energy and anticipation. The anticipated event has not yet happened, but it is sufficient to make one very happy now. Similarly, when someone looks back and cherishes fond memories of things that happened in the past, one may also feel sweetness and contentment. Just as a future happy event can make one happy, so a future unhappy event that is waiting to happen can engender fear and anxiety. Just as a past happy event can make one happy now, so a past unhappy event can make one depressed, regretful or traumatized.

Mental goods and motivation

The fact that human beings value mental goods a lot is well recognized in everyday life, although economists tend to ignore mental goods in their formal analysis, which is a pity. Failing to recognize the importance of mental goods, economists tend to place an excessive emphasis on material incentives. Singapore pays its senior civil servants and ministers the world's highest salaries because it is believed that money will attract the best people to serve the country. If the CEOs of top corporations are paid around $\$x$ to be commensurate with the private sector, and if the country's prime minister is considered the CEO of the country, then certainly the pay has to be commensurate with private sector pay in order to be competitive, so goes the logic. However, many outstanding people are willing and happy to render their services and even make giant sacrifices without demanding a huge pay package. This is because they can achieve the mental good of knowing that they are serving the country.

Mental goods, then, have much to do with "intrinsic motivation," which is driven by an identified goal deemed highly desirable. It should be noted that intrinsic motivation may be stimulated *from without* since an effective motivator may help the subject identify a desirable goal. In a sense, this motivator ignites the internal engine of the subject (hence *intrinsic*). While a good pay package is usually considered to provide an extrinsic motivation, a decent pay package also offers a mental good in the form of knowing that one is well treated and that one's contribution is well recognized. People may accept a small pay package working for someone who they know cannot afford to pay more if they can get job satisfaction, but are unlikely to accept an unfairly small pay package working for someone who can well afford to pay at the market rate.

Mental goods, therefore, are not completely divorced from material goods or money; rather, they may represent command over material goods. Material goods or money often provide a medium to create or destroy mental goods. Excessively low pay may signal to employees that they are not well appreciated by the employer, which is a mental bad. On the other hand, mental goods sometimes do not require a material good or money as a medium. The trust that an employer expresses to employees may be sufficient to motivate them to perform better. On the other hand, distrust could ruin their motivation and undermine their performance.

While intrinsic motivations are often even more effective than extrinsic motivations, much depends on the circumstances of the worker. For someone who desperately needs money, extrinsic motivation may be quite effective. But for those who do not need money so badly, paying money to get things done could be counterproductive, because this could signal that the worker was just working for the money and not for a more noble goal. Roland Benabou and Jean Tirole (2003) cited the experiment of Edward Deci's (1975) that showed that college students who were paid to do a puzzle were less motivated and less engaged than those who were not paid, suggesting that the pay could "debase" the value of an activity.

Ageing and the economics of life

One of the key aspects of the economics of life is that decisions are made at some points in one's life and that once made they are completely irreversible. Life is fleeting, and with each day gone we inevitably grow older, and we can never go back to the time of the initial decision. Most of us regret our earlier bad decisions, but we still have to face the consequences of those decisions. We can at most try to figure out what is the best thing to do given the foregone decision. With ageing, our physique changes and our health conditions change. Our values and our perspective on life change. We have become "experienced" in many things and our brains have been "programmed" in such a way that it will affect our future decisions, for better or for worse. What we have learnt will affect our perspectives and our ability to learn new things. As a result of all this, our *household production functions* will change. We need to be aware of these laws of ageing early in life so we can achieve what gerontologists call "successful ageing."

Successful ageing consists of several elements: maintaining our physical and mental health in top form as far as possible by reducing the rate of depreciation of the health stock (Ho, 2012). This requires adopting a healthy, active and purposive lifestyle *early in life*, physically, mentally and socially. Interestingly, the brain improves rather than depreciates with use.[4] It would be too late for prevention if we have allowed our health stock to depreciate beyond repair and if we have accumulated too much negative mental capital[5] early in life! Regret is of no use and is even counterproductive. Adopting the right lifestyle and attitude early in life is probably the most important message from the economics of life.

Conclusions

We are distinct individuals in that our personalities and traits are quite different. Our genes are different and we come from different backgrounds. Yet we share many things in common. Despite the differences, we have very similar needs and similar emotions, to the extent that translation from any language to any other is possible. It is often pointed out that needs are different from wants. Wants are supposed to be things that we can do without, but actually, many of the things that "we can do without" fill a real "mental good" need.

Most people who opt for plastic surgery do not "need" the plastic surgery physically. But they spend huge amounts of money and often go through much trouble and even physical pain to receive the plastic surgery. Similarly, we certainly have no physical need for jewelry, but attending certain kinds of occasions without any might make some women feel impolite or unworthy as it might be for men attending a certain kind of function without a tie and a suit when all the other men are wearing them. All these cases may show evidence of mental goods involving a perception of "acceptance by others" and that of "self-acceptance." Perhaps it is more accurate to say that there are many different ways of filling similar needs. Some ways are far more costly than others. But for some people their mentality is such that they can only get their mental good needs fulfilled in specific ways that may prove very costly. We will explore what determines this mentality in the next two chapters.

Another similarity that we all share is the laws of nature that govern us. We all grow old, for example, and we share very similar emotions, to the extent that the vocabularies of totally different languages are strikingly similar. In every language and culture that we know of, there are words for anger, for jealousy, for love, for sorrow and for pain. As we look back into history, events that are long gone stir similar emotions even today, and all the literature that depicts different aspects of humanity continues to find resonance now.

Recognizing our common constraints, particulary the laws that govern our physical and emotional lives, making the most out of our limited lives given those constraints is the most rational thing to do. It appears self-evident that the economics of life is an economics for everybody.

Key points to note

- The economics of life is the economics of making the most out of life through optimization.
- Optimization requires knowing what we want, what the true constraints are, and then using whatever resources available effectively and efficiently.
- In a sense, over the long run, previously impossible things can become possible. Constraints can be pushed out. But there are laws that govern how and how much constraints can be pushed out.
- LIFE—i.e., Love, Insight, Fortitude, and Engagement—can push out many constraints that we face today and will enable us to realize our dreams so that life becomes fulfilling.

Some questions to ponder

- What may be the reasons why people apparently "choose to be unhappy"?
- What is success in life? Is making a lot of money equivalent to success in life?
- People are born different. But the American Declaration of Independence says all men are created equal. What does this mean? What kind of institutions should we build up to further the cause of equality?

- Is equality a mental good? Is equality of opportunity more worth pursuing than equality of outcomes? Why?

Notes

1 The Center for Health Protection warned that expectation of life at birth in 2022 should be interpreted with care as the figures are affected by exceptionally high mortality rates in 2022 during the COVID-19 epidemic. Provisional figures for 2023 for male and females at birth are 82.5 years and 87.9 years respectively.

2 For ease of reading, from this point on, I shall simply use "his" and "he" instead of he/she without gender bias implication.

3 A 2011 French movie, *Declaration of War*, told the story of a couple taking the hard reality of their newborn baby afflicted by brain cancer cheerfully and making the most out of their lives through love and wisdom. Widely acclaimed, it touched the hearts of many. It won the Grand Prix Asturias for Best Film at the Gijón International Film Festival.

4 Carl Sherman, Patrick Griffith and Laura Reynolds (2017) offer an introduction to neuroscience and some very good tips for successful ageing.

5 Some examples of negative mental capital are envy and other forms of obsession. Mui (1995) studied envy using economic theory and how it led to harmful behavior.

2

HUMAN NATURE

Human needs, character strengths and weaknesses

This chapter explores the dimensions of human nature. Humans share similar human needs, strengths, and weaknesses. Although humans may not realize it, self-actualization or following one's heart and realizing one's life potential offers life satisfaction of the highest order, as testified by Bertrand Russell (1968) and suggested by Abraham Maslow (1943). Self-actualization will be enhanced by character strengths and impeded by weaknesses. Building character strengths and overcoming weaknesses is a form of self-actualization and forms the essence of personal growth.

Introduction

According to Maslow's hierarchy of needs, a lower or more basic need must be more or less satisfied before one seeks to satisfy the next higher level of needs. Maslow (1954, p.370) thus stated: "Human needs arrange themselves in hierarchies of pre-potency. That is to say, the appearance of one need usually rests on the prior satisfaction of another, more pre-potent need. Man is a perpetually wanting animal." Following the grand master, Tara Well (2021) wrote in *Psychology Today*: "The lower level needs, sometimes called deficiency or ungratified needs, have more power over us and must be met before the (gratified) or higher levels of need emerge." Saul McLeod (2024) in *Simply Psychology* wrote:

> Maslow's hierarchy of needs is a motivational theory in psychology comprising a five-tier model of human needs, often depicted as hierarchical levels within a pyramid. From the bottom of the hierarchy upwards, the

DOI: 10.4324/9781003507093-2

needs are: physiological (food and clothing), safety (job security), love and belonging needs (friendship), esteem, and self-actualization. Needs lower down in the hierarchy must be satisfied before individuals can attend to needs higher up.[1]

This sequential interpretation of human needs may sound reasonable, but it has not been empirically supported (Soper, Milford and Rosenthal, 1995, and Banerjee and Duflo, 2011). Ancient Chinese shared the same sequential view: "When one is adequately fed and clothed, then one will begin to know the worth of a good name and the detest for shame."[2] However, the fact is that many people would end their lives upon being cyberbullied! Cyberbullying does not do a thing to a person's physical freedoms or hurt access to one's basic material needs. The evidence clearly implies that self-esteem and being respected as a human being to many may be more important than survival.

A recent study funded by the National Institutes of Health and published in JAMA Network Open on June 27, 2022 found that the young respondents in the study who experienced cyberbullying were more than four times as likely to report thoughts of suicide and attempts as those who hadn't.[3] This association diminished but remained significant when the researchers adjusted for other factors known to affect thoughts of suicide and attempts. Banerjee and Duflo wrote, in *Poor Economics*, "It has been widely documented that poor people in the developing world spending large amounts on weddings, dowries, and christenings, probably in part as a result of the compulsion not to lose face" (p.35). Evidence shows that many people rate survival lower than self-esteem. Similarly, evidence shows that children crucially need love, and could suffer developmental defects and may even die if they never sense affection or love.[4]

Maslow put "self-actualization" at the top of the needs hierarchy. In his words,

> It refers to the desire for self-fulfillment, namely, to the tendency for him to become actualized in what he is potentially. This tendency might be phrased as the desire to become more and more what one is, to become everything that one is capable of becoming.

Maslow is right to put self-actualization at the top of the hierarchy to underscore the fact that the satisfaction from self-actualization is of a "higher order" than the satisfaction from food and shelter. Maslow thinks that this desire is extremely strong, saying "What a man can be, he must be" (1943, p.382).

Interestingly, actualization does not require one to be a refined achiever in the arts or in any field. Although Maslow did use poets, artists, and musicians as examples of people successful at self-actualization, this interpretation is a bit narrow. The quest for self-actualization is human nature and starts very young. Toddlers having fun exploring the environs is a way of self-actualization. Kids playing with one another is a form of self-actualization. Mentally handicapped people singing and having fun is self-actualization. Of course, self-actualization can also be at a very high level. Virtuoso musicians and great artists, great poets, and great scientists self-actualize in ways that are beyond the imagination of most common folks. But this does not mean that common folks do not self-actualize. Mothers doing their best and out of their inner nature to care for their kids are not only loving but are also self-actualizing. To self-actualize, one simply follows one's mind and be honest with oneself. Because self-actualizing is so important, we all treasure freedom.

Self-actualization, in plain language, is to follow one's heart. This may sound simple enough, but following one's heart requires self-discovery. This is particularly true of those with strong cognitive powers. For these intelligent people, self-reflection enables self-discovery. Bertrand Russell described his self-discovery process thus:

> In adolescence, I hated life and was continually on the verge of suicide, from which, however, I was restrained by the desire to know more mathematics. Now, on the contrary, I enjoy life ... This is due partly to having discovered what were the things that I most desired and having gradually acquired many of these things. Partly it is due to having successfully dismissed certain objects of desire ... as essentially unattainable. But very largely it is due to a diminishing preoccupation with myself ...
>
> *(Russell, 1968, p.6)*

For those with weaker cognitive capability, such as the mentally handicapped who may lack the ability to self-reflect, following one's heart is instinctive. They would simply do what comes to mind that they like to do at the time.

Two kinds of needs

It is fruitful to see two kinds of human needs as essential to a good life. I would call these "mental good" needs and "physical good" needs. Physical good needs are well known and are represented in the bottom tier in Maslow's hierarchy. Maslow's upper tiers all have to do with "mental goods." Regrettably economists have traditionally focused on physical goods as goods and until recently economists almost totally ignored human needs for mental goods. Physical goods satisfy physiological needs, which include such things as air, food, drink, shelter, clothing, a comfortable weather or at least protection against extreme hot or cold), sex, and sleep. Mental goods satisfy mental needs, which include self-esteem or self-acceptance, love, peace of mind, sense of security, sense of autonomy, sense of achievement, and self-actualization. Putting this in everyday language, we may say that physical goods satisfy the needs of the body, while mental goods satisfy the needs of the soul.

In psychology literature there is a lot of talk about eudaimonic and hedonic well-being. Hedonic well-being is associated with physical goods and physiological well-being, including different kinds of sensual pleasures. These sensual pleasures are provided by nature so we have the instinctive drive for reproduction, food, and the comfort and security of a home. Eudaimonic well-being is associated with mental goods that range all the way from just having fun and a happy get-together with friends and family (which reflects love and friendship) to reading a great novel or poetry, watching a great movie (which offer deeper understanding of humanity), attending a concert or artistic performance (which offer aesthetic satisfaction), to self-actualization in the sense of following the heart's calling. Realizing one's full potential (which may include among many other things intellectual, artistic, or athletic accomplishments) of course is nice, and setting this as the life goal is wise, as it helps personal growth. Mental goods give meaning to life. Maslow's hierarchy of needs suggests that hedonic well-being based on physical good needs is of a lower order, while security, self-esteem, love, and self-actualization are of a higher order. Maslow talked about "strong people" with admiration. They "can swim against the stream of public opinion and … can stand up for the truth at great personal cost." Maslow also expressed admiration for those "who have loved and been well loved, and who have had many deep friendships" because they "can hold out against hatred, rejection or persecution" (Maslow, 1943 p.388).

Some would propose that there are also spiritual needs, but spiritual fulfilment should be regarded as a form of self-actualization. The progression from the more mundane mental well-being to spiritual well-being is gradual, and always represents a shift away from focusing on the self. Spiritual fulfilment is achieved when one transcends and rises above the dictates of one's ego. Albert Schweitzer is widely recognized as a humanist and a philosopher. But he was also a theologian, musicologist, and physician. He spent much of his life serving people in Africa, primarily in the area now known as Gabon, helping people of another ethnicity and whom he had never met before. His formal religious affiliation notwithstanding, his fervent belief in "Reverence for Life" transcends religious and ethnic boundaries. For this he earned the Nobel Peace Prize in 1952.

Utility or happiness? The joy of self-actualization

Economists have always used the term "utility" to refer to a measure of success in achieving what humans seek. If happiness is what is sought, economists would not object to calling happiness utility. After all, economists try to understand human behavior and decision-making in terms of "utility metrics." But seeking utility is not necessarily selfish, because economists are always ready to define utility so it also depends on altruistic acts.[5]

Quite apart from defining the utility function in the way that allows economists a handle on the analysis of behavior, it is commonly admitted that the elevator, the washing machine, the computer, the car, etc., all provide utility. Indeed any "good" that makes life more comfortable, that saves our time, or that is enjoyable contributes to utility. If so, can we equate well-being with utility? If not, what is the distinction between utility and well-being?

I have been making the point that life is the most precious and truly scarce resource that human beings have. As we strive to make the most out of our lives, however, we face constraints. One constraint is time. Another is our energy. If we have to spend much time and energy moving from one place to another place, going up to the twentieth floor, washing clothes, and cooking, we will have less time and energy to do other things. Thus, all those gadgets that humans have invented, which save our energy and time, also serve to relax the constraints that prevent us from realizing our life potential. So it does make sense to say that gadgets like the car, the train, airplanes, elevators, washing machines, etc. relax our constraints. We can call the utility derived from such gadgets "instrumental utility," as they allow us to have more time and save us energy so we can enrich our lives with desirable activities that can elevate our "ultimate utility."[6]

We go back to the distinction between mental good needs and physical good needs. If we have more time and after we have already more or less satisfied our physical good needs, we can do much more to satisfy our mental good needs and that includes self-actualization.

This is indeed what highly productive and self-motivated scientists, musicians, artists, and scholars would do. But when people have more time, they may also spend more time drinking, gambling, partying, taking drugs, quarreling with one another, fighting with one another, or watching TV. There are of course many other things people can do, like touring, swimming, jogging, cycling, tennis, golf, etc. It is a matter of honest assessment as to what is the most rewarding thing to do. But "honest assessment" about what the most rewarding thing to do is, unfortunately, often the last thing that comes to mind for many people. Inertia is part of human nature. Many people, without thinking about it, simply spend each day following the same routine, and staying within the comfort zone. In general, only those who have a habit of self-reflection will escape the loop of inertia and get to know what they truly value. Lacking self-reflection, the "perceived utility function" that they try to maximize limits their pursuit and their level of self-actualization. In a sense, materialistic people also "self-actualize," but the scope and extent of self-actualization are limited by their narrow and shallow perspective of what life can offer.

For those who consciously do something for a purpose, often they may not realize that they are striving for are often just an "instrumental goal" rather than their final goal. For example, many of us think that making money is their final goal, but money is at most a means to ends. Many students study in order to get a qualification, or to win a place in a renowned university. Again, however, a qualification or a place in their dream university cannot be the ultimate reward in life. Life has much more to offer.

Self-actualization simply means realizing what life has to offer. Notwithstanding the fact that human nature is universal, we are differently endowed with different abilities and different backgrounds. Self-actualization thus varies from person to person. Instrumental goals like making money or graduating from a renowned university or getting a professional qualification can never give us satisfaction that can compare with discovering and realizing what one is capable of doing. Confounding means and ends is a serious and common weakness of human nature. When people fail to achieve their instrumental goals, which they had presumed to be final goals, some become so disheartened that they may even kill themselves. Similarly, sensual pleasures represent motives Nature gives to humans so they will survive and reproduce. These can be looked upon as "nature's instrumental motives" installed in the animal kingdom. On the other hand, eudaimonic pursuits satisfy the needs of the "soul" or one's true self.

George Ainslie (1989), a pioneer in behavioral economics, proposed the concept of picoeconomics that depicts the competition for resources within a person, as opposed to the competition among market participants in the marketplace. He coined the term picoeconomics for this micro-microeconomics. This competition within a person is about the pursuit of long-term goals versus the pursuit of short-term goals. We can say that the self that pursues long-term goals is the true self or the soul, while the self that betrays the long-term interest of the person is the false self.[7]

Alternative theories of needs

Other than Maslow's, there are several alternative theories of needs. David McClelland's (1985, 1987) Human Motivation Theory suggests that individuals have three main needs: the need for achievement, the need for power, and the need for affiliation. McClelland was an expert on achieving success. He identified the motivation to achieve and competence as the keys to success on specific tasks. It is notable that achieving success, power, and affiliation are all related to mental goods. Being successful in accomplishing what one has set out to do is naturally a mental good. Power by itself is not a mental good, but with power, one may feel that one has better access to the means of getting what one wants. So power is an "instrument" that some people strive to get so they can get what they want. Power may be seen as an end in itself because it boosts one's self-esteem but it is still just a means to an end in the sense that if someone has already achieved a strong sense of self-esteem there is no need for power to serve that purpose. Affiliation is related to being accepted by one's peers. Humans are a social animal and they need other people's recognition or acceptance. Being accepted by others is, to many, conducive to self-acceptance and self-esteem, which is an important mental good.

Richard M. Ryan and Edward L. Deci (2000) think that humans have three common psychological needs: autonomy, competence, and relatedness. A sense of autonomy, self-efficacy, and being part of a community are all important mental goods. These needs form the basis for their Self Determination Theory and underlie the observation that intrinsic motivation is often more effective than extrinsic motivation. In short, intrinsic motivation is like an engine from within. When we want to do something driven by our inner nature, it is a form of self-actualization and it offers us a degree of ultimate utility. When we are induced to do something with a monetary reward, we are unlikely to be really interested in that something. The monetary reward at best offers us instrumental utility.

Human weaknesses

As noted above, it is rather common that people mistake means for ends. Human perception is often flawed. For this reason, people's choices might not reflect what they truly prefer. Paul. A. Samuelson (1938), a Nobel Laureate in Economic Science, proposed the Theory of Revealed Preference, which, at the time, appealed very much to fellow economists because inferring preference based on behavior appears much more scientific than accepting a stated preference as a true preference. However, the theory is flawed because humans are subject to many inherent weaknesses. These weaknesses include flawed perception, lack of self-control, lack of information, and lack of wisdom.

Flaws in perception are inherent in human nature. With choice based on perceived opportunities and perceived constraints, and given that perceptions may not be the reality, inferring preference based on choices may be a serious mistake. Many drivers believe that they can control their cars and so will not run into an accident. But this perception is often mistaken. We cannot say drunk drivers are irrational. They decide to drive only because they believe they have the ability.

Humans are rational in the sense that their acts are all for a reason. Human behavior is not random and is mostly driven by purpose. However, lack of self-control and flawed perception are commonplace.

The seven "deadly sins" are well known to Westerners. They are pride, greed, wrath, envy, gluttony, lust and sloth. Pride is arrogance; greed is possessiveness and a unstoppable instinct to keep craving for more; wrath is anger and is driven by one's wishes being dashed; envy is an unhappiness due to other people having something that one lacks; gluttony is excessive indulgence; lust is a strong sexual desire that is out of control; and sloth is laziness and lack of drive. These "deadly sins" are all related to a strong ego that dominates one's best interests. A strong ego is often the cause of a lot of trouble. It is behind many mistaken decisions or choices. A drunken driver chooses to drive because he thinks he can control the car as well as when sober, intake of alcohol notwithstanding.

When one is arrogant, which happens when one refuses to admit one has any faults, the door to personal development is shut; the chances for one to realize one's full potential are sharply reduced. When one is greedy, which has to do with possessiveness, not only does one keep craving more wealth, but one also tends to be mean and worried about losing what one already has. The fact, regrettably, is that human life is short and one really cannot possess anything. Greed only condemns us to become slaves to material wealth and takes away our peace of mind and freedom from anxiety. Wrath, or anger, is the result of things turning out to be the opposite of what we would wish. When this happens, we may "lose our mind" and become destructive. This always translates to our losing more—on top of what has already been lost if the turnout is perceived as a loss. We would lose health, and we may even hurt those we love. Envy is a trait that humans and many other animals share.[8] We tend to show displeasure on seeing our peers are treated better or fare better than ourselves. But the fact is that we all have different lives and different circumstances. Envy will not help us get better treated by life. Only our own effort can change our fate. Lust (excessive indulgence in sex), gluttony (excess in eating and drinking), and sloth (laziness) are just different dimensions of excess. Sexual desires are needed for the preservation of the species, but excessive indulgence in sexual or sensual pleasures make us lose sight of other rewarding ventures in life. Eating and drinking without restraint harms our health and undermines our most valuable resource, which is life. Rest or relaxing is a way of preserving our energy so we have the energy to do things that we need to do or that are more rewarding over the long term. But sloth or excessive rest and unwillingness to go beyond one's comfort zone deprives us of the opportunity to develop life's full potential.

Character strengths and values in action

While humans have weaknesses, many humans show spectacular strength. Christopher Peterson and Martin Seligman (2004) came up with 24 character strengths that can be grouped under six headings: wisdom, courage, humanity, justice, temperance, and transcendence. The character strengths are qualities that can be nurtured so we will be in a position to meet the challenges in life and to capitalize on the opportunities that life offers. It is important to note that "sins" and "virtues" are the terms that moralists use, but for our purposes the more important question is whether the qualities foster personal growth and human flourishing or undermine personal growth and human flourishing. In fact, personal growth is an important aspect of self-actualization. Not only will this produce a strong sense of self-worth, but by building character strengths and overcoming human weaknesses one gains a sense of accomplishment and self-efficacy.

Albert Schweitzer was, no doubt, an example of a man with practically all the 24 character strengths that Peterson and Seligman listed. We will go through the first six on their list to illustrate his way of life:

Appreciation of beauty and excellence: Schweitzer was a musician and musicologist.

Bravery: Schweitzer spent years in Africa. He was not intimidated by the risks and the hard life that living there, then often referred to as the Dark Continent, would pose.

Creativity: Schweitzer developed a technique for recording the performances of Bach's music; wrote notable books; and invented the philosophy known as Reverence for Life.

Curiosity: Schweitzer never stopped exploring new ways of doing things and offering new perspectives that often challenged mainstream views.

Fairness: Schweitzer was vocal in denouncing colonialism.

Forgiveness: Schweitzer denounced wrongs, but, as a theologian, he followed the example of Jesus, who had on the cross asked God to forgive the sinners "for they know not what they do."

The other character strengths are: gratitude, honesty, hope, humility, humor, judgment, kindness, leadership, love, love of learning, perseverance, perspective, prudence, self-regulation, social intelligence, spirituality, teamwork, and zest.

The list is long, which is why the character strengths are grouped under six headings, which are Wisdom, Courage, Humanity, Justice, Temperance, and Transcendence. I prefer a shorter list, and propose that Love, Insight (or Wisdom), Fortitude, and Engagement encompass most of the 24 character strengths and virtues. With the acronym LIFE, it is also easier to remember, and it reminds us of Schweitzer's philosophy "Reverence for Life."

There can be some debate about which heading a character strength belongs to. I would prefer grouping humility under Insight (wisdom), since it is wise to be humble so we can keep learning and correcting our mistakes. Similarly, although it is correct to regard prudence and self-regulation as temperaments, these qualities certainly are also intrinsic to wisdom. It would be hard to imagine someone without prudence and self-control to be wise.

Wisdom needs to include the realization that one has to be on top of oneself through self-discipline before one can learn and achieve anything.

Conclusions

Humans have similar aspirations and fears. Humans obviously share similar emotions, so that novels written in the West are widely read and appreciated in the East, and vice versa. The human weaknesses and strengths discussed above are as common in the East as in the West.

However, people obviously adopt a huge variety of lifestyles. Their ways of life reflect their cultural differences. But what exactly are cultural differences? We argue that cultural differences generally do not represent different values. Rather, they merely represent different ways of pursuing the same values that are represented in the hierarchy of human needs.

We need similar nutrients and energy needs, but different peoples cook differently and eat differently. We have similar "mental good" needs, including self-acceptance or esteem, acceptance by one's peers, sense of autonomy, sense of achievement, freedom from anxiety and worries, sense of security, etc. But people with different "values" (they think so) may act totally differently to achieve similar mental goods. Warren Buffet is known to live a rather simple life notwithstanding his wealth, while a lot of people with far less wealth might flaunt their luxurious lifestyle. Tim Kasser had written a lot on materialism and referred to such lifestyles as reflecting a materialistic culture. Kasser et al. (2004) propose that a Materialistic Value Orientation (MVO) develops through two main pathways: (1) from experiences that induce feelings of insecurity, and (2) from social modeling. But materialistic people and those who prefer a simple life have similar needs. Their differences lie in the ways they seek to satisfy those needs.

Between the two pathways that Kasser and his coauthors mentioned, we would argue that social modeling is the main drive behind the particular choice chosen by those with a MVO, and not the former. People with feelings of insecurity will seek to free themselves from such insecurity. But many opt to live a simple life even though they can afford to spend much more on luxury goods. Many opt for a life of service and giving. As Kasser and his coauthors pointed out, MVO is often counterproductive, as people dominated by such "values" are likely to see their personal well-being decline. An MVO also damages interpersonal and community relations as well as the ecological health of the planet. The true reason behind an MVO lifestyle is social modeling. Social modeling is also the reason why the French cook the French way, the Chinese cook the Chinese way, and the Indians cook the Indian way. This observation gives us the hope that we can search for lifestyles that are environmentally and ecologically sustainable and still allow us to seek the ultimate values that we cherish.

If human nature is universal, the more important implication is that there really should be no clash of civilizations as Samuel Huntington had ominously proclaimed. With human ingenuity and the resources that we are endowed with, we should be able to free ourselves from hunger, from water shortages, from war, and from human-caused climate change. With an open mind, all countries would seek the form of government that best serves their peoples. We would all put ourselves in the shoes of others when we design our public policies and educate our children. This way the world would become peaceful and prosperous.

Notes

1 See Saul McLeod, "Maslow's Hierarchy of Needs," available at: www.simplypsychology.org/maslow.html. Accessed June 4, 2025.
2 The orginal text is from Guanzi (725 BC to 645 BC) and was cited by Sima Qian in his Shi Ji (Historical Records), around 91 B.C.
3 See Arnon, Brunstein-Klomek, and Visoki (2022), available at: https://jamanetwork.com/journals/jamanetworkopen/fullarticle/2793627
4 René Spitz, a psychiatrist who studied infants and children in orphanages and prisons in the 1930s, discovered infants and children could die if they were not connected with or touched, even if they received adequate nutrition and healthcare. See "Infancy and early childhood matter so much because of attachment" in *The Conversation.com*. Published: May 29, 2019.
5 See for example Bell, D.E., Keeney, R.L. (2009). Altruistic Utility Functions for Joint Decisions. In: Brams, S.J., Gehrlein, W.V., Roberts, F.S. (eds) *The Mathematics of Preference, Choice and Order. Studies in Choice and Welfare*. Springer, Berlin, Heidelberg. https://doi.org/10.1007/978-3-540-79128-7_2
6 Sex offers instrumental utility so that a couple can be better bonded and connected. Excessive indulgence in sexual pleasures, however, could distract one from self-actualization.
7 See George Ainslie, *Picoeconomics in a Nutshell: A hyperlinked overview*, available at www.picoeconomics.org/Nut2/Nutshell2.html. Accessed June 4, 2025.
8 See Nell Greenfieldboyce, "Dogs Understand Fairness, Get Jealous, Study Finds," published December 9, 2008, available at www.npr.org/templates/story/story.php?storyId=97944783. Accessed June 4, 2025.

Key points to note

- Human nature is universal in that humans have similar needs and similar weaknesses. They are all "rational" in the sense that their choices and decisions aim at achieving what they value at the time.
- Human needs include physiological needs and mental good needs. Mental good needs and physical good needs are both important for human flourishing.

- The hierarchy of needs is about the "level of fulfilment." "Self-actualization" offers the highest order of life satisfaction but does not necessarily come last in the sequence of pursuits. It is possible that people prefer to go hungry to pursue what they value.
- While all humans are subject to human weaknesses, human strengths and virtues can be nurtured.
- Nurturing human strengths and virtues allows people to have resilience, a high degree of self-efficacy, and cherish hope and optimism in their lives.

Some questions to ponder

- Why do we often hear: "We are our own worst enemy"? Is there any truth to this?
- Can human strengths and virtues be taught? If so, how?
- What are the reasons for people to engage in criminal activities?
- Can adults who are arrogant be converted into people with virtues such as humility?
- What do you think are the most important strengths and virtues? Why?

3

LOVE AND THE ECONOMICS OF LOVE

Love is both a mental capital and a mental good. A loving person is a loving person because he has accumulated the mental habit of loving to genuinely care for the well-being of others. We may say loving others and loving oneself has become that person's second nature or, alternatively, we may say that person has rediscovered his inner nature. A loving person "produces love as a mental good" so people that he loves experience love as a receiver while he also experiences love as a giver. The economics of love is the study of how to love most effectively given whatever resources are available.

Introduction

Gary Becker (1965) pointed out that "utility" does not come about simply by purchasing market goods and services. Similarly, Kelvin Lancaster (1966) suggested that consumers are not really interested in the goods bought in the market *per se* but are looking for certain "characteristics" offered by the goods. What Becker called "basic commodities" Lancaster called "characteristics." Both Becker and Lancaster attempt to go behind the market goods to discover what really matters to utility. It was Becker, however, who pioneered the concept of *household production*. In contrast, Lancaster thought the "characteristics" of goods were inherent in the goods purchased and represent what is desired.

Unfortunately, both Becker and Lancaster missed one really important point: that "utility" is not derived from "physical attributes" or "physical characteristics" alone. Life would be too dreary if "value" were derived only by people acting like consumption machines that gobble up goods and services in the marketplace. Unfortunately, this has been the mainstream economics narrative. Nobel Laureate J.R. Hicks (1939) titled his highly acclaimed book

DOI: 10.4324/9781003507093-3

Value and Capital: An Inquiry into some Fundamental Principles of Economic Theory. The focus of his analysis was the consumption of goods purchased in the marketplace. But value certainly goes beyond the goods and services that money can buy; and the value of the goods and services that money can buy is not derived just from the physical attributes associated with those goods. Those who are familiar with marketing know very well that consumers are in pursuit of *mental goods* as well. For example, marketing professionals try very hard to have potential consumers associate certain products with a glamorous lifestyle, self-confidence and success. Most advertising does very little in conveying to consumers the physical qualities of the products. Instead, it usually focuses on glamor, confidence, style, recognition, caring, love—all of which are mental goods. Marketing professionals also pay much attention to packaging. Good packaging for some goods allows the same product to sell at a much higher price, even though much packaging is already excessive: it does not serve any purpose other than marketing and is bad for sustainable development.

An important observation about mental goods is that, although physical goods sometimes serve as inputs in producing the mental goods, physical goods cannot really substitute for mental goods. For example, a life full of love is a fulfilling one. So, love is clearly a mental good. But even though money can buy care in the marketplace, it cannot buy true love from one's alienated or unloving family members, for example. Some people are incapable of loving and may have seldom experienced love. They can be quite rich and yet unhappy, because all the physical goods that money can buy may not bring them love. While some mental goods are easier to obtain—or example, through the purchase of an insurance policy one can enjoy greater peace of mind against some feared scenarios—the capacity to love has to be nurtured and cultivated over a long period of time and can only come naturally in an environment that is favorable to its natural development.

Mental goods as outputs of household production

Why do people pay hundreds of times more for one watch than for another one, when the other one can tell time just as well and may even have many more functions? One might say it is more beautiful. But is it really the more beautiful design that makes it command that much higher a price? If the answer is yes, how can we explain the huge effort made on designing an advertisement to promote it? Why is "brand building" so vital in marketing?

In an affluent society, people are particularly used to using commercial goods as a means to acquire mental goods for oneself and to deliver mental goods to others. Buying some luxury good may affirm one's success and status. A bundle of flowers on Valentine's Day may convey one's care and love for one's lover. On Mother's Day and Father's Day, and on someone's graduation, as well as many other occasions, a well-designed card with nice words carries a message of love, celebration or congratulations. The cards that people receive are of absolutely no use, and certainly do not fulfill any physical need, but they deliver mental goods, which make the physical objects (a card or a gift) very much treasured. When a couple in love go to a movie or a concert together, the movie or the concert could be secondary. The mental good derived from spending an evening together may be far more important.

But mental goods do not always have to cost anything. A letter may not cost anything in money terms, but the mental good delivered to the recipient may be far greater than that delivered by a card that costs quite a few dollars, though it takes time and effort to write. Kind words and encouragement also do not cost anything, but they may be deeply appreciated and may even change a person's life. Being together with someone we love and walking casually and relaxing in the park or along the lakeshore could be very nice, and it need not cost anything. But over the ages there have been many sceptics about love without lavish spending. To wit:

> Daisy, Daisy, give me your answer true! I'm half crazy, all for the love of you;
> It won't be a stylish marriage.
> I can't afford a carriage.
> But you'll look sweet upon the seat of bicycle made for two.
>
> Michael, Michael, this is my answer true:
> I can't cycle half as well as you;
> If you can't afford a carriage, there'll be no bloomin' marriage,
> For I'll be blowed
> if I'll be towed
> On a bicycle made for two.

The fact remains, however, that there are costly and not so costly ways of procuring mental goods. There are limits to how much or how many physical needs people have to fill, but there is virtually no limit as to how much one can spend to procure the mental goods that we need. The efficiency of the household production function varies greatly from person to person. By efficiency is meant the output-to-input ratio. Spending a lot but getting little out of the spending is inefficient. As we will see in the next chapter, the efficiency of household production in generating mental goods has much to do with culture. *Culture plays a key role in the economics of life and sustainable development.*

Mahatma Gandhi has been quoted as having said: "There's enough for everybody's need and not for anybody's greed." But we do not have to be moralistic in interpreting people's "greedy" behavior. In a sense we are all the same in that we all have similar mental good needs, even though we are vastly different in our efficiency of procuring them. We all want to be respected and accepted by those we associate with. We all want peace of mind and freedom from anxiety. We all want a sense of freedom and autonomy, and do not like being told what to do and what not to do. We all want to feel strong and dignified. We all want love and "self-actualization": discovering and realizing the potential that lies within, in our different ways. The challenge is how we can procure all this without leaving too much ecological footprint, so that our needs can all be fulfilled, and that the fulfilment of these needs today will not undermine the fulfilment of the same needs for our progeny.

Nature of love

This brings us back to the subject of love. First, we would stress that love is both a mental capital and a mental good. If one is a loving person, that means one has a lot of love stored up, so one has an instinctive inclination to care for the well-being of others. The life experience featuring loving and being loved translates into a loving nature that is a mental habit or a mental capital. There is a likelihood that mothers are by nature mostly loving. People are, however, not all born naturally to love.[1] Most people need to accumulate love as a mental capital before love becomes second nature to them.

All forms of mental capital, including skills of all kinds that one has acquired, are basically a form of habit. A musician, for example, must have spent years playing some musical instrument and learning music. A mathematician or a basketball player, similarly, must have spent years training and refining his skills.

In the beginning, one experiences love as a mental good and is happy because one enjoys love. There is a loving person at one's side, and that person serves as a role model. Through social modeling one begins to act in a loving way. Generally, this engenders positive feedback that enforces that loving behavior. Behavior that is repeated many times becomes habit. The loving habit is Love mental capital. There is thus a "love–love virtuous circle": love as mental good reinforcing love as a mental capital; love as a mental capital generating more love as a mental good.

In this book, love strictly refers to *a yearning from inside to realize the best that life can offer for those for whom we care*, including ourselves. I would not distinguish the love between a couple "in love" from the love between parents and children. I would regard the romantic passion between a couple "in love" as distinct from the love between them. John who loves Mary from his heart expresses that love through a genuine concern for the well-being of Mary and a readiness to offer *emotional support* whenever needed. Rick who "loves" Mary passionately just wants her to be at his side and treats her like something that he possesses. John could sacrifice his life for Mary if this sacrifice would somehow help Mary get through difficult times. Rick could kill himself if Mary rejects him. I would define the former as love and call the latter simply an *obsessive possessiveness*[2].

Relational psychotherapist J. Richard Cookerly[3] defined love thus: "Healthy real love is a powerful, vital, natural process of highly valuing, desiring for, often acting for, and taking pleasure in the well-being of the loved."

This definition corresponds to mine (**Box 3.1**). He points out that true love involves a respect for life and is a truly potent force, and that true love is spontaneous and natural. **Box 3.2** shows an excerpt from his website (with minor adaptations). Although love is natural and spontaneous, it can be overpowered by other equally potent forces, in particular *egocentrism* and *possessiveness*. But even the most egocentric and possessive person needs to be loved. This is why some very rich people are unhappy, their huge wealth notwithstanding. Without love one may feel lonely, betrayed, insecure and angry, and lacking in self-esteem. Money certainly can buy care from a commercial caregiver, but if the care is purchased you know deep in your heart it is not love. Rich people can get all the care they need by paying for it, but they will still be yearning for that someone who cares for them from the heart.

Thus, love is one of the very crucial mental goods that enrich one's life and make life meaningful and thus worth living. Indeed, love is a very strong driving force, not only for individuals in pursuit of their dreams, but also for the transformation of society and, in particular, the economy (Richard and Rudnyckyj, 2009).

BOX 3.1 LOVE: A BLESSING FROM THE HEART

Have a Reverence for Life, loving yourself as much as you would love others.
Love starts with loving yourself ... your life ...
Then extending to your immediate family ... Then extending to other forms of life.

Love is an aspiration from deep inside:
An aspiration that the loved one will live a life free from worry;
A wish that the loved one will realize one's full potential and will enjoy a rich life:
Away from danger and ever joyful.

A pure love is free from self-interest considerations;
A broad-minded love benefits all;
An enduring love is ever so new;
A selfless love knows no sacrifice too big.
Love always stems from identifying with Life. There are no other kinds of Love.
Love is unconditional and certainly not an exchange.
Love requires nothing in return.

Love is the strongest motive.
Love often begins with a relationship.
Yet it must transcend that relationship.
Love is a Blessing from the Heart.

(Ho, 2012)

BOX 3.2 MAJOR ELEMENTS OF LOVE

High valuing – treasure, cherish, respect, appreciate, affirm the worth of, admire, see as fine, excellent, unique, special. Healthy real love consistently highly values the loved.

Powerful – strong, vigorous, effectual, energy-filled, dynamic, ascendant, prevailing. Healthy real love is amazingly powerful.

Vital – important and necessary to life process and function, of paramount importance to continued existence, having to do with the life force and its cardinal process, a biological, neuro-chemical, psycho-neurophysiological phenomenon. Healthy real love is a great, vital force for healthy life.

Natural – of nature, part of essential existence, inherently of fundamental reality, intrinsically part of the cosmos, especially essential to the processes of nature and natural existence, in life a biological, neuro-chemical, psycho-socioneuro-physiological phenomenon. We are naturally constructed to thrive via love.

Process – an active succession of systematic, changing operations with a developing progressive, onward organized flow. Healthy real love is a growth process.

Desiring for the well-being of the loved – a state of thriving, championed by those who love healthfully; a loved one's well-being is paramount so one is always ready to lend a helping hand when needed or useful, with a view to the continuance of well-being and realization of the loved one's potential.

Acting for the well-being of the loved – behaving often or when possible to nurture, protect, assist, support, affirm, heal, cause improvement and otherwise promote the well-being of the loved.

Taking pleasure in the well-being of the loved – experiencing joy, happiness and many other positive emotions when the loved is perceived as doing well, thriving, succeeding, growing, healthfully happy and ascendant; this often involves pleasure sharing with the loved.

Adapted from: whatislovedrcookerly.com/97/the-definition-of-love/
(courtesy of Richard Cookerly)

Love without excessive attachment

Love as discussed here is to be distinguished from "romantic love," which social psychologist Zick Rubin (1970) says is characterized by:

1 Attachment: The need to be cared for and be with the other person. This encompasses a desire for physical contact and approval by this other person.
2 Caring: Valuing the other person's happiness and needs as much as one's own.
3 Intimacy: Sharing private thoughts, feelings and desires with the other person.

Rubin developed a Romantic Love Scale based on responses to 13 questions, which fall under the above three categories. As readers can see, "caring" in the sense of *caring from the heart* is one of the three hallmarks of romantic love according to Rubin, and this is no different from true love under our earlier definition. But Rubin additionally requires *attachment* and *intimacy* as telling signs of romantic love. Consider his questionnaire, from which the romantic love scale is to be derived. Respondents are asked to answer to what degree they agree to the following statements:

- I find it easy to ignore his (her) faults.
- I feel very possessive toward him (her).
- If I could never be with him (her), I would feel miserable.
- It would be hard for me to get along without him (her).
- When I am with him (her), I spend a good deal of time just looking at him (her).
- I would do almost anything for him (her).

Being attached to and feeling possessive about a person who has attracted one's romantic love is quite natural. A degree of attachment is not only natural, but also healthy for developing healthy interpersonal relations. In particular, physical contact and intimacy are very effective in communicating love and support. This is as true for parental love as for the love between two spouses or lovers. But *excessive* attachment goes counter to the purpose of true love: you would not want the one whom you truly love to be too attached to you, since excessive attachment diminishes the possibilities that one can make of one's life. In the animal kingdom, some animals force their offspring to be independent because otherwise they will not be able to survive.[4] You would also like your loved one to have the courage and the ability to live and thrive even without you. Excessive attachment is unfortunately often highlighted and lauded in romantic dramas, and *Romeo and Juliet* is an example of a Shakespearean tragedy founded on excessive attachment. We really should break the often taken-for-granted but totally misguided notion that greater is the love when the attachment is greater (**Box 3.3**).

BOX 3.3 ROMANTIC LOVE

From Romeo and Juliet in the West,
To the Butterfly Lovers in the East,
Literature romanticizes love with death,
As if only this is the truth we know best.

'I love you so much,' the lover tells his beloved:
'If you die first,
I want to die too,
So I can be with you.

'Since I love you so much,' the lover continues:
'So if I die first,
I want you to die too,
So that I can be with you.'

But can't we see love and romance are different?
If my beloved dies first I would tell her:
'I should live on,
So I can think of you, and live out your dreams.

'And if I die first,
You should live on and live well,
Tell me in your dreams what love is and what love is not.
Remember that I love you no matter what.'

(poem by Ho, circa 2023)

Loving economically and parenting with wise love

Economists talk of the diminishing utility of a good. Within a time period, the more a good is consumed, the smaller becomes the marginal utility—the utility derived from an additional unit of consumption. As far as physical goods are concerned, this is clearly true. Within a specific time period, there is only so much food that can be eaten; only so much clothing that can be worn; only so much accommodation that one can call a home. Our lives are finite, so the claim for "insatiable wants" would not make much sense if only physical goods matter. Some may counterargue that there is no limit to the quality of physical goods that can be coveted. But, in truth, such clamor for *ever higher* quality is often more in the nature of a clamor for a mental good, such as an assertion that one is only satisfied with having the best products.[5] Knowing and letting others know that they are getting the best that is available makes one feel good.

When it comes to mental goods, the law of diminishing return apparently does not apply. One will not be "fed up" with too much love, too much peace of mind, or too much sense of self-worth. Parents would never need to worry about giving too much love to their children. But they should really worry about giving them too much material goods. Spoiling children with too many toys and giving them too much pocket money will run into diminishing returns and even negative returns. They will then not learn to value what they have and may consume resources without any regard for sustainable development or for the welfare of others. If we want our children to become loving individuals, we need to nurture in them an understanding about scarcity. Giving children too much material goods will make them selfish. Providing a role model for sharing, for giving, for caring for the underprivileged will help them become less self-focused and become more compassionate. People who are too self-focused and selfish can never be strong because they easily succumb to temptations and overlook the merit of inner strength.

Of all the mental goods that are important to children, self-actualization and self-worth are probably the most important. Loving parents will convey their love to their children effectively if they give children the room to develop their interests and to find their dreams, and remind them how much they love them—regardless of their school results or how they perform in competitions. Instead of focusing on results, successful parenting must involve applauding children's efforts and encouraging them to tackle challenges patiently and seriously. Sadly, many parents fail to understand that focusing on results always leads to unwanted pressures and may undermine the sense of self-worth of their children. They *must not* alienate their children with language or behavioral abuse even when children "misbehave." In any case, "misbehave" is not the same as disobeying orders. Only when a child acts in a way that will cause harm should a behavior be called misbehavior. In these cases, try reasoning with them at an appropriate time privately (**Table 3.1**).

Rebecca Strong (2022) distinguishes self-worth from self-esteem. In her view, self-worth is one's own affirmation of one's value as a person. It generally comes from within. Self-esteem, on the other hand, is one's opinion of one's traits and abilities. It often comes from without. Someone with a strong sense of self-worth "knows his worth" that will not be easily undermined by adversities or other people's opinions about him. He has developed a strong sense of direction, self-discipline, confidence, and courage. Sense of self-worth is an important aspect of growing up.

TABLE 3.1 Keys to good parenting

Basic principles	Love your children by nurturing their confidence and sense of self-worth, so from an early age they learn to love themselves and others and want to become the best of what they can through being truthful to themselves and self-discipline.
Build trust through respect and love	Avoid alienating them with abusive words and behavior. Praise them for their effort regardless of results so children would love to talk to you.
Build independence	Let children share housework from an early age.
Give children challenges that fit their stage of development	Manageable challenges make life interesting. A sense of achievement is an important mental good.
Take good care of yourselves, both physically and mentally	This serves as a role model for self-love.
When children "misbehave," reason with them respectfully and clearly. It is not for you to convince them but for them to work out what is right	Children need time to turn around. No need to repeat your message. Give them plenty of time to reflect. Avoid forcing them to act against their will.
Listen to your children attentively	This shows your respect for them. They will learn to listen to you attentively.
Relax, and appreciate life's delights	Be a role model for children in appreciating life's delights.
Keep learning with self-reflection	Be a role model for children in lifelong learning.
Have a sense of priority: nothing is more important than life, and LIFE is the way to let life shine.	Be a role model for children in wise, positive living.
Never argue with your partner or with your children. Always only make your point clearly.	Arguing with your partner or with your children hurts relations. Never try to convert your children or your partner to your point of view. Let them decide.
Have fun with the kids	Parents and children are equals as human beings and should be best friends who can share lots of fun, as well as joys and sorrows.

These days a decline of fertility has raised alarm in many countries, from Japan and China to France and the United States. Many countries have offered economic incentives for prospective parents but they do not seem to work. The cost of raising children is, of course, one concern, but not knowing the art of parenting may be the more serious concern. Many prospective parents do not know how to raise happy children. Should they adopt Amy Chua's "tiger mother" way, or should they respect and nurture children's individuality? In point of fact, parents do not own their children. They should not dictate the way children live as they grow up. However, they should nurture in children a sense of self-worth through communicating parents' love and helping them acquire a habit of self-discipline. Parents who role-model as individuals with a strong sense of self-discipline will go a long way. The fact is: without self-discipline there can never be achievement of any kind. Sharing housework at an early age is a good start. (More on this under the "Attracting love and 'tough love'" section below.)

Many of us have heard of the Taj Mahal story. The Taj Mahal was built in the seventeenth century by the fifth Mughal emperor and grandson of Akbar the Great, Shah Jahan, in memory of his beloved wife Mumtaz Mahal, who died giving birth to their 14th child. The construction was said to have taken 22,000 workers toiling 22 years. The Taj Mahal did not fill a physical need of the loved person nor that of the lover, but rather a mental need. The emperor purportedly wanted to tell the world how much he loved Mahal, or, more romantically, he wanted to tell the dead Mahal how much he loved her.[6] His mind would not be at peace until the most beautiful monument in the world was built in her memory. The Taj Mahal story may suggest that the love between a couple is not the same as the love between, say, a mother and a child, or that between two siblings, or that between two friends. Surely the way love is expressed may vary from one relationship to another, but this does not detract from the universal nature of true love being a genuine desire for the loved one to live a good life, to live in peace, to die in peace, and to enjoy eternal bliss, if that is possible.

I have observed that "Love often begins with a relationship. Yet it must transcend that relationship." When true love is lit up between a couple "in love," the partner who is loved must be recognized as an individual and loved as an individual. A husband does not own his wife, nor does a wife own her husband. A parent does not own his children. Loving someone as a person means wishing him or her all the best in his or her life flourishing in his or her own way. The true lover, regardless of the relationship, will be prepared to make sacrifices for the loved person for his benefit. When the love is sufficiently strong the true lover may even lay down his life for the loved one.

It is indeed rare that a father would build a Taj Mahal for his daughter, but building a monument such as the Taj Mahal for one's deceased wife is also quite rare. But there are parents who would buy a car for their child, just as there are husbands/wives who would buy a car for their spouse?

But you would agree with me that building a Taj Mahal or buying a car or a house is in truth not a requirement in love. Indeed, excessively pampering the loved person is often not the best way to love the person. The economics of love tells us that we need to love effectively and efficiently. We would be loving effectively if the acts of love produce the intended effect of enhancing the well-being of the beloved. We would be loving efficiently if we could make the most out of what we have, to enhance the well-being of the beloved. Excessively pampering the loved person is neither an effective nor an efficient way of loving that person. You can spoil a spouse just as you can spoil a child. When humanity is facing an existential threat because of climate change and environmental degradation, loving efficiently and effectively is important.

In contrast to spending big, taking delight in simple things can often bring huge rewards. There are many examples of this: taking a walk in the park, bird-watching, star-gazing, listening to music, singing, calligraphy, writing a poem, writing a diary, making bread, taking pictures, playing chess, playing table tennis, swimming, arranging flowers, learning to play a musical instrument, and so on. Some of these might be expensive too, but most need not be that expensive. Many of these things we can do with our loved ones; others we can do alone. But all the same, they add color to our lives, and often food for conversation, and fun. The interesting thing is that most people have talents that they have not yet discovered. Being involved and getting active allows us to discover our true values and capabilities.

Although the heading in this section states "Loving economically," when the time comes for spending big, such as when big spending really can improve quality of life, saving money would be the last thing on the mind of the true lover, since, compared to life, money will always be secondary. "Loving economically" means maximizing the welfare of the beloved given whatever resources are available. Since money is only a means to an end, money is never to be saved at the expense of the welfare of the beloved. Love needs to be complemented with wisdom or Insight in order to produce the most benefits.

Interspousal spillovers and division of labor

But "the beloved" should include both the lover and the loved. A lover can love others effectively only if he knows how to love himself. Suppose a couple truly loves each other, both will consider his or her partner's well-being equally worthy.

So, in the case of a couple who truly loves each other, economically loving would require maximizing the welfare of the couple with the resources available. This generally would require a division of labor between the couple to enhance the welfare of both. As is often pointed out, this would require specialisation according to comparative advantage. Comparative advantage theory requires us to think in terms of opportunity costs, or what is given up when we take up something.

Suppose a husband is a better cook than his wife. But one day he feels inspired and needs to compose music at the time when he usually cooks. His wife knows that composing the music at this time means so much to her husband. She goes to the kitchen and cooks. This makes economic sense because her husband's best use of the time is composing music. The value of his improved well-being is much greater than the value of his cooking. If his wife really loves him, she should do the cooking. The dinner may not taste as nice, because she is not as good a cook as her husband, but this is secondary.

Apart from division of labor, emotional support and sharing of learning are also important in a love relationship. In Chapter 5 we will discuss at length the concept of mental capital. At this point it is sufficient to point out that each person owns some "mental capital" that could be a true asset but could also be a liability, depending on whether that mental capital is positive or negative. In general, someone with strong positive mental capital is better able to offer emotional support, advice and other forms of help to his or her spouse. For that reason, for someone who is married to someone with a lot of mental capital it is a real blessing, because the person will enjoy the positive spillover from the marriage partner.

Being married to one who has much less mental capital or even a lot of negative mental capital could be a pain. In general, trying to convert someone who has little Love mental capital into a loving person is a huge challenge and is normally not advisable; I can only say that this is normally very difficult. If you love a person a lot, you probably can put up with snoring or bad manners. But if that person has negative mental capital, such as a strong ego, lack of self-discipline or an abundance of grumbles all the time, there is little hope that that situation would turn around. Marrying such a person is likely to be a recipe for an unhappy marriage.

Attracting love and "tough love"

If one wants to improve the quality of life of the beloved, one should try to nurture love in the beloved, since the evidence that will be presented in the following chapters shows that love provides purpose and meaning to living and is significantly related to happiness. In order to nurture love, not only is it necessary to offer the person whom you love things that offer utility, such as good food, but also what may appear to cause disutility, such as hard work. As mentioned above, asking children to share some of the household work is an example, and this should be done at an early age, before they have learned to refuse. Young children will not be able to do things that require strength and skill and may not do well what they are asked to do, but that is not important. What is important is for them to learn that sharing the housework is the natural thing to do. It is important not to reprimand them for doing a bad job. Quite the contrary, even if they do a lousy job we should still commend them for their effort. Such words of encouragement and recognition provide a mental reward. By seeing how difficult it is to do a good job, they will learn to appreciate what other people do for them. This is the idea of "tough love."

Asking children to share the housework sometimes becomes a problem, since they may complain about "uneven sharing of the workload." This is potentially a problem with siblings who could be overly concerned about "fairness." Remembering that a sense of unfairness is a mental bad, reprimanding them for this may be inappropriate and ineffective. Instead, teaching by example—showing one's readiness to help without worrying if one has done more than one's fair share, and offering a mental good in the form of encouragement or appreciation for an uncalculating attitude—will work, especially when the children are still young.

Some parents pay children to do housework. This has both advantages and disadvantages. Working for pay is the way of the market, and children will have to learn the ways of the market sooner or later. However, within a family where love is treasured, the way of the market is not really the most appropriate.

Children need to learn to take work as driven by a desire to do good, and particularly by love. A loving person attracts love when he goes about his day-to-day activities thinking about doing good to others and to himself. As Erich Fromm (1956) explains in *The Art of Loving*, self-love is synonymous with loving one's own life and this is a precondition for loving others. Parents who know self-love will inspire self-love in the children. The corollary, obviously, is that parents who do not love themselves will *never* inspire self-love in their children. Loving parents will *always* inspire love in their children, even though patience will be needed. A seed, provided it is alive, will *always* germinate under the necessary conditions, provided that sufficient time is given for the germination to take place. Similarly, a loving husband/wife will inspire love from his spouse. Human emotions are such that they tend to attract and draw out the same kind. In psychology there is already a huge amount of literature on *emotional contagion*. So hate begets hate, and love begets love. This is a constraint that rational decision-makers have to accept as a fact of life.

Doing something together (such as working on the house or working on a fun project), enjoying something together (such as singing, dancing, cooking, or hiking), learning something together (such as learning a musical instrument) is an aspect of sharing. All this sharing—working together and sharing the fun together—can be looked upon as an investment in mental capital. From time to time parents may share their insights with children, and marriage partners may share their insights with each other on life and on other things. In this way they are companions in their life journeys.

It is common for parents to save the best foods and best of everything for their children. But we should resist this, and instead insist on the spirit of sharing, because sharing inspires mutual respect and consideration.

Self-love and personal growth

Learning to love oneself is the best way to learn how to love others effectively. This is an example of *learning by doing*. To the extent that human beings are tied by a common bond and share broadly similar characteristics, if we know how to love and take care of ourselves we also know how to love and take care of others. This is why both Western and Eastern cultures teach: "Don't do unto others what you don't want others to do unto you."

Consider the case of addiction. Consumption of addictive substances like tobacco, alcohol and drugs is very common, and some behaviors, like gambling and playing computer games, have also been found to be addictive. Becker and Murphy (1988) came up with the idea of "rational addiction," and stipulate that the goods are addictive because consumption of these goods leads to the accumulation of "addictive capital" or "addictive stock." This "addictive capital" is obviously a "negative capital," as it undermines the addict's long-term welfare. The central tenet of their paper is that, while the addictive stock momentarily increases utility as the addict engages in the addictive act, it has a negative impact on utility over the longer run. The "rational addict" has to find an optimal trade-off between the benefit from the short-term gain and the cost from the longer-term loss. The reduction in marginal utility over the longer run is due to increasing tolerance—a kind of "adaptation" or getting used to the excitement so that what excites becomes less exciting. However, Becker and Murphy ignore or forget the sense of loss of autonomy that afflicts the addict. This sense of loss of autonomy is a truly serious "mental bad." Drug addicts are not able to rationally achieve the optimal trade-off because of the "addictive stock" that has been accumulated.[7] Because the substance is addictive, addicts eventually discover that they are "hooked." When the time comes for another thrill there is little they can do but surrender to the biological clock that tells them this is the time for another intake of the substance. Typically, we find addicts frustrated with their loss of autonomy and therefore unhappy. Self-love would require steering oneself away from addictive substances.

Consider the related case of adopting a healthy lifestyle. This is important to ward off or postpone the onset of diseases that can debilitate or kill us. A healthy lifestyle is most effective when adopted at a young age. When our health stock has already been depleted, it is too late for prevention. But young people may not be aware of the adverse consequences of an unhealthy lifestyle, because they do not notice any immediate effect on their health. They are cheated by their apparently unaffected "functional health"—a health condition that allows bodily functions to go on, to ignore the depletion of the "stock of health"—a health condition such that functional health cannot continue very long (Ho, 2013).

Self-love is the key to personal growth. Personal growth is a process of self-discovery, so one gains independence and develops a "self-authoring mind"[8] and a strong sense of direction. One begins to feel more and more "on top of oneself," enjoying self-efficacy, resilience, hope, and optimism. Psychologists have called these four "psychological capital," but they are more like mental goods than mental capital and are grounded on Love, Insight, Fortitude, and

Engagement. Apart from resilience, which is synonymous with fortitude, self-efficacy, hope, and optimism are possible only because of the accumulation of LIFE mental capital, namely the mental habits that are synonymous with "increasing resources for wellbeing" (Maurer et al. 2023, p. 3). Maurer et al. explain that well-being is "a multidimensional concept, entailing both eudaimonic and hedonic aspects, including authenticity (the integration of self or integrity), harmony (Kjell et al., 2015), and life satisfaction (Diener 2009)."[9]

Thus self-love requires a forward-looking perspective. When we can take good care of ourselves and keep investing in positive mental capital and divesting negative mental capital, we help our beloved ones to do the same by example. We will revisit the subject of mental capital in Chapter 5.

Conclusions

The economics of love is about how to love effectively and efficiently, and a starting point of this is to understand that human beings do not live on bread alone, and to realize that our lives and those of our dear ones are the most valuable things in the world. We need to know that we all have mental good needs as well as physical good needs. Both needs have to be fulfilled for you to live a happy, fulfilling life. If you love someone—whether that someone is your lover, your spouse, your child or your friend—you would naturally care for his mental good needs as much as his physical needs, and you would like to love most efficiently and effectively given the limited span of your and his lives and the resources available. The resources include not only financial resources, but also the capability that one has accumulated over the years in the form of skills, wisdom and temperament, and the time invested in cultivating and nurturing this capability.

Box 3.4 is titled LIFE as the Happiness Formula. But it is meant not to replace Seligman's well-known happiness formula. It is meant only to spell out the most important voluntary factor in his formula, which is the accumulation of LIFE mental capital.

BOX 3.4 LIFE AS THE HAPPINESS FORMULA

Life is Wonder.
Living is to give Life a chance,
    the best chance, to show its true colors.
Fill your living with Life and Love.
Love yourself and others.

Insight is Wise Living.
Considerate, congruent, and contemplative:

Keep an eye on the big picture.
For what you see is all relative.

Fortitude is to Persevere.
Never worry about setbacks, which could be a Godsend.
For setbacks teach us,
So we can carry through and triumph in the end.

Engagement is to be passionate,
Passionate about things we do.
So we find meanings
And be to ourselves true.

Notes

1 Many parents, especially mothers, instinctively love their babies. Some do not. Evolution by natural selection suggests that babies whose mothers do not love them are more likely to die young and thus will not carry the "unloving gene" to the next generation.

2 Beth Sissons and Zawn Villines (2023) noted that "obsessive love disorder," a condition that is known to exist among some people, is not currently listed in the *Diagnostic and Statistical Manual of Mental Disorders*, 5th edition (*DSM-5*), and that obsessive love can be a sign of other mental health challenges and conditions. I would refrain from calling this possessiveness "love."

3 D. Richard Cookerly (2018), "The Definition of Love," available at www.whatislovedrcookerly.com/2018/02/the-definition-of-love_15.html. Accessed June 4, 2025.

4 See Sophy Thyn and Dabria Yiong (2022), "Article: Mothers in the Animal Kingdom," published May 8, available at https://theanimalwelfarestation.wordpress.com/2022/05/08/article-mothers-in-the-animal-kingdom/. Accessed June 4, 2025.

5 Yew-Kwang Ng coined the term "diamond good" to describe goods that are treasured because they are considered high-quality and precious. Paying a premium price on diamond goods could make the consumer feel good because the high price creates a perception of higher quality. For a discussion, see Xin Deng and Yew-kwang Ng (2004).

6 It is difficult to tell if he wanted to tell the world how much he loved his deceased wife or simply craved for the honor of being a great lover.

7 Becker coined the term "addictive stock", which is clearly a negative capital according to our definition because it undermines the pursuit of happiness.

8 See Forbes Coaches Council (2017) "What Having A Self-Authoring Mind Means," published Jan. 27, available at www.forbes.com/sites/forbescoachescouncil/2017/01/27/what-having-a-self-authoring-mind-means. Accessed June 4, 2025.

9 "Integration of self" or integrity is "Congruent" as in Ho's poem in Ho (2020, p.7), reproduced in Box 3.4. Needs for both physical goods and mental goods are

implicit in the reference to "eudaimonic and hedonic aspects"; authenticity and harmony are implicit in "considerate, congruent, and contemplative" and "be to ourselves true."

Key points to note

- Love is both a mental capital and a mental good.
- Love means a genuine and natural desire to give the best life to those that one loves.
- Since all humans need mental goods and physical goods to thrive, loving someone means that you want him or her to enjoy such mental goods as a sense of self-worth, peace of mind, self-efficacy, and sense of autonomy, etc., apart from having adequate material goods.
- Romantic love is romance plus love. Romance without love is possible. But it cannot compare with love in terms of life fulfilment.
- Lack of parenting skills and the daunting emotional requirements for parents are a key factor behind falling fertility around the world.
- Different relations may imply different ways of expressing or conveying love. But the nature of love is the same.

Some questions to ponder

- What is the relationship between personal development and love?
- What are the common mistakes parents make?
- Self-discipline is very important for wellbeing. How would you nurture self-discipline?
- Must lovers be "honest" with one another? Why or why not?
- Should young people have a dose of parenting education at school? Why or why not?
- Why is love important to sustainable development?

4

THE ROLE OF CULTURE IN HOUSEHOLD PRODUCTION AND SUSTAINABLE DEVELOPMENT

Culture is a way of life. Different peoples have different ways of life, but they have similar dreams and aspirations because human needs are universal: we all have similar physical needs to sustain life and the perpetuation of the human species; we all want peace of mind, a sense of self-worth, freedom, respect and acceptance by others, and "self-actualization." How we go about meeting these needs for physical and mental good needs are conditioned by culture. The efficiency or lack of efficiency of "household production" to produce the "end goods" we need matters a lot to the important subject of sustainability. Choice of culture matters a lot to sustainable development.

Introduction

It is a pity that modern economics takes culture and values as given. As a result, each individual is considered as a "utility-maximizing" decision-maker given his values and culture. This approach is fine if we want to explain how people behave, but counterproductive if economics is meant to offer advice so we can make the most of our lives and achieve sustainable development.

Actually, the most important choices in life relate to choices about culture and values. The economics of life differs from the economics of everyday life in that it confronts cultural choices explicitly. Choices about culture and value determine what kind of person we will be, and thus play an important role in our long-term well-being.

From an early age we are told that there is no right or wrong about culture and values. But to the extent that different norms and values lead to different well-being outcomes, and since we do care about well-being outcomes, we

DOI: 10.4324/9781003507093-4

need to be choosy about culture and values. Most cultural practices and norms that are associated with ethnicity do not matter much about welfare outcomes and do deserve our respect as merely a different way of life, but cultural influences such as excessive materialism and competition will undermine the quality of our lives.

Culture consists of all the implicit norms and values and ways in which people conduct their lives. Take what we eat for example. Pork is eaten by many people but not by Muslims or Jews. Jews only eat kosher foods, which excludes many foodstuffs, some of which must be prepared in specific ways in order to be kosher, as instructed in the book of Leviticus.

Take another example: in some communities, spiders, scorpions and worms are delicacies, which would be unthinkable in other communities. How we clothe ourselves is another example. Certain kinds of attire would be perfectly acceptable in some societies but utterly unacceptable in others. Despite all the differences, however, all human beings have to eat, and they need essentially the same nutrients in order to stay healthy; and all human beings need to be dressed in such a way as to be acceptable in their respective communities, and to be clothed to protect against cold and heat.

People of different cultural and ethnic backgrounds may prepare their food and eat differently, dress differently, worship differently, communicate with one another in different languages, and they may live in different kinds of homes. But despite all the differences, they are all human beings and are subject to the same physical and psychological laws that govern their lives as humans. We procure our different needs in different ways, but we share similar needs, emotions and aspirations. Although there are shades of meanings that are different, all languages, surprisingly, have similar words that convey very similar meanings, so that translations of novels, poems and speeches are possible and meaningful. Moreover, apart from the new words that have appeared in recent years on account of the technological revolution, most of the vocabulary that we have today has existed for a long time.

Human nature is by and large universal, the diversity of cultures and ethnicities notwithstanding.

It is important to note that culture crucially affects how we procure our needs, both mental and physical. Using the terminology of Gary Becker, we buy various goods and services in the marketplace, and through "household production" turn them into various "basic commodities" (my preferred terminology is "end goods") that enhance our well-being. My extension of Becker's hypothesis is that these "end goods" include both mental and physical goods, and that the technology of our household production or *household production functions* is conditioned by our cultural backgrounds and our past activities. More importantly, however, how different people procure the mental goods that they need has significant resource implications and matters a lot to sustainable development.

Culture is not value; ideology is not value

Culture determines how we procure our needs. Many people associate culture and ideology with values. But this is confusing means with ends. Humans share similar *ultimate values*, which are the fulfillment of the needs that Maslow identified. We all want a good life, to fulfill our physiological needs and our mental good needs, and to "self-actualize": making the most out of our lives. Culture has to do with the way we conduct our lives to procure our common needs. People naturally identify with their cultural heritage and the ideology that they cherish. But these "instrumental values" are not ultimate values. We hold on to these as values because they are like instruments that allow us to meet our identity and self-esteem needs as different peoples.

Because a sense of belonging is an important mental good, it is natural for us to identify with a culture that we are used to. In general, different ethnic groups have different cultural identities, and there is no right or wrong, or better or worse among different cultures. In a significant sense, cultural diversity is much valued for its own sake, because it testifies to the richness of life. Most governments today have learnt to preserve the cultural heritage of minorities.

Although our cultural heritages are all worth preserving so we know better how today's human society has come about, not all cultural heritages are good for humanity. Still, even the darker side of our heritages and history need to be remembered. Notwithstanding the differences in cultural heritages, humans have values that are common to all. We all want a good life; we all like our children to live in peace and happiness; we all treasure peace, freedom, respect, and self-actualization. These are our ultimate universal values. On the other hand, religious wars were human conflicts based on clashes of misconceived values. Historically, apart from plundering, humans have fought others trying to convert them to "their own kind." This desire has to do with humans' need for self-esteem and for identification. Although momentary success in these endeavors may make people feel safer or more secure, true security is possible and sustainable only when everybody feels safe and secure. Humans in the twenty-first century should be civilized in the sense that dialogues and reason should trump brute force and self-proclaimed ideological, racial, or cultural supremacy. We all need to be open-minded and be ready to seek what is needed for sustainable development and for world peace. Christopher Weber (2019, p.1) pointed out that "ideology has unique consequences in contemporary politics, as evidenced by increased political polarization, partisan-ideological sorting, and ideologically divisive rhetoric." The reason is that different camps holding different ideologies hold on to these ideologies without much examination or scientific doubt. Ideologies are often mistaken for values.[1] Obsession about an ideology prevents us from finding the best ways to organize our social, economic, and political activities and may lead us into unnecessary wars. Indeed, a culture of allowing one's perspective on the world to be dictated by one's long-held ideology without questioning is creating artificial constraints on personal growth.

In this context, we should re-examine the claim, made by Samuel Huntington (1993), that the "clash of civilizations" between the West and the East cannot be resolved because they cherish deep-seated values, reflecting

> views on the relations between God and man, the individual and the group, the citizen and the state, parents and children, husband and wife, as well as differing views of the relative importance of rights and responsibility, liberty and authority, equality and hierarchy.
>
> *(p.25)*

As "the products of centuries," any hope for reconciling the clash of civilizations would be slim, Huntington claims. From the perspective that different "civilizations" differ in culture and that different cultures are just different ways to achieve the same ultimate values, all that is needed for reconciling the clashes is humility and an open mind. For example, people may practice their religions in different ways. Why should this matter? People eat different foods. Can we respect people's choices? Much more fundamental are things like the Stoic virtues of wisdom, courage, temperance or moderation, and justice, which have their counterparts in the East. They are not much different from the Confucian virtues of wisdom, benevolence, courage and moderation.

Neither cultural arrogance nor ideological arrogance is helpful in our pursuit of a good life. Instead, there is always a need for humility and for self-examination over our ways of life to assess if and how we can do better. Some ways of life need to be abandoned because they produce undue suffering on some subgroups among us. For example, there was a time in China when it was believed that girls should bind their feet. There was a time in India that the caste system was legal because that was the accepted practice for many centuries. There was a time in America that women did not have the vote. There was a time in Europe, spanning over three centuries, when "witches" were hunted down, routinely tried, and burnt to death as if this was the will of God. Today the prevalent culture in America is for preservation of electoral democracy as an American value. But the ballot box is only a means to realizing equal political rights. Many authors, particularly Jason Brennon (2012, 2016), have called for a re-examination of the ballot-box based democratic system. We need to be open-minded and scientific in the search for a better alternative political system or an improved version of the election-based political system. In becoming more tolerant of alternative political systems, perhaps we could avoid a major confrontation between China and America, the world's two major powers. Cultural clashes, if they lead to a nuclear war, could end any prospect for sustainable development.

Cultural environment and personal culture

Depending on where we live and with what people one is associated, we are exposed to different cultural environments. However, even though, generally, the cultural environment in which we live has influences on us, we may, as individuals, respond in different ways to the same cultural environment and adopt totally different ways of life or personal cultures. For example, Warren Buffet and Donald Trump are both Americans and they are both extremely wealthy. Yet they have adopted totally different ways of life or "personal culture." Warren Buffett is reputed to still live in the same house he bought in 1958. Although the house is quite roomy, its market value in 2024 was not much more than $1.43 million according to one source.[2]

Donald Trump has many properties. His New York City residence is a gilded, three-level penthouse 66 stories up at the top of Trump Tower, his skyscraper at 725 Fifth Avenue. Trump told a *Forbes* reporter that his penthouse was the "best apartment ever built" and had an estimated value of at least $200 million. *Forbes* found that his estimate was inaccurate and the actual market value was probably around $54 million. Still, $54 million is many times more than Buffet's $1.43 million. While Trump loves to brag about his wealth and opts for a glamorous life Buffet prefers to be low key and lives a thrifty way of life. Trump opts for politics; Buffet has little ambition to advance within politics.

Still, the dominant cultural environment does have a huge influence on most people. In a society in which teachers, parents, and principals of schools all focus on examination results, it is difficult for students not to worry about grades. In a highly competitive environment, it is inevitable that students feel tremendous pressure trying to be at least above average. Yet, by definition, not everybody can be above average. Paradoxically, even though these days in Hong Kong a much bigger percentage of students in each cohort can enter university, pressures are higher than in the old days when just about 2 to 3% of the student population could be admitted to the only university that existed then, pressures on students have climbed tremendously. The reason is that, at that time, since the vast majority of students failed to get into university, not being admitted to a university was not a big deal.

When the cultural environment is toxic, it is not easy to stay aloof and maintain one's preferred way of life. It takes tremendous wisdom and strength not to be "infected" by the "cultural virus." Yet with a strong sense of direction and insight, it is possible. Those who have independent thinking deserve applause and serve as an example for the rest of us. Parents and teachers, please note.

The culture of the *nouveau riche*

China is now known to be a rapidly emerging luxury goods market, and many Chinese who belong to *nouveaux riches* want to display their newfound wealth to prove their worth.[3] They may be a small minority in a population of 1.4 billion. But they have attracted the ire of others. Yet they apparently take heart at others' anger, as if such anger were synonymous with envy, and other people's envy was the telling sign of their success. This kind of thinking is not unique to the Chinese. Kenneth Galbraith in *The Affluent Society* (1958) had already depicted the tendency of Americans to spend and spend, in order to "keep up with the Joneses," not in order to satisfy any "true needs." A more recent book by John de Graaf, David Wann and Thomas H. Naylor (2002) described the same phenomenon, and the authors aptly called it "affluenza," to underscore that the mentality is contagious, like influenza. In recent years I have come across the term "gigayacht" and discovered that this is the name of the game for the super-rich, who like to measure their success by the size and luxury content of their boats. This is how a CNN story described the nature of gigayachts[4]

> for the billionaire who has everything, sometimes a superyacht just isn't enough—that's why the world's wealthiest are buying "gigayachts."
>
> These boats are the ultimate status symbol—a sign of eminence, power and a seemingly limitless supply of cash. And when it comes to showing off wealth and status it seems the rule is 'the bigger the better'.
>
> 'There's definitely a "mine is bigger than yours" syndrome in this industry and there is a desire to have the best. That's the great thing about these yachts,' said Jonathan Beckett, CEO of Burgess Yachts, one of the world's leading yacht brokers.

It is interesting to note why some people need to spend so much to feel dignified, while others do not have the same need. To put it differently, some people can achieve the same mental good, that of feeling dignified, with very few resources, while some can achieve the same mental good only with a huge demand on the Earth's scarce resources. Indeed, some people feel dignified and particularly proud of leaving only a very small ecological footprint on Earth, while others feel dignified only by consuming hundreds or even thousands of times what the average human being on this planet consumes. Yet, as far as mental goods are concerned, extravagant people do not necessarily enjoy more. While rich people do consume more of the physical goods, they have long gone past the point of physical satiation. This is the key to understanding the Easterlin paradox (1974),[5] namely that while higher incomes apparently bring more happiness in cross-section studies in any single year, higher per capita incomes from decades of economic growth from after WWII to the early 1970s did not make Americans any happier. To acquire the mental goods that support mental health, one needs mental capital. Without progress in mental capital, the average happiness of Americans did not show any increase. The culture of out-competing one's peers or the "keeping up with the Joneses" culture is self-defeating due to the "treadmill effect."[6]

Inefficient household production

When I first learnt economics, I was confronted with the proposition of "non-satiation" that was presumed to be true. "Resources are limited, but human wants are unlimited, so human beings have to confront the perennial "economic problem of scarcity." The youthful mind in me wanted to challenge this view, and I came up with a concept akin to relative humidity: "in a given period of time, for any given good, there must be a physical limit to how much we consume to reach satiation, so relative satiation can be defined as a percentage, much like relative humidity is defined." But then I was told: "People may keep demanding better quality, and there is no end to the quality that people demand."

I would argue that the craze for the marginal improvement in quality of the musical sound or that of fine wine that comes with huge costs has more to do with "mental good needs" than with physical good needs. "Refined taste" is a sign of status and "high culture." From the sustainable development or the human welfare point of view, it just does not make much sense.

A book came out recently that directly challenges the concept of non-satiation. In the introduction of *How Much is Enough: Money and the Good Life*, Edward Skidelsky and Robert Skidelsky (2012) wrote:

> The premise of what follows is that the material conditions of the good life already exist, at least in the affluent parts of the world, but that the blind pursuit of growth puts it continually out of reach. Under such circumstances, the aim of policy and other forms of collective actions should be to secure an economic organization that places the good things of life—health, respect, friendship, leisure and so on—within reach of all. Economic growth should be accepted as a residual, not something to be aimed at.

The phrase "blind pursuit of growth" begs the question: why do people pursue growth blindly, and not for the good life? Why is there a rat race rather than a genuine pursuit of the good life? The simple answer is: people do not live on bread alone. There are things that money cannot buy (Sandel, 2012). People also want pride, recognition, a sense of success, love, peace, security, freedom from fear and autonomy. Many of the material goods that we buy are really aimed at filling our mental good needs, and not our physical needs. People spend huge amounts of money on luxury goods not so much because of the additional physical comfort or enjoyment derived from them but largely because they can then procure a sense of success, of superiority, of recognition. They join the rat race because they want to stay ahead of others.

But some people have freed themselves from the rat race, and they feel great success and joy, and, at the same time, a strong sense of being in command and at ease with themselves, without having to commit so much of our global resources.

Using the language of economics, we can say that those who seek greater wealth blindly have very inefficient household production functions. Remarkably, these inefficient production functions have to do with a materialistic culture. T. Kasser (2003) and Kasser et al. (2004) explained that such materialistic culture may have to do with "social modeling" and "insecurity." Social modeling, put simply, is following the example of others with whom one associates. Insecurity drives materialism because insecure people may believe that commanding more resources will offer them more security. Clearly, it is natural for people to be influenced by their peers, and desiring a greater sense of security is not morally wrong. But once acculturated to materialistic thinking, people tend to lose their sense of judgment. They tend to give up their ethical sense when it gets in their way as they seek greater wealth.

Paul Piff et al. (2012) found that rich people tend to be more tolerant of unethical behavior. The study consists of carefully designed experiments and observations of behavior in real life involving people from different backgrounds as test subjects. One experiment recruited 195 adults using Craigslist to play a game in which a computer was supposed to roll dice for the chance of winning a $50 gift certificate. The numbers each participant rolled were the same without the participants knowing it; anyone self-reporting a total higher than 12 was lying about their score. Those in wealthier groups were found to be three times as likely to lie as others.

Another test invited 108 adults, who were found through Amazon's Mechanical Turk (MTurk), to assume the role of an employer negotiating a salary with job seekers. They were told several things about the job, including that it was temporary. Upper class individuals were found less likely to disclose the temporary nature of the job.

Still another set of tests, which involved 426 cars, found that wealthier people tended to be less concerned about others' safety. First, about one third of drivers in expensive cars were found to cut off other drivers at an intersection watched by the researchers, about double those in cheaper cars. Second, almost half of the more expensive cars did not yield when a pedestrian entered the crosswalk while all of the lowest status cars did.

According to the authors, this could reflect "a set of *culturally shared norms* among upper class individuals." In particular, their wealth and status may disconnect them from others and make them less sensitive to other people's well-being. "It really shows the extreme lengths to which wealth and upper-rank status in society can shape patterns of self-interest and unethicality,"

Piff remarked.[7] An interesting question is: what drives unethical behavior? One study suggests that envy could be at work. Francesca Gino and Lamar Pierce (2009) reported how subjects working under an honor system to pay themselves according to the number of correct answers in an anagram task behaved differently when they were presented with the sight of two different piles of cash from which the payout was to be made. They found that participants were far more likely to overstate their performance when they had seen the bigger pile of cash than when they had seen the smaller pile. This suggests that people may be tempted to become unethical at the sight of a big pile of cash. Another experiment included questions assessing the propensity for envious feelings under different situations. The authors found that those whose responses to some questions suggested that they were more prone to envy and who saw the big cash pile cheated more, suggesting that envious people were stimulated to cheat by the sight of the big cash pile.

It seems that the "culturally shared norms" of the rich in part may have something to do with the fact that they are rich, in part with the greater diversity of wealth among the rich, and in part with certain ways and practices that are common to the business world in which they happen to live. If some are much richer than others, their lives become more and more detached from those of others. At the same time, within the relatively small circle of the rich, diversity of wealth is much bigger than that within the circle of ordinary working-class people. As the relative rise or fall may be quite rapid within this group the pressure to keep up with one's peers is quite intense among the rich, while among the circle of ordinary working-class people, getting ahead or falling is not such a big deal, because the number of ordinary folks is huge, and the relative rise or decline within this ocean of ordinary folks is often not even noticeable. Finally, in the business world where exchange of favors is often taken as good for mutual benefits, it is easy to develop an increasing tolerance of corrupt practices.

It would of course be wrong to think of rich people as all sharing similar norms and values. Again, Warren Buffett is vastly different from Donald Trump, for instance. One is low-key and does not care much for a luxurious life; the other is all for glamor and the high life. A good question is: what makes them so different?

Actually Warren Buffett and Donald Trump, as well as you and me, are the same in that each of us tends to make reference to a group as our peers. In general, everyone has a strong desire not to fall behind one's peers in the dimensions considered important by those peers. Besides, everyone has an inclination to act in a way that is regarded as acceptable by people in the reference group. Warren Buffett and Donald Trump are different in large part because they see different people as their peers. Very often, this makes all the difference in the formation of culturally shared norms, and here, crucially, choice comes in. Choosing whom we associate with and take as peers determines what kind of people we will be. As much as "affluenza" is contagious, some people can get immunized, largely through their prior choice of models for emulation. Then, even though they are quite affluent, they may not share the same norms as those who contract the "affluenza virus."

Efficient household production

There is thus such a thing as acculturation through social modeling. If we socialize and associate with people who are ethical, who believe in conservation, who love nature more than the high life, we tend to adopt similar values, because that is how we gain recognition by those we are associated with. Then the "production" of crucially needed mental goods through various household activities will become much more efficient. In a fundamental sense, people acculturated to a simpler, less extravagant lifestyle are no less happy than those who leave a very costly ecological footprint every day of their lives, because, like them, they are able to achieve the respect and recognition of those that they associate with. In Figure 4.1, we can see that just because the household socializes and identifies with people who prefer to leave a small ecological footprint in their activities, the "household production function" has become different. Less input is required, and yet the mental goods aren't that much different from those in Figure 4.2.

One may, of course, query the definition of luxury goods and non-luxury goods. We know that many of the goods that were considered luxury goods in the past may not be considered luxury goods at all today. Air conditioners, televisions (particularly color televisions) and refrigerators are today considered

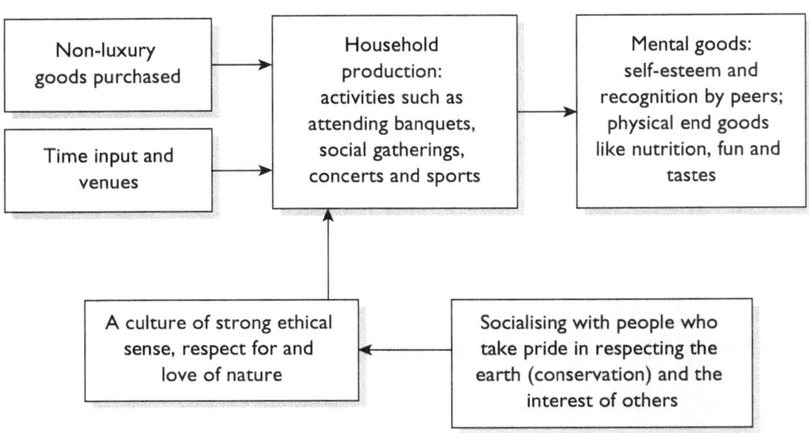

FIGURE 4.1 Efficient household production.

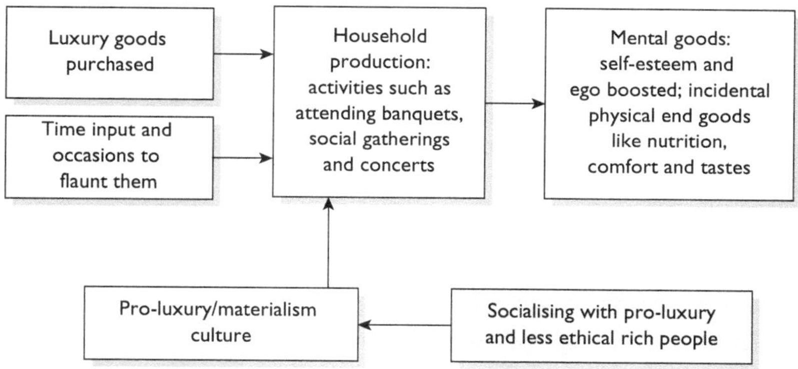

FIGURE 4.2 Inefficient household production.

necessities in many places. In the present context, however, "luxury goods" refers specifically to goods that are acquired to show off one's wealth and status, and so they are synonymous with conspicuous consumption. Conspicuous consumption is intended clearly not just for the physical benefit of the actual goods, but, more importantly, for the benefit of the mental good derived—the thought that one is somehow better placed than others in wealth or in lifestyle. Professor Yew Kwang Ng (1987) coined the term "diamond goods" to refer to goods that offer consumers utility beyond the utility from the physical qualities of the goods, in particular utility based on the knowledge that the good is scarce and costly—sufficient to put their owners in a class distinct from others.

While "diamond goods" and conspicuous consumption in general certainly contribute to utility, and rich people certainly can afford and normally do consume more luxury items, a huge body of literature now suggests that incomes above a certain level may not bring much additional happiness at all. Recent examples include Daniel Kahneman and Angus Deaton (2010), and Richard Easterlin et al. (2010). Kahneman and Deaton noted that "when plotted against log income, life evaluation rises steadily. Emotional well-being also rises with log income, but there is no further progress beyond an annual income of $75,000." Life evaluation is a measure of "total life satisfaction" with respondents evaluating their current life on the Cantril Self-Anchoring Scale, in which 0 is "the worst possible life for you" and ten is "the best possible life for you." Given the way "satisfaction" is normally understood, the respondent is likely to interpret more in terms of material well-being and then only secondarily in terms of mental goods. As such it is no wonder that higher income leads to a higher rating. But Kahneman and Deaton's plotting of positive affect, "stress-free," and "not blue" (i.e. not sad nor worrying), against income shows that these dimensions of well-being clearly level off roughly around an annual income of around $75,000. These aspects of "emotional well-being" reflect mental goods and suggest that people with very high incomes typically do not enjoy mental goods any more than people with an "adequate income," which would have amounted to approximately $75,000 in the United States in 2010.

Easterlin and his coauthors (2010) found that the "happiness–income paradox" holds not only for developed countries, which was the earlier finding, but also for developing countries and such transitioning economies as the Eastern European countries that were previously socialist planned economies as well, if one looks at data over ten years and beyond. In particular, while China doubled its real per capita income in less than ten years, and South Korea and Chile in 13 and 18 years respectively, "one might think many of the people in these countries would be so happy, they'd be dancing in the streets." But Easterlin and his coauthors were surprised to find nothing like that. Although these countries have made big advances in procuring the physical goods for their compatriots, apparently they have been extraordinarily unsuccessful in improving the lots of their compatriots in terms of advancing "emotional well-being" through procuring the mental goods that their compatriots aspire for. Keeping up with the Joneses somehow produces only a fleeting increase in utility, an increase that evaporates into thin air in no time, because not everyone can be ahead of others.

Conclusions

Culture plays a key role in the efficiency of household activities in generating the mental goods that all people need to live a happy life. Culture is related to the decisions, often made without our awareness or careful deliberation, as to whom we associate and socialize with. Once we have identified whom we regard as our peers, we seek their acceptance and recognition by trying to perform according to the standards and value system of this peer group. If our identified peers all value a luxurious life, we will tend to be like them and strive to live a luxurious life so we can achieve self-esteem and recognition by our peers. Household production of the mental good "self-esteem" will then become very costly. On the other hand, if our identified peers all value a simple life, we will not need to spend much, and yet we will still enjoy the same mental good.

In general, the cultural environment in which one lives tends to mold our thinking and way of life. However, there are always individuals who are somehow "immunized" and unaffected by "affluenza" or other toxic influences, such as bigotry and discrimination, that prevail in society at large. They have developed a "pro-LIFE culture," able to live a life with Love, Insight or Wisdom, Fortitude, and Engagement.

There are even spiritually inspired individuals whose love extends to all humanity and even other forms of life. Instead of identifying with people who live around them, they identify with certain spiritual teachers who may be historical figures or legendary spiritual teachers. Their self-esteem then is based on the standards set by their spiritual teachers. Their sense of self-worth cannot be corrupted.

As we will see in the next chapter, personal culture is an aspect of ***mental capital***, and mental capital can be positive or negative. We should invest in positive "mental capital" that dramatically increases the efficiency of the production function and avoid building up negative mental capital.

Notes

1 Jost et al. (2003 and Jost, 2017) did mention "ideological needs" but considered that ideological preferences as a means to bolster a group's standing in society.
2 See Jeannine Mancini (2024), "Warren Buffett Still Lives in the Home He Bought Back in 1958 for $31,500—It's Worth $1.43 Million Today and He 'Couldn't Imagine Having a Better House'—But Says He Would Have Made 'Far More Money' Renting Instead," published February 20, available at https://finance.yahoo.com/news/warren-buffett-still-lives-home-173015366.html. Accessed June 4, 2025.
3 After Covid-19, there seems to be a change. It is not clear if this is due to an awakening or a result of the weak housing market.
4 The rise of the "gigayacht": Why size matters to the super rich | CNN September 15, 2011. https://edition.cnn.com/travel/article/rise-gigayacht/index.html
5 Easterlin (1974) explained this paradox by alluding to reference to social norms. In his words, "In judging their happiness, people tend to compare their actual situation with a reference standard or norm, derived from their prior actual situation with a reference standard or norm" (p.118). In a more recent article Easterlin et al. (2010) showed that the paradox also applies to developing countries. See www.pnas.org/content/107/52/22463.abstract?sid=6699db95-04ed-45af8450-074fe609aa6f
6 See The Hedonistic Treadmill: Understanding Its Role in Human Well-Being, available at www.all-about-psychology.com/the-hedonistic-treadmill-understanding-its-role-in-human-well-being.html
7 See "Rich people more likely to take lollies from children: study," Australian Broadcasting Corporation, Tue 28 Feb 2012, available at www.abc.net.au/news/2012-02-28/upper-class-people-more-likely-to-cheat-says-study/3856172. Accessed June 4, 2025.

Key points to note

- Culture is a way of life. Values are what are desired and cherished.
- Ultimate values are the final values that humans seek. Instrumental values are values that people seek largely to satisfy identity needs, but they can stand in the way of ultimate values.

- Household production transforms inputs into outputs. Inputs include time, market goods, and mental capital. Outputs are physical end goods and mental goods which are counted in the well-being of the household.
- Culture affects the way we transform inputs into outputs in household production. It is a way of life.
- Sustainable development is development based on taking a long view so that our progeny can enjoy what the planet offers us today.
- Sustainable development requires humans to scientifically assess the opportunities and constraints they face without being biased by ideology or misperceived values.

Some questions to ponder

- Why is culture an important consideration to achieve sustainable development?
- Is politics inevitably divisive? Why or why not?
- What is the greatest threat to sustainable development?
- Can you name some misconceived values? Explain why they are misconceived values.
- Is the clash of civilizations inevitable? What is the nature of this "clash of civilizations"?
- Are western and eastern civilizations intrinsically different?

5

MENTAL CAPITAL AND HABIT FORMATION, WITH A DIGRESSION TO SPIRITUAL CAPITAL

The formation of good habits is the key to a good life. Good habits are good because they help us achieve our dreams. Bad habits are bad because they undermine self-actualization and success in life. Habits take time to form and take time to break. Forming useful habits is an investment in our lives. Useful mental habits are called mental capital. Habits that inhibit personal growth are called negative mental capital.

Introduction

As discussed in Chapter 3, the psychological term "psychological capital" refers to four qualities that serve as an asset to individuals, allowing them to overcome difficulties and achieve better outcomes. These include *self-efficacy*, *optimism*, *hope* and *resiliency* (Luthans and Youssef, 2004). Self-efficacy is a "belief in one's capacities to organize and execute the course of action required to produce given attainments." Optimism is a belief that any negative factor is likely to be temporary and specific to a situation while the positive factors are permanent and more general. Hope is "having the will power and the pathways to attain one's goals." Resilience is the ability to tough it out through adversity and to bounce back from disappointments and failures. These qualities are seen to contribute to better work performance and psychological health.

In this chapter, I shall discuss an alternative but related concept called "mental capital," which is more akin to the concept of "capital" as used in economics. Economists define "capital" as a produced means of production. Thus, firms invest to acquire the machinery and equipment and buildings to

DOI: 10.4324/9781003507093-5

help them produce, while individuals acquire human capital to become more productive and competitive in the job market. "Investing" is accumulating capital. The services of capital assets form a "factor of production" or an input used in the production of outputs. So mental capital is the mental capability of an individual that accumulates over the years and that contributes to production, which may be in a commercial or household setting.

When the mental capital is in the form of skills and a capacity that contribute to commercial/economic production it is called human capital, and the pertinent skills can be called "job skills." When the mental capital is in the form of skills and a capacity that contribute to household production, it can be called life capital, and the pertinent skills can be called life skills. Two of the most important life skills are "reflective skills" and "learning skills," which are related and which will be further discussed below. Four types of life capital are fundamental to personal growth. They are Love, Insight, Fortitude, and Engagement, collectively called "LIFE mental capital" (Figure 5.1).

In household production the end goods include physical end goods and mental goods. The former include nutrition, what we see, hear, and taste, and sense with our body. The latter include good company, a sense of autonomy, self-efficacy, confidence, self-esteem, composure, sense of success and sense of self-actualization. The household production activities could be dinners, watching movies, picnicking, and other activities.

Figure 5.2 shows that ***mental capital can potentially grow into spiritual capital.*** As an individual gains more mental capital and benefits from it, a wish

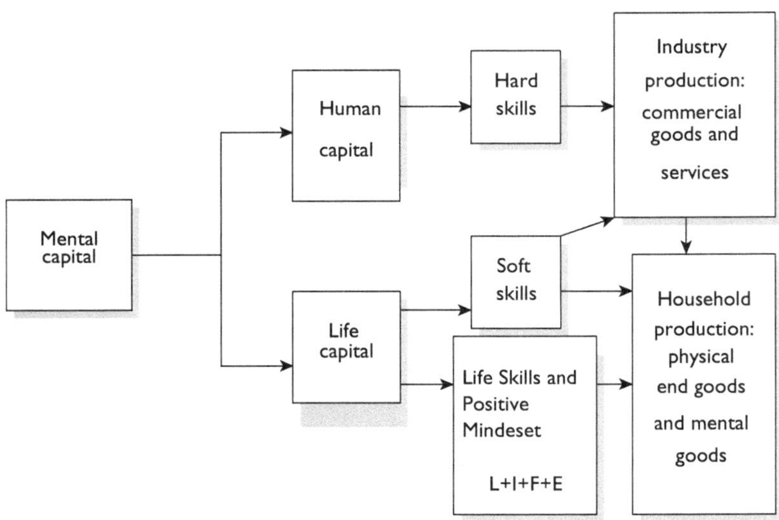

FIGURE 5.1 Mental capital.

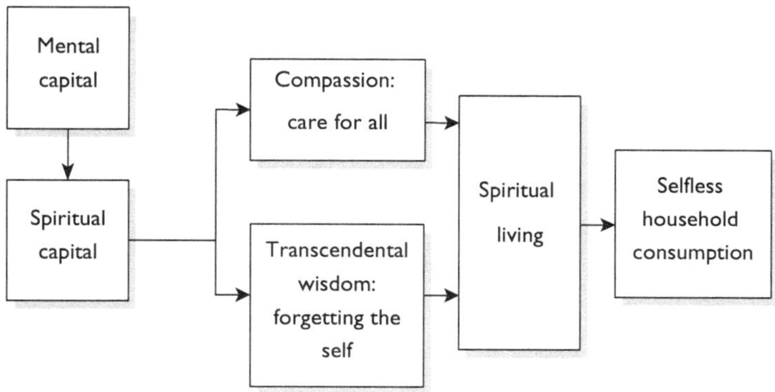

FIGURE 5.2 Spiritual capital.

that the same benefit can be enjoyed by others may grow. As this wish grows, the individual gradually broadens his perspective, eventually transcending the ego, and develops a compassion for all others. Forgetting him-/herself, he simply goes about doing everything that needs to be done and within his capacity. In so doing he maximizes the welfare for humanity to the best of his ability without thinking about himself. Even as he eats and drinks to maintain his survival and keeps his health, he does that because that is his duty. Using the Kantian terminology, his *categorical imperative* is to serve humanity selflessly.

The concept of spiritual capital has attracted research from mainstream economists and other social scientists. According to the John Templeton Foundation:[1]

> The specific term 'spiritual capital' refers to that aspect of social capital linked with religion and/or spirituality. In the last ten years, Robert Fogel (University of Chicago and 1993 Nobel Laureate in Economics) and others have explored and used the term. In one sense, then, spiritual capital might be seen as a significant subset of social capital. According to Robert Putnam's influential work on social capital, religion is by far the largest generator of social capital in the United States, contributing to more than half of the social capital in the country.

Ho (2012) distinguished *social spiritual capital* from an individual's spiritual capital.

> Social spiritual capital does not refer to the number of churches, mosques, temples, and other worshipping places that can be found in a country.

> Social spiritual capital refers, rather, to the interconnectedness of the human existence that awakens each individual to the common roots of humanity. *(p.47)*

An individual's spiritual capital, on the other hand, refers to an individual's capacity to think beyond him-/herself and even to forget him-/herself, simply devoting his life to making life a bounty rather than a burden for everyone. Fully developed spiritual people do this as part of their nature, because they have transcended the ego into human beings beyond their physical being[2] (Figure 5.2).

Formation of habits

As we live, the thoughts and activities we go through each day have an impact on us. As we keep repeating certain waysof thinking, speaking, or behavior, we form habits, and as habits form, our responses to stimuli become automatic, and gradually out of our conscious control. At this point we have effectively programmed ourselves to respond to certain tasks or responses as if this is our second nature. These automatic, reflexive responses can be good for us or bad for us. Without these automatic or reflexive responses, musicians cannot possibly play their music, for example. It would then be virtually impossible for performers to play their pieces and be able to express their emotions. There is simply no time to think between one note and the next note, or one group of notes and the next group of notes. The training of the musical performer consists of many years of repetitive training so that, in the end, music-making becomes almost automatic. Musical sense and musical playing skills are a form of mental capital.

On the other hand, there are reflexive and habitual responses that may be bad—not because moralists call them bad but because they end up undermining our personal growth and well-being. For example, if children grow up living in an environment in which they are criticized in an unfriendly manner that makes them hate to be criticized, their self-defense mechanism may build up so that they automatically reject even friendly criticisms and spontaneously give excuses when anything goes wrong. This might prevent them from learning from their mistakes. Other bad habits include procrastination, not fastening the seatbelt in cars, losing our temper at irritations, and carelessness. Some may disagree that losing our temper is a habit. But it is indeed a habit, meaning that people can train themselves not to lose their temper.[3]

Ann Graybiel, the Walter A. Rosenblith professor of neuroscience in MIT's Department of Brain and Cognitive Sciences, saw some physiological reasons behind why bad habits were hard to break. She noted that, when habits are formed, often through repetitive behavior in certain contexts that offer specific stimulations, such as smoking and gambling, neural activity patterns in a specific region of the brain are changed. "It is as though, somehow, the brain retains a memory of the habit context, and this pattern can be triggered if the right habit cues come back."[4] As much as we may like to kick a habit, the sight of a trigger, such as the sight of a piece of chocolate for someone who wants to control their weight, could ruin all previous effort. When a bad habit is formed, it becomes a negative mental capital that keeps undermining our well-being, because we would then effectively lose control of ourselves, and succumb to the potentially ruinous inertia that prevents us from reaching greater goals that we have identified.

On the other hand, when good habits are formed, they keep benefiting us, and they become part of our (positive) mental capital. This mental capital benefits us in several ways:

- We will be able to draw on it when we need it, and the reflexes that we have acquired allow us to do things that we otherwise cannot accomplish, so we gain self-efficacy.
- As we gain more mental capital, we also gain more confidence, which is a mental good. Confidence allows us to realize our potential and gain optimism.
- An important aspect of mental capital is that we become better organized and able to plan ahead to achieve specific goals. This gives us the promise of a better future which we reckon to be within our reach. So we gain hope.
- We also gain resilience in due course. Since learning from a mistake has become a habit, we reckon that mistakes and failures contribute to our growth. Instead of being beaten by the failure or hurt by the mistake, we will learn and gain more skills and confidence. This contributes to a virtuous circle of learning and growth.

As was noted in Chapter 3, self-efficacy, optimism, hope, and resilience are all components of psychological capital, and it has been demonstrated that they are related to self-esteem.[5] Moreover, psychological capital and self-esteem may affect mental health among adolescents. Given that sense of self-worth is more related to self-evaluation, while self-esteem is often related to other people's evaluation, "core self-evaluation"[6] is really about a sense of self-worth. We can say that good habit formation is essential to our sense of self-worth. A strong sense of self-worth protects us from anxiety due to unfavorable judgment by others or fear of the loss of something that we initially gain and cherish but cannot hold on to.[7]

Charles Duhigg, in his bestseller *The Power of Habit: Why We Do What We Do in Life and Business*, published in 2012, recounts dozens of real stories of people transforming their lives from chaos to order, from flop to success, from lack of direction to meaningful and fruitful pursuits. And every time a

TABLE 5.1 Self-esteem and self-worth: a comparison

	Self-Esteem	*Self-Worth*
Meaning	It is self-acceptance in a broad sense. This is a universal need identified in Maslow's hierarchy of needs.	It is self-acceptance that is based on a growth mindset and is synonymous with "core self-evaluation."
Source	Often based on evaluation by one's peers.	Always based on a growth mindset that keeps building up LIFE mental capital.
Effects on mental health	Self-Esteem makes one feel good, but self-esteem that is based on recognition by one's peers may lead to anxiety and may weaken resilience.	Self-Worth makes one feel good, and the growth mindset strengthens resilience. Self-worth helps self-efficacy, hope, and optimism.

miracle happened, it is because the person, at a crucial point in life, decided to change one of his old habits and focused his mind on it. As Duhigg demonstrates, entire organizations and even societies can be transformed when habits change. Like Graybiel, Duhigg pointed out that changes in habits ultimately lead to physical changes in the brain, which at once informs us of the daunting task of breaking a bad habit and the desirability of forming good habits.

If Duhigg convinces you about the importance of habit formation, James Claiborn and Cherry Pedrick (2001) and Travis Bradberry and Jean Greaves (2009) offer clues as to how to break old habits, most importantly by raising our self-awareness, or mindfulness—realizing that we are slipping back to the old habits whenever we do so, and by constant self-reminders about the desirability of the goal that we have set for ourselves. Self-reflection through writing a daily journal about our own failures or successes at handling our habits is a strategy of raising and reinforcing such awareness. Habits that undermine personal growth and the endeavour for self-actualization can be called negative mental capital.

Just as the four dimensions of psychological capital are direct outcomes of habits, so are the five dimensions of Seligman's PERMA, which stands for Positive Emotion, Engagement, Positive Relationships, Meaning, and Accomplishments or Achievements. Achievements are never fortuitous. They require identifying goals, working out a strategy, learning from mistakes, overcoming mistakes, hard work, all with the requisite skills that are themselves the results of habit formation. Meaning is possible only when people have a strong sense of purpose, which love and learning and active living (Engagement) offers. Relations among people always need to be built up through interactions and the cherishing of those interactions. Engagement as mental capital is the habit of active or purposive living. Active living with Love, Insight, Fortitude, and Engagement produces Positive Emotions like self-efficacy, confidence, optimism and hope. Accumulating habits that are truly useful and good for us (positive mental capital) and emptying out habits that stand in the way of personal growth, offer the pathway to personal growth and form the basis of self-efficacy, optimism, hope and resilience—the psychological capital that psychologists talk about.

Reflecting, imitating, drilling, and learning

Human behavior is mostly driven by desires and *motivations*. This means that there are certain goals that people want to achieve, and then they go about trying to achieve them. Sometimes people do not consciously identify the goals yet pursue them instinctively; sometimes they consciously pursue what they want. When individuals succeed in achieving those goals they reckon that they have done the right thing, and tend to take the same strategy or act the same way the next time they want to achieve their goal. A crucial question is: what will they do if they fail?

There are two diametrically different responses to a failure. A common response is to be upset. We could let out our anger in an outburst that could be very destructive. Without being aware of the consequences, we could hurt people close to us, and damage relations between them and us. If those near to us are themselves emotionally vulnerable, serious consequences could occur. When we are upset we might blame others or the circumstances for preventing the achievement of our goals. In focusing on the blame game, we lose sight of the mistakes that we may have made, and the opportunity for self-correction. Once we have developed a habit of getting angry and blaming this and that for our failures, negative capital forms, and then it will be very difficult to break away from this. People can fall into a very miserable life.

On the other hand, we could conduct a careful and systematic assessment of why we failed. This is called *reflection*. Realizing what was not done right, we would learn how we could do better next time. Good reflective skills would involve an objective, systematic assessment of the circumstances and the reasons for the failure. Perhaps we may not have been well enough prepared; perhaps we may have missed signs that would have warned us not to do what we did; perhaps we should have been better organized, and so on and so forth.

One still can never guarantee success the next time. Often there will be uncontrollable factors that cannot be anticipated in advance. But with reflection and learning, the chances for success the next time will be that much higher. More importantly, even if we still fail, the reflection and learning imply that we are "growing up," and not just "growing old." "Growing up" is itself a huge success and makes our lives that much more meaningful and fun.

In a sense, learning is the gradual formation of an appropriate reflex to a situation. For some people, reflecting has become a habit. Whenever they have gone through a new experience, they automatically look back to assess what they have done right and how they could have done better. The habit of reflection is a tremendous mental capital.

Learning a musical instrument or a new language is obviously the acquisition of new reflexes. In learning a language, for example, simply understanding how a foreign language works and its grammar will not allow you to use it. To use a new language requires a reflexive response whenever it is used. There is no time to think through the sentence structure and the vocabulary. All that needs to be spoken must be spoken spontaneously. When a new language habit is formed, the mental capital will be enhanced. To acquire a new language, considerable drilling is required, consciously or unconsciously. The same applies to learning a musical instrument. Without acquiring the needed reflexes, and just relying on logic and understanding, it is like learning to swim onshore. It will never work.

Usually it takes a lot of effort, and it needs motivation. For adults who clearly know what they want, the motivation will be there, but then they could easily succumb to laziness or the curse of "not having enough time," which often reflects a habit of making an excuse. Overcoming excuses is a big challenge that promises personal growth.

For children who may not know what they want, often it is the parents who want them to learn something. Sometimes parents like to offer material rewards as a lure to motivate. But psychologists have long found that material rewards may not be very effective, and they certainly are not reliable. They can only motivate for some time, but they seldom become an engine that keeps giving the child the energy and enthusiasm to learn. The greatest motivation for children is always intrinsic: when they find learning brings mental good rewards, such as the satisfaction of achievement, the joy of mastering a skill, the joy of cracking a puzzle, etc. Parents who want to spark children's enthusiasm in learning should try to make learning a source of fun or at least not a punishing experience. Too many parents unknowingly make learning a punishing experience. Imagine a child starting to learn a new task being yelled at when he cannot do it well. Imagine you are the child, and Mom keeps saying that you are not doing it right and demanding that you do better. That is a punishing experience that you will never forget. Such a punishing experience will haunt a child for a long time. Learning will then be associated with the punishing experience. Can we blame the child for his lack of enthusiasm and interest in learning?

On the other hand, if a child is not doing so well but the parent expresses appreciation for the child's effort and tells him that he is already pretty good for a beginner, and that he shows great promise at being quite good at it before long. The child is likely to be motivated.

Habits and the genius within

There is another sense in which habits can become a negative mental capital or a positive mental capital. When we have become so used to a way of thinking that we automatically forget the possibility of an alternative we will have lost the possibility of creativity. When we are so used to our personal experience we may simply rule out the possibility of anything that is out of our experience. Before human beings ever flew, flying was considered impossible. Humanity had to wait until 1903 when the Wright brothers invented, built and successfully tested the world's first airborne vehicle. Before the telephone was invented, no one took Alexander Graham Bell seriously when he claimed he could make a gadget that would allow people to converse over a longer distance than the human voice could naturally travel. We could easily assume we could not do this, and even ridicule the inventor for being silly. Humans tend to be conditioned by their limited experience and lack of an open mind. Those who have imagination and an open mind make history.

Breaking from a way of thinking that has become a habit is sometimes just what it takes to become a genius. We cannot live without reflexes. But we must not be confined by our reflexes. We are so used to logical and linear thinking—step-by-step arguments and derivations—that we automatically follow such lines of thinking. Thinking "out of the box" is needed to break new ground. This is sometimes called lateral thinking.[8]

Conclusions

Mental capital, consisting of good habits and useful reflexes, benefits our lives and allows us to achieve our dreams. But people can accumulate negative mental capital in the form of bad habits that undermine the pursuit of our dreams. The habits and reflexes are good or bad not because a moralist tells us they are good or bad, but because they benefit or harm our longer-term interest. In a substantive sense, as we try to make the most out of our lives subject to constraints, mental capital pushes out our constraints, while negative mental capital creates additional constraints.

Interestingly, as we accumulate more and more mental capital we automatically gain confidence in ourselves and enjoy a sense of autonomy, a sense of self-worth that is not dependent on other people's judgment of ourselves. We become immensely happier. With a strong stock of mental capital, we are more at ease, because we know that we have become masters of ourselves, which is the basis of our self-worth. We will have gained self-efficacy, optimism, hope and resilience, which comprise what psychologists call "psychological capital." We will be better able to do what we want, be less affected by anxiety and stress, and we will know our limits and avoid creating excessive pressures for ourselves. The world for that reason has become wonderful!

Notes

1 See "Spiritual Capital," avilable at templeton.org/2004/horiz03.html. Accessed April, 11, 2012.
2 See Ho (2020) for a fuller discussion of human spirituality.
3 Steven Stosny, "The Anger Habit," *Psychology Today*. November 24, 2019, available on Psychology Today website, accessed June 4, 2025.
4 Cathryn M. Delude (2005) "Brain Researchers Explain Why Old Habits Die Hard" | MIT News | Massachusetts Institute of Technology, published October 19, available at https://news.mit.edu/2005/habit. Accessed June 4, 2025.
5 Christina Hibbert (no date). "Self-Esteem Is a Myth," available at www.drchristina hibbert.com/5-reasons-self-esteem-is-a-myth/. Accessed June 4, 2025.
6 Paloş R, Samfira EM, Vîrgă D and Purić D (2023) "The Core Self-evaluations, Psychological Capital, and Academic Engagement: A Crossnational Mediation Model." *Front. Psychol.* 14:1189665. doi: 10.3389/fpsyg.2023.1189665
7 This is called fear of happiness or cherophobia.
8 See De Bono (1970).

Key points to note

- Positive mental capital comprises all mental habits, which include skills of all kinds, including job skills, the life skills of reflections and learning, social skills, homemaking skills, and LIFE mental capital.
- Negative mental capital, like positive mental capital, is accumulated over time. Negative mental capital includes procrastination, arrogance, addiction to gambling, etc.
- Habits take time to accumulate and we virtually become someone that is the result of our habits. Choosing what habits to develop in our formative years are especially important. Parents and aspiring take note.
- LIFE, i.e., Love, Insight, Fortitude, and Engagement can push out constraints and enable us to realize our dreams so life becomes fulfilling.

Some questions to ponder

- Can we all "choose to be happy"?
- What is the nature of self-efficacy?
- What makes people over-confident?
- What is overthinking? Why do some people overthink?
- Which specific mental capital is the most important for personal growth? Why?

6

THE HAPPINESS FORMULA, THE ROLE OF VOLUNTARY ACTION, AND VALUES IN ACTION[1]

Martin Seligman pointed out that happiness is the result of what is set by nature (genes), circumstances, and voluntary factors. Because among these three only voluntary factors are within our command, we should focus on these factors and in particular on how we can accumulate the qualities that are favorable to achieving a fulfilling life. Investing in our Love, Insight, Fortitude, and Engagement mental capital becomes the formula for the enduring level of happiness. It feeds personal growth and builds a strong sense of self-worth that will prevail over adversities and difficulties. The LIFE formula happens to correspond to the Values in Action proposed by Peterson and Seligman and has the additional pedagogical advantage of being easy to remember and more coherent.

Introduction

We equate happiness with subjective well-being (SWB). Thus, a person's happiness is not for anyone else to define except the person him-/herself, whose personal experience for good or for ill is the litmus test for its validity. Still, we need to distinguish between a moment's joy or excitement and a more "enduring level of happiness," which was the subject of discussion in Martin Seligman's book *Authentic Happiness* (2003). It is also exactly this enduring level of happiness that is the subject of study in this book.

Seligman, widely considered the father of positive psychology, asked us to consider the equation:

$$H = S + C + V \qquad \text{[equation 6.1]}$$

DOI: 10.4324/9781003507093-6

where, according to Seligman, H is "the enduring level of happiness," S is "your set range," C is "the circumstances of your life," and V represents "factors under your voluntary control."

The "enduring level of happiness" is not just about happiness "these days." Unfortunately, this is the way the key happiness question is often asked in many questionnaires in happiness studies.[2] The enduring level of happiness is certainly not the same as the mood of the moment; neither is it the "utility" derived from a smartphone or an experience or that from an episode in life. The enduring level of happiness is "taking everything together, and looking at your life as a whole, how happy or unhappy you are."

This *enduring level of happiness*, by definition, does not change from moment to moment, even though one's assessment of it may vary somewhat from time to time, and measurement error could exist as the respondent may perceive the question differently from what is intended. Moreover, these assessments will unavoidably be influenced by situational factors. Still, in asking a person to assess his life as a whole, you are inviting him to take a holistic view of his life, or in other words, assess his Total Life Satisfaction.

Since people's subjective reports of well-being or Total Life Satisfaction do vary from time to time while the true enduring level of happiness should be quite stable, we would amend the interpretation of that equation and propose that S mirrors the real enduring level of happiness and is unobservable while H is the reported happiness score that includes deviations from the enduring level due to various factors. Because S is the enduring level of happiness, it does not have a range. Moreover, while S is stable, it is not set in stone. This stable enduring level of happiness S will change with the accumulation of mental capital, which can be positive or negative.

We would propose, therefore, that the reported happiness score H consists of a score on the enduring or stable level of happiness that depends on both inherited genes G and voluntarily accumulated mental capital $V1$, and a short-term deviation from that more stable level that depends on circumstances beyond one's making t and voluntary actions $V2$. Thus we can write:

$$H = S(G, V1) + C(t, V2) \qquad \text{[equation 6.2]}$$

In responding to an interviewer who asks for an assessment of overall happiness, it is expected that the circumstantial effects will also be reflected in the answer. So, again, the set point or enduring level of happiness is unobservable. Overall happiness is expected to include deviations due to circumstances. H should be reported happiness while the enduring level of happiness should be S.

Moreover, given the imprecision of language, in responding to a question on "Total Life Satisfaction" respondents will likely assess if there is something in their life that they would consider not totally satisfactory. Most blind people would prefer that their eyesight could be restored. Inevitably no one will be fully satisfied with everything. As mortals we make mistakes and we cannot be totally satisfied with everything that we have done. Yet a blind person can still be "perfectly happy," not in the sense of being in "perfect bliss" but in the sense of being genuinely happy. A parent with a mentally handicapped child cannot be "totally satisfied," and yet again he or she can be "perfectly happy." I met a parent with a mentally handicapped child who told me that their child was a great gift from God.

If happiness is taken as "enduring level of happiness," there can be no "fear of happiness" as is discussed in the literature (Joshanloo et al, 2014). In many cultures, people fear a high level of momentary happiness may be followed by disappointment and a sense of loss. Thus, even those who "fear happiness" do so in order to achieve a higher level of sustainable or enduring happiness.

Set range or set point?

Seligman used the term "set range," suggesting that even the genetically determined level of happiness (called "set point" earlier) may vary over a range randomly.

Our blood pressure may go up or down with changes in activities and changes in the level of intensity of these activities. Similarly, the "set range," according to Seligman, refers to a range of happiness that we are born with. It is a range because it may not be a definite value and may cover a range of values. It is believed to be "set" by biological factors that determine the personal traits or personality that ultimately affect our subjective well-being.[3] According to Seligman, we could work to lift up our happiness, but "The best you can do with positive emotion is you can get people to live at the top of their set range." It is held that we could deviate from the set range from time to time, as happy events or unhappy events take place, but we would return to the set range in due course.

David T. Lykken (2000) did a lot of work on identical twins and, based on that research, proposed his set point theory of happiness, which affirms the role of genes in determining a person's well-being. According to this theory, individuals may experience temporary increases and decreases in well-being in response to major life events, but they will quickly adapt and their subjective well-being will return to its genetically determined set point. Lykken himself, however, never dismissed the role parents can play in children's well-being and even proposed that prospective parents should meet specific requirements before giving birth to or adopting a child. Richard Redding (2002) found merit in his proposal but thought it would be unconstitutional in America. Instead, he recommended:

> "mandatory parenting education classes in the schools, tougher child abuse laws, improved child protective services, and more research on

> the effectiveness of the effectiveness of public policies and intervention programs aimed at enhancing parent-child relationships and decreasing the rates of divorce and father absence."
>
> *(p. 988)*

Anusic et al. (2014) tested the set point theory using a large, nationally representative panel data of Swiss households, and found that some major life events are associated with substantial changes in one's levels of life satisfaction and that "in some instances, these changes persist in the years following the event." Moreover, Lindqvist et al. (2020), with the assistance of Statistics Sweden, collected a large dataset that enabled the study of the effects of large prize lottery wins on the well-being of the winners against controls. They found that these winners experienced sustained increases in overall life satisfaction that persisted for over a decade and showed no evidence of dissipating over time. They also found evidence suggesting that the wealth impacts of a lottery win lift people's satisfaction with their lives more than their affective well-being. The findings of these authors do not disprove the significant role played by genes but affirm the possibility that the effects of genes need not be overriding.

More importantly, these authors found evidence confirming our hypothesis that "mental goods" or affective well-being may not rise with material well-being. Lykken's affirmation of the benefits of parenting education shows his belief that mental capital can be nurtured and can enhance well-being. Anusic et al., importantly, found the "set point of happiness" is not set in stone. Major life events can impact the enduring level of happiness. Recent development in neural science has found that some switches to genetic messages to behaviour and emotions can be turned on or off through habits and the environment, particularly the cultural environment, in a process called epigenetics.[4] This supports our thesis that the accumulation of mental capital will change the enduring level of happiness. With early intervention, patience, a strong will, and perseverance, negative mental capital can gradually be reduced, and positive mental capital can accumulate. A person's personality is only in part determined genetically, so people can build mental capital *by working sufficiently hard, methodically, and over a sufficiently long stretch of time consistently.* This is the role of *V1* in equation [6.2]. Some people may need to work harder to accumulate their mental capital; others may acquire it more easily. Although some people may need to make a greater effort to be happy, they need not be less happy than others once they have accumulated the requisite mental capital.

C and V

Seligman notes that circumstances may affect a person's reported SWB. But the circumstances that may make a person happier are subject to change and their effects are transient. While extreme poverty makes a person unhappy and a higher income will make a person happier, the effects of income changes tend to be transient, and incomes may not have as much effect on enduring happiness as one's mindset. While a disabling illness could produce a more enduring effect on happiness and life satisfaction, unless there are "five or more [health] problems," Seligman noted that the negative effect is "not nearly as much as you might expect." My own observation is that people with chronic pain can indeed be very unhappy, but people with a disability (such as blindness, loss of the use of a limb or deafness) need not be unhappy at all. Chronic and severe pain invariably makes people very miserable because it cannot be easily dismissed or forgotten. But there are many examples of people overcoming even severe disabilities cheerfully. Nick Vujicic, evangelist and motivational speaker, born without arms or legs in Australia to a Serbian immigrant couple, is one. Hirotada Ototake, a Japanese bestselling author, who was also born without arms or legs, is another. Both *V1* and *V2* in equation [6.2] play important roles in determining the turnout of the life experience.

V1 is in the form of accumulating positive mental capital (including both human capital and LIFE and other skills) and reducing negative mental capital. Many experiments, involving subjects going through appropriate training sessions, have proven that a positive attitude can be acquired, and that is the *raison d'être* of positive psychology. *V2* has to do with decisions made in the past that change one's circumstances in the present, and decisions that are made today that will change one's circumstances in the future. Examples of *V2* include marriage, career choice, the decision to migrate, etc.

Thus there are always things within our control and things that are outside our control. Things that are within our control are "decision variables." Things that are outside our control are "constraints." Recognizing the true constraints and focusing on the decision variables will allow us to make the most out of our lives. This is the essence of the economics of life and the real meaning of positive living.

It is futile to grumble or complain or dwell on the real constraints. That would just be a waste of time and would certainly undermine our happiness. Sadly, one's arrogance, which is a lack of humility and an unwillingness to self-reflect and to change, is actually a self-created constraint that prevents personal growth. Distinguishing between the real constraints and the false ones is an important challenge and does require constant honest reflection. Unfortunately, for some people, the idea never occurs to them that some constraints are real and that the best strategy then is to take them as given. Similarly, it never occurs to some people that some constraints can be overcome provided that they approach the problem wisely and make a sufficient and enduring effort.

The key strategy under *V* is acquiring LIFE mental capital in our day-to-day lives. This is the key to a positive "growth mindset." The four-pronged approach building Love, Insight, Fortitude and Engagement mental capital will lift our enduring level of happiness. It is also based on a vast literature in psychology, philosophy, and religion. In stipulating LIFE as the key voluntary element in the happiness formula that we should focus on, I merely bring these ideas together in an easy-to-remember formula. We have, of course, discussed this formula throughout the book but it is worth a reiteration.

LIFE

Love

I have already cited Fromm's *The Art of Loving* (1956). Among religions, Christianity explicitly espouses "Love thy neighbor as thyself," and Buddhism explicitly preaches "compassion." Confucianism, the main school of philosophy in traditional Chinese society, asks us to put ourselves in the shoes of others. Love connects us. Life connects us. Albert Schweitzer, the practitioner of Reverence for Life, practices love through his life.

Insight

Insight, or wisdom, includes several elements, but all these elements stem from seeing the big picture. Only when one sees the big picture can one develop a sense of proportion or a sense of balance. Only when one sees the big picture can one know the difference between ends and means. Bertrand Russell referred to this in *The Conquest of Happiness* (1996). Only when one sees the big picture can one understand the need for sustainable development, which requires a culture or living style that effectively allows "efficient production of mental goods." For example, many people have learnt to achieve a sense of dignity without conspicuous consumption. Explicit reference to "thrift" or "avoiding excesses" is made in the philosophical classic, the *Daodejing*. Still another aspect about Insight is humility. Here is an excerpt from the *Daodejing* (Chapter 67).[5] Only when one sees the grandeur of life and the limits of human senses will one learn to be humble.[6]

> I have three treasures that I keep and adhere to always.
> The first is compassion.
> The second is thrift.
> The third is humility.

In psychological literature much research has been done on the distinction between extrinsic and intrinsic motives and how different motivations affect happiness (Kasser and Ryan, 1993, 1996, 2001; Schmuck et al., 2000; Schmuck, 2001). A common conclusion is that overemphasis on materialistic or extrinsic goals tends to lead to unhappiness. We can say that extrinsic goals have to do with pleasing our physiological senses. Intrinsic goals have to do with enhancing our sense of self-worth. Realizing one's potential or rediscovery of life is critical for human flourishing. The Templeton website states:

> We flourish by maintaining a sense of wonder, curiosity, and humility about the world we all share and our place in it. Our focus on flourishing is concerned with studying how an extension of these interior traits, habits, and behaviors can impact social goals.[7]

Fortitude

Fortitude is just another word for resilience, which is again a subject in psychology with a vast body of literature. The common term for it is "inner strength." People with fortitude are not afraid of difficulties and are never intimidated by difficulties. They have a sense of self-worth that will not be affected by other people's opinions.

Engagement

Engagement is purposive and active living and, again, has been widely discussed in the psychological literature and is a central theme in Zen (or Chan) Buddhism. Seligman has explicitly emphasized engaged living as a key to happiness, along with the pleasant life and the meaningful life.

Consider the following well-known prayer of Saint Francis of Assisi, which is often considered to represent the epitome of spirituality:

> Lord, make me a channel of thy peace;
> that where there is hatred, I may bring love;
> that where there is wrong, I may bring the spirit of forgiveness;
> that where there is discord, I may bring harmony;
> that where there is error, I may bring truth;
> that where there is doubt, I may bring faith;
> that where there is despair, I may bring hope;
> that where there are shadows, I may bring light;
> that where there is sadness, I may bring joy.
>
> Lord, grant that I may seek rather to comfort than to be comforted;
> to understand, than to be understood; to love, than to be loved.
>
> For it is by self-forgetting that one finds.
> It is by forgiving that one is forgiven.
> It is by dying that one awakens to eternal life.
>
> Amen.

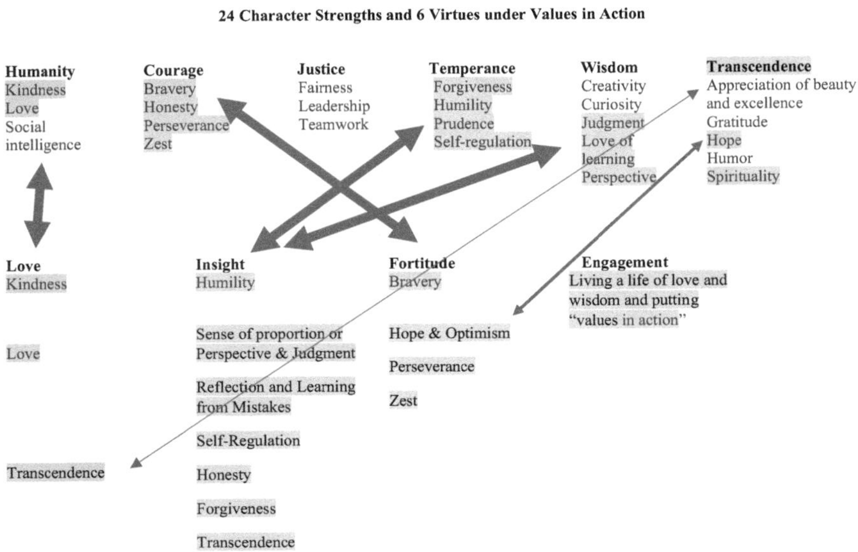

FIGURE 6.1 Commonality between Values in Action and LIFE.

Note: The bi-direction arrows indicate the similarity or overlap between the two frameworks. Justice is subsumed under Transcendence, as transcendence implies abandoning the concept about the narrow self and putting oneself in others' positions.

Here we find that Love, Insight, Fortitude and Engagement are all highlighted: Love (where there is hatred, I may bring love; where there is sadness, I may bring joy; grant that I may seek rather … to love, than to be loved); Insight (where there is error, I may bring truth; grant that I may seek rather … to understand, than to be understood; it is by self-forgetting that one finds); Fortitude (faith, hope); Engagement (to bring harmony, to bring truth, to bring faith, to bring hope, and to love; to console, to understand, to forgive—all in active rather than passive voice, all with a clear purpose).

In short, to get the most out of life we need to nurture more Love, Insight (wisdom) and Fortitude, and to live with a sense of purpose and devotion (Engagement). This is the essence of spirituality, and in what follows, I shall present some evidence about the effectiveness of LIFE in elevating happiness.

Personal growth and values in action

As we accumulate LIFE mental capital, we develop a strong sense of direction and a strong sense of self-worth that will prevail over adversities and other people's judgments. We will notice a clear change in our lives. As explained in Chapter 5, we will have PERMA: blessed with positive emotion, engaged in our daily living, cherish relationships, find meaning and personal growth, and achievement in life. Figure 6.1 shows that LIFE is values in action.

Testing LIFE, the happiness formula, using Hong Kong data

We have talked extensively about mental capital. Building up mental capital allows us to become happier, because mental capital allows us to enjoy more mental goods like love, a sense of autonomy, freedom from anxiety and self-esteem. We need to make love into a habit, insight into a habit, resilience into a habit, and purposive activity into a habit. Once we have developed these habits, we will find our lives much more fulfilling, because then each day offers a new opportunity for personal growth and self-actualization. Apart from presenting some evidence to support the use of LIFE as the happiness formula, we will also discuss how these mental capitals relate to one another and hang together.

Over the years I have tested and confirmed this happiness formula based on Love, Insight, Fortitude and Engagement, each of which may be considered to be a dimension of mental capital essential for positive living. These different aspects of LIFE mental capital are not completely distinct. For example, Fortitude is typically grounded on a very strong Love, which in turn may generate a strong sense of purpose and purposive activity that is the essence of engagement. However, Love, Insight, Fortitude and Engagement form an easy-to-remember "quartet" and remind us that, after all, LIFE represents the basic value of all activities, and this gives good educational value. The LIFE scores were all measured on an 11-point scale (from 0 to 10) to describe the extent to which the respondent agrees with a statement. After much reflection and making reference to the existing literature we have slightly amended the questionnaire so there are three questions under each element in L, I, F, and E, which is more balanced and more coherent, with one additional optional question under each mental capital heading.

Love is measured using responses to questions about the respondent's propensity to care for oneself, for one's family, and for others in the community. Love helps generate a sense of purpose and meaning in life. It is about the "Why" of Life.[8]

- I take good care of my health and my life.
- I care for my family.
- I am happy to help people in need.
- (Optional) I care for other living things.

Insight is about the "how" or the "art" of love.[9] It is measured using responses to three questions about the respondent's sense of proportion and priorities, ability to distinguish between means and ends, understanding that success in life is not so much about outperforming others as realizing the potential within, willingness and preparedness to reflect on one's decisions and to learn. Insight thus helps generate a sense of self-efficacy and autonomy, and a sense of achievement that is not dependent on others. We have added a third question, one about the environment and sustainable development to the original two questions, given the importance of having a long view, which is also an aspect of seeing the big picture. Only when we see the big picture and take the long view can we make the most of our precious lives.

- Success to me is achieving my best within my ability.
- I maintain a good balance over work, rest, and spending time with my loved ones.
- I take the environment and sustainable development seriously.
- (Optional) I keep humble in my daily living.

Fortitude is all about perseverance, which requires learning from mistakes and failures, calmness, and maintaining hope. Questions about Fortitude consist of the following:

- I face adversity without being discouraged.
- I reflect and learn from my mistakes and disappointments.
- Regardless of what happens I always stay hopeful.
- (Optional) I have gained strength through disappointments and failures.

Engagement is measured using responses to questions regarding the respondent's putting thoughts into action. Engagement is all about living with Love and Insight on a day-to-day basis and never giving up (Fortitude). Engagement generates a sense of self-actualization.

- I have clearly identified goals and purposes in life.
- I always look for opportunities to realize my potential.
- When I decide to do something, I will do my best to do it well.
- (Optional) I always have a strong sense of drive.

Lingnan University started conducting annual happiness surveys in 2005 and in 2008 began its LIFE score surveys, each time using the randomized digit dialing method (a telephone survey), on the Hong Kong population aged 21 and above. The Wofoo Group took over the population-wide annual survey from 2019 while I focus on school children's happiness and life education.

We averaged the scores[10] under each category and called these LIFE mental capital scores or simply LIFE scores. We discovered that reported happiness, which is rated on a scale from 0 to 10, can be explained by these LIFE scores very well, and that the LIFE scores generally rise with age. The LIFE scores from 2008 to 2011 from the randomized telephone survey are presented in Table 6.1. Two striking results are apparent. First, female LIFE scores are

TABLE 6.1 LIFE scores by sex and age groupings: telephone survey data from Hong Kong

Age	*Sex*		*2008*				*2009*				*2010*				*2011*				
			L'	*I'*	*P'*	*E'*	*L'*	*I'*	*P'*	*E'*	*L'*	*I'*	*P'*	*E'*	*L'*	*I'*	*P'*	*E'*	*HI*
50 years	Male	Mean	7.20	6.21	6.48	6.28	7.17	6.94	6.57	6.77	8.00	7.11	7.12	6.32	7.18	6.76	7.21	7.06	6.68
		n'	225	225	223	226	213	197	183	213	176	176	176	173	183	183	183	*183*	
	Female	Mean	7.75	6.70	7.07	6.51	7.62	7.11	7.01	6.88	8.37	7.28	7.10	6.50	7.94	7.43	7.39	7.47	7.39
		n'	315	318	311	316	307	279	267	310	303	305	305	302	275	275	275	*275*	
50 years	Male	Mean	7.81	7.15	7.17	5.88	8.02	7.09	6.43	6.54	8.28	7.62	7.33	5.87	7.27	7.31	7.04	6.74	6.98
		n'	107	108	104	102	114	110	92	113	119	119	118	115	140	140	140	*140*	
	Female	Mean	7.97	7.45	7.52	6.11	8.19	7.29	7.38	6.67	8.67	8.03	7.65	6.31	7.96	7.68	7.37	7.25	7.28
		n'	132	137	129	128	161	142	141	159	211	214	208	203		204	204	*204*	

L, Love; I, Insight; F, Fortitude; E, Engagement; HI, Happiness Index.

[1] Notice that females enjoy higher LIFE scores in almost every year from 2008, for both the younger group and for the 50 and above group.
[2] Notice that for both males and females the older groups generally have higher scores in L, I and F, but a lower score in E.

Average for the years.

almost always higher than those of males. Second, LIFE scores clearly tend to rise with age, with the exception of the Engagement score, which does show an eventual decline with age. The increases in the Love, Insight, and Fortitude scores over the life cycle for both males and females are all quite consistent. This result corroborates a recent finding by Mogilner et al. (2011) that "Whereas younger people are more likely to associate happiness with excitement, as they get older, they become more likely to associate happiness with peacefulness." Older people are less focused on the joy or excitement of the moment and tend to take a more holistic view toward life.

Table 6.2 presents the results of a statistical test with the happiness score regressed against the LIFE scores and various demographic and economic status variables. It shows that LIFE variables all carry statistically highly significant coefficients, all with the right signs, suggesting that higher LIFE scores are associated with higher happiness. Moreover, with the age group below 30 left out (to serve as the benchmark, so the coefficients reported are relative to this group), the age group coefficients show a drop in happiness for the 30–49 age

TABLE 6.2 Regression results using 2008–2012 telephone survey pooled data (with yearly dummies) from Hong Kong

Dependent variable: happiness	*Coefficient*	*t-statistic*
Love	0.18	6.71
Insight	0.20	6.83
Fortitude	0.14	6.35
Engagement	0.25	9.91
Age 30–49 years	-0.23	-2.68
Age 50 up	-0.26	-2.62
Female	0.11	2.01
Married	0.16	2.09
Divorced	-0.47	-1.84
Widowed	0.45	1.39
Financial stress	-0.30	-7.41
Household income lower than HK$10K	-0.10	-0.88
Household income HK$40K or more	0.08	1.22
Monthly income not reported	-0.04	-0.65
2009	0.09	1.06
2010	-0.20	-1.82
2011	-0.24	-2.35
2012	-0.23	-2.71
Constant term	2.28	11.31
Number of observations = 2,999		
$F(18, 2980) = 61.75$ Probability > $F = 0$		
R-squared = 0.3642		

Dummy for 2008 has been left out and serves as the benchmark for year effects.

group relative to the younger cohort and then an even bigger drop for the 50 and above group, which is different from the result commonly reported about a cited U-shaped happiness profile (Blanchflower and Oswald, 2007; Stone et al. 2010). The different result is likely to be related to the fact that the effects of LIFE scores have been controlled in the equation, and both Love and Insight scores tend to rise with age. Female still carries a positive coefficient, and so does married. Financial stress carries a significant negative coefficient. Income categories carry the expected signs, with the lowest income group least happy but the highest income group" those with HK$40,000 monthly income (around US$61,500 annual income)—not enjoying any noticeable increase in happiness. Given Hong Kong's lower tax rate and taking purchasing power parity into account, HK$40,000 monthly pre-tax income is rather similar to an annual pre-tax income of US$75,000 in the United States in real purchasing power after tax, which was the threshold beyond which Americans' emotional well-being leveled off in Daniel Kahneman and Angus Deaton (2010).

Here again the LIFE variables all carry highly significant coefficients, and once again, the Engagement variable carries the biggest coefficient, followed by Insight, Love and Fortitude, in that order. Ageing is here seen to have a negative effect on happiness, after the LIFE variables have been controlled for. It should be noted that in this sample there are more females than males, and female happiness tends to be more negatively related to age. Both Female and married again appear to have positive effects on happiness. Unemployment and financial stress carry the expected negative signs. In this sample, the high household monthly income variable (for HK$40,000) even carries a negative, though insignificant coefficient. Similar results are obtained from an online survey that was conducted in 2011 (Table 6.3).

Testing the LIFE formula using the World Value Survey

In order to test the validity of the happiness formula as Love, Insight, Fortitude, and Engagement, we use the data from the World Value Survey that covers many countries across different cultures. We compiled indices of Love, Insight, Fortitude and Engagement based on some subsets of the questions asked. It should be noted that the questions are not custom-designed for my research, and are chosen on the basis of their bearing some resemblance to the central concepts of Love, Insight, Fortitude and Engagement.

The questions in the World Value Survey on which the LIFE scores are constructed, as well as the way the scores are compiled, are laid out in Appendix Table 6.7.

Table 6.4 shows the results on the baseline model, with happiness regressed on only the LIFE variables. The estimation is based on a sample of 52,693 observations, each of which represents one person who responded to all the

TABLE 6.3 Regression results using online survey (2011) data from Hong Kong

Dependent variable: happiness	*Coefficient*	*t-statistic*
Love	0.16	14.14
Insight	0.29	19.91
Fortitude	0.15	10.38
Engagement	0.33	24.23
Age 30–49	-0.26	-7.27
Age 50 up	-0.36	-5.93
Female	0.25	8.31
Married	0.40	10.92
Divorced	-0.26	-2.88
Widowed	0.07	0.45
Education	-0.08	-7.51
Unemployed	-0.33	-3.59
Financial stress	-0.44	-19.8
Household income < HK$10K	0.12	2.67
Household income ≥ HK$40K	-0.04	-1.06
Constant term	1.07	9.83
Number of observations = 8,523		
$F(15, 8507) = 609.10$		
Probability > $F = 0.0000$		
R-squared = 0.5178		

Notes
Education is a scale variable from no formal education to university. Income earners in the HK$10,000 to HK$40,000 per month range are left out as benchmark. The low-income group benefitted from a statutory minimum wage that took effect on May 1, 2011. Cronbach's alpha for the LIFE scores are 0.7736, 0.7723, 0.8615, and 0.8371 involving 3, 5, 3, and 3 items respectively for Love, Insight, Fortitude, and Engagement.

The dataset is available for download at www.ln.edu.hk/serc/en/happiness_index.php for anyone interested in the surveys.

TABLE 6.4 Baseline regression on World Value Survey data with wave 5 data (2005–2008)

Dependent variable: happiness	*Coefficient*	*t-statistic*
Love	0.18	19.34
Insight	0.08	8.77
Fortitude	0.10	20.12
Engagement	0.13	22.1
Constant term	3.68	40.45
Number of observations = 52,693		
$F(4,52688) = 441.68$		
Probability > $F = 0.0000$		
R-squared = 0.034		

Note: Data available for wave 5 at the time of writing was only up to 2008 though the full dataset was eventually made available up to 2009.

relevant questions. The regression shows how the happiness index is related to the LIFE scores statistically.

The figures in the coefficient column show the estimated effect of each of the LIFE variables on the happiness score. It shows that Love carries the biggest coefficient, followed by Engagement (Figure 6.1). Given that all scores have been converted to the 0–10 scale, someone with one point more in the Love score will on average enjoy 0.18 points higher on the happiness scale. All coefficients on LIFE score variables are statistically significant at 1%.

Table 6.5 shows the results of a bigger model, with demographic and economic variables included along with the LIFE variables. Again all LIFE variables carry statistically significant coefficients. The sample is reduced to 42,514 observations. Females are found to be happier, as are the married and the relatively high-income people. Age has a U-shaped effect on happiness, first declining and then rising.

TABLE 6.5 World Value Survey results (wave 5) with effects of demographic variables and other variables added

Dependent variable: happiness	*Observations = 42,514* *F(19,42494) = 204.28* *Probability > F = 0.0000* *Adjusted R-squared = 0.0893*	
	Coefficient	*t-statistic*
Love	0.16	15.47
Insight	0.10	9.99
Fortitude	0.07	13.83
Engagement	0.12	17.61
Female	0.12	5.38
Age	-0.06	-12.07
Age squared	0.00	11.27
Education	0.08	3.68
Education squared	-0.01	-3.64
Married	0.22	5.98
Cohabitation	0.3	6.38
Divorced	–0.3	–4.14
Separated	–0.26	–2.82
Widowed	–0.54	–8.32
With child/children	0.06	7.76
Self-employed	0.05	1.54
Retired	–0.28	–5.92
Unemployed	–0.49	–11.18
Relative income	0.18	33.33
Constant term	3.89	26.62

Note: Coefficient for Age squared shown as 0.00 is correct. Digits for additional decimal places are not shown for readability reasons.

Finally, we add country dummies, and the results are presented in Table 6.6, where the country coefficients are not reported. Standard errors are recalculated to be clustered at country level and thus allow for intercountry variations.

We may observe that the LIFE variables continue to be highly significant. Happiness is seen to be positively associated with marriage and (self-reported perceived) relative income. Age appears to have first a negative effect on

TABLE 6.6 World Value Survey results (wave 5) with country variables included and year dummies added (2005–2008): ordinary least squares result (errors clustered at country level)

Dependent variable: happiness	*Observations = 42,514* *F(18,42495) = 405.48* *Probability > F = 0.0000* *Adjusted R-squared = 0.1715*	
	Coefficient	*t-statistic*
Love	0.13	7.81
Insight	0.06	3.59
Fortitude	0.05	4.82
Engagement	0.09	6.52
Female	0.09	2.21
Age (excluding those below 18)	-0.06	-7.2
Age squared	0.00	6.34
Education	0.09	2.01
Education squared	-0.01	-1.86
Married	0.45	6.96
Cohabitation	0.22	3.98
Divorced	-0.16	-2.22
Separated	-0.32	-3.11
Widowed	-0.19	-2.5
With child/children	0.02	1.87
Self-employed	-0.07	-1.59
Retired	-0.09	-1.29
Unemployed	-0.39	-4.26
Relative income	0.17	7.95
Year 2005	-0.31	-9.64
Year 2006	-0.74	-20.2
Year 2007	-0.63	-7
Constant term	5.28	15.14

Notes: The year 2008 has been dropped and serves as a benchmark for the year dummies. Country variables are subject to data availability and include: Andorra, Australia, Brazil, Bulgaria, Burkina Faso, Chile, China, Cyprus, Egypt, Ethiopia, Finland, Georgia, Germany-East, Germany-West, Ghana, India, Indonesia, Malaysia, Mali, Mexico, Moldova, Norway, Peru, Poland, Serbia, Slovenia, Spain, Romania, Rwanda, South Africa, South Korea, Sweden, Taiwan, Thailand, Trinidad, Turkey, Ukraine, Uruguay, Vietnam, Zambia).

happiness and then a positive effect, confirming the well-known result of a U-shaped profile of happiness over the life cycle.[11] This result appears to be at odds with the earlier results reported based on Hong Kong data, but the specification of the equation is slightly different as age squared is now adopted instead of age bracket dummies. The effects of ageing on health may just not yet show up under this specification. Interestingly, education brings benefits in terms of benefits initially but higher education appears to result in lower happiness. Unemployment has a significant negative effect on happiness. Adjusted R-squared goes up to 17.15%.

Conclusions

It takes time and effort to build up mental capital. The scores on Love, Insight, Fortitude and Engagement reflect people's mental capital and have been found to be associated with a happy, fulfilling life. The qualities underlying these scores are related to personality and are in part inborn. But they are certainly not immutable. Most people learn to love more as they age and tend to find new meanings in life (Mogilner et al., 2011), acquire a new understanding of what success in life is all about and become wiser. The Hong Kong surveys suggest that among Love, Insight, Fortitude and Engagement, Engagement is the only element among the four elements in LIFE that does not seem to grow with age. The same surveys suggest that women appear to have higher LIFE scores than men, especially among those before 50. Women in particular appear to be naturally more loving than men, but with age men gradually learn to love more, and also become wiser.[10]

The LIFE happiness formula focuses on the key mental habits that we need to build up in order to live a life of fulfilment. It is not only easy to remember but also reverberates with Albert Schweitzer's Reverence for Life philosophy. The LIFE happiness formula also overlaps with PERMA and Peterson's and Seligman's Values in Action. Empirically, using World Value Survey data in a regression with Total Life Satisfaction as the dependent variable, it has been found that once the effects of LIFE mental capitals have been captured, the coefficient on Meaning turned significant and negative, suggesting that those with strong LIFE no longer needs to search for meaning. The Epilogue to this book will present evidence showing that those still searching for meaning tend to be short in LIFE and are less happy because they cannot find meaning in their day-to-day lives.

Notes

1 This chapter is jointly authored with Prof. Simon Ching Lam (School of Nursing, Tung Wah College, Hong Kong SAR).

2 For example, the key Eurofound happiness question is: "How happy would you say you are these days?" www.eurofound.europa.eu/surveys/smt/eqls/2eqls_03_13.htm.

3 Traits are usually taken to be those characteristics in a person's disposition of a person that one is born with, while personality is more inclusive, comprising "the entire mental organization of a human being at any stage of his development." "It embraces every phase of human character: intellect, temperament, skill, morality, and every attitude that has been built up in the course of one's life' (Warren and Carmichael, 1930, p. 333). We are using the terms more loosely to refer to what Warren and Carmichael called "personality."
4 "Epigenetics functions as a set of molecular switches that can turn genes on or off without altering the DNA sequence. These switches are influenced by various environmental factors, such as nutrition, stress, lifestyle, and environmental exposures." See https://phys.org/news/2024-03-biologists-secrets-gene-traits.html
5 Translation from: Lok Sang Ho in *Human Spirituality and Happiness,* 2nd edition (2020).
6 Stellar et al. (2018) show that awe, such as that over the grandeur of life, offers an important pathway to humility.
7 See "What is Human Flourishing," available at www.templetonworldcharity.org/our-priorities/launch/building-field-human-flourishing/what-is-human-flourishing#:~:text=For%20us%2C%20human%20flourishing%20begins,lead%20with%20empathy%20and%20virtue. Accessed June 4, 2025.
8 Love pertains to the Personal, Communal, and Transcendental Domains as identified by Fisher (1998).
9 Insight pertains to the Environmental and Transcendental Domains of Fisher (1998). More elaboration will be offered in the Epilogue.
10 The surveys then were mostly based on an 11-item measure: Love (2 items), Insight (5 items), Fortitude (2 items), and Engagement (2 items) but in some cases we used a shorter version with Love (2 items), Insight (2 items), Fortitude (1 items), and Engagement (2 items) in order not to have an excessively long questionnaire.
11 Frijters and Beatton (2012) challenged the U-shaped happiness profile as a result of researchers not having controlled for fixed effects and for age-related selectivity and reporting problems. Once the effects were properly controlled, they found "quite a sharp decline around the age of 75'.

Key points to note

- As humans, we can only work on what is within our control, and we have to accept what is truly beyond our control. We should focus on the voluntary factors in Seligman's happiness formula.
- Love, Insight, Fortitude, and Engagement are mental capitals that we should invest in, so we have self-efficacy, resilience, optimism, and hope.
- LIFE is the formula for personal growth, and experiencing personal growth is a source of joy and achievement.
- LIFE overlaps with the inventory of character strengths and virtues, and Engagement for someone strong in LIFE mental capital is Values in Action.

Some questions to ponder

- What constitutes the most important choices in life?
- Between hedonism and eudaimonia, is there a middle way? If there is a middle way, what is it?
- What is the keyword that makes life meaningful?
- What is "burnout"? What causes burnout?

APPENDIX TABLE LIFE score definitions based on World Value Survey wave 5 data

Question	*Love*	*Insight*	*Fortitude*	*Engagement*
1.	Putting more emphasis on family is:	I seek to be myself rather than follow others	Hard work in the long run brings success	Important in life: to be creative to and to do things one's own way
Scale	A bad/a neutral/ a good thing (scale 1–3)	Strongly disagree ... strongly agree (scale 14)	Not true at all ... usually true (scale 1–10)	Not like me ... very much like me (scale 1–6)
2.	Progress toward a less Impersonal and more humane Society is of:	I make a lot of effort to live up to what my friends expect	Belief in one's ability to change destiny	How important in life: politics
Scale	Lowest rank ... highest rank among several choices (scale1–3)	Strongly agree ... strongly disagree (scale 1–4)	Total belief in fate ... total belief in ability to shape destiny (scale 1–10)	Not important ...very important (scale 1–4)
3.	I consider my family as:	I decide my goals in life by myself		Importance in life: work
Scale	Not important ... very important in life (scale1–4)	Strongly disagree ... strongly agree (scale 1–4)		Not important ... very important (scale 1–4)
4.	I consider friends as:			
Scale	Not important ... very important in life (scale 1–4)	Not like me ... very much like me (scale 1–6)		
5.	I consider helping others in need as:	Importance in life: to look after environment		
Scale	Not like me ... very much like me (scale 1–6)	Not like me ...very much like me (scale 1–6)		

LIFE, Love, Insight, Fortitude, Engagement.

All scores as well as their components are rescaled to the 11-point 0–10 scale and are averaged to obtain the LIFE scores using the equation specified below.

New variable= (original variable-1) *[(new scale number of points-1)/ (original scale number of points-1)]

The original variable is assumed to take on values starting from 1. If it starts from zero, there would be no need to subtract 1 before multiplying with the conversion factor.

7

MARRIAGE, MENTAL CAPITAL, AND HAPPINESS

Empirically, married people tend to be happier than unmarried people. This does not mean, however, that marriage will always enhance happiness. Granted, marriage *may* enhance happiness, but it is also likely that causality runs the other way. People with more mental capital are not only happier but also more likely to find marriage partners. Romantic love does not always lead to marriage, and romance does not necessarily mean there is love. Marriage can breed love, but it can also breed discordance. Successful marriages do not come fortuitously, and always require LIFE mental capital.

Introduction

Many studies have indicated a positive "marriage premium" on happiness.[1] That is to say, married people often report to be happier. Tables 6.5 and 6.6 in the last chapter, based on the World Value Survey, also confirm this. The causality between happiness and marriage, however, may work the other way. In principle, people with strong mental capital tend to be happier and more sociable and they stand a better chance of finding a marriage partner. So happier people are more likely to get married than unhappy people. This is similar to the argument that, while success makes people happy, happiness may also breed success.

A large on-line survey from Hong Kong (2011, 8,523 observations) indicates that, in that sample, for males the marriage premium tends to fade with age. That is, older married males do not appear to be much happier than single males of the same age. This suggests that, even if marriage does lift

DOI: 10.4324/9781003507093-7

happiness, for men marriage may not matter that much to happiness over the long run. Interestingly, adult females generally trump males in LIFE mental capital, but males in that sample tend to catch up with age.[2] Both married men and single men saw their mental capital rising faster than females. With mental capital surpassing that of females (**Table 7.2**), older single males enjoyed happiness that almost matched married males. Females married to males, who appeared to have gained much mental capital, likely through the marriage, tended to enjoy a clear marriage premium in happiness compared to single females.

Still, marriage is not always a blessing, and mental capital does not always rise with age. Marriages may fail. A crucial question therefore is how to enhance the chances of a "successful" marriage, in the sense that it enhances the happiness of the married couple. At the very least, marriage should not make people less happy. What is the key?

Mental capital is the key to happy marriages

Table 7.1 shows a comparison of LIFE scores and happiness indices from a large-scale online survey conducted in 2011 between single and married people.[3] As explained in the last chapter, the LIFE scores are the averages of the responses to the questions asked under Love, Insight, Fortitude, and Engagement. It is quite clear that married people consistently have higher LIFE scores and happiness scores than single people, for both the below 45 and the 45-and-above groups.

Table 7.2 shows LIFE and happiness scores among single and married people by sex and by age. It shows that younger females have much stronger Love than males, and that is true both for married and for single female. But males quickly become more loving as they age, to the extent that older single males have higher Love scores than single females, while married older males have Love score that match older females.

TABLE 7.1 LIFE scores between single and married by age (online survey 2011)

Both sexes	*Below 45*		*45 or above*	
	Single	*Married*	*Single*	*Married*
	(4,710)	(2,370)	(184)	(953)
Love	7.27	7.80	7.62	8.07
Insight	6.57	7.08	7.20	7.42
Fortitude	7.37	7.66	7.59	7.84
Engagement	7.03	7.45	7.23	7.67
Happiness Index	6.79	7.56	7.23	7.67

LIFE scores are indices of LIFE mental capital. Figures in brackets are number of observations.

Interestingly, a similar pattern of males' LIFE scores rising faster than females' with age applies to other LIFE mental capitals, with Fortitude for singles being the only exception. Following the hypothesis that people with higher LIFE scores tend to be happier, we would predict that the age premium (i.e., how much older people are happier than younger people) of happiness for older single men (7.59-6.71=0.88) will be higher than that of women (7.06-6.83=0.23). Following the hypothesis that the marriage premium is likely to be higher the higher the marriage partner's LIFE scores, older women married to men benefit from the husbands' increasing mental capital and enjoy a larger marriage premium than men's marriage premium, which is rendered smaller because single men's LIFE mental capital also grew faster. We also observe the pattern of greater marriage premiums for older females than for younger females (older husbands have much more LIFE mental capital than younger

TABLE 7.2 LIFE scores and Happiness in Hong KongBy sex, age and marital status 2011, online data

Male

		below 45	*45 or higher*	*Change with Age*
Love	Single	7.14	7.77	0.63
	Married	7.62	8.07	0.45
Insight	Single	6.75	7.53	0.78
	Married	7.09	7.51	0.42
Fortitude	Single	7.49	7.68	0.19
	Married	7.6	7.82	0.22
Engagement	Single	7.18	7.6	0.42
	Married	7.41	7.72	0.31
Happiness	Single	6.71	7.59	0.88
	Married	7.19	7.61	0.42
Marriage Premium		0.48	0.02	–0.46

Female

		below 45	*45 or higher*	*Change with Age*
Love	Single	7.34	7.55	0.21
	Married	7.89	8.06	0.17
Insight	Single	6.47	7.05	0.58
	Married	7.08	7.33	0.25
Fortitude	Single	7.32	7.55	0.23
	Married	7.69	7.86	0.17
Engagement	Single	6.95	7.06	0.11
	Married	7.47	7.63	0.16
Happiness	Single	6.83	7.06	0.23
	Married	7.75	7.72	–0.03
Marriage Premium		0.92	0.66	–0.26

Note: Underlined indicates higher than the measure for the other sex.

husbands). Because unmarried men also experience a surge in LIFE mental capital, the smaller marriage premium for older men than that for younger men is also expected. (**Table 7.2**).

Table 7.3 allows us to see the effects of gender and marital status on happiness through interpreting the results in a statistical model with interactive variables. First, we find that female singles' gender premium disappears for those aged above 45, corroborating with the surge in LIFE mental capital for males as they age. For married females, the marriage premium narrowed for the same reason. In the event of a divorce, younger males, who had benefited from their mentally strong wives, appear to suffer more than females with a broken marriage. Similarly, older females with a broken marriage appear to suffer more than older males. (Second line from bottom, **Table 7.3**)

The marriage premiums for younger people (Row D) appear invariant with respect to gender. The marriage premium for males disappears as they age, but females keep their marriage premiums, which get higher. (Row I)

Younger males suffer much more from divorce than females (Row L); older females suffer more than males from divorce (Row Q). The pattern again is consistent with the hypothesis about the importance of the mental capital of the marriage partner.

When there is a divorce, it is likely that it is because of a deficiency in mental capital, and under the circumstances breaking up may be wise for the one with stronger mental capital, but it probably hurts more for the spouse with weaker mental capital, in part because he or she would be less able to cope with challenges, and because losing someone with stronger mental capital means losing the benefit of someone who could give emotional support.

Types of marriages

People get married for all kinds of reasons. A marriage can be a natural result of a romantic relationship, but it may also have nothing to do with romance. There are marriages for convenience, such as for the purpose of gaining the right of abode in a country. Some people marry to gain wealth or status. Historically, marriages have been used to gain political ties. In China, marriages were for a long time simply a way to perpetuate the family line. As late as the twentieth century in China, arranged marriages were common. Families sought marriages for their offspring with families with comparable wealth and status. Most women were married before the age of 20.

Today, involuntary child marriages have persisted around the world. According to the United Nations, more than 41.6 million women in Bangladesh were married under 18 years old, accounting for 51% of all married women. Child marriages today are often a result of poverty. School age girls who are married off are then deprived of the opportunity for education, and a vicious cycle continues. The surprise is that child marriages are still allowed

TABLE 7.3 Gender and marriage status effects on happiness/discounts (online survey)

	Dummy Variable	*Coefficient*	*Dummy Variable*	*Coefficient*
Row A	Female	0.28342	Male (excluded dummy)	0
Row B	Female married	0.22016	Male married	0.22553
Row C = A + B	Full effect female and married below 45	0.50358	Full effect male and married below 45	0.22553
Row D=C-A	<45 Female marriage premium	0.22016	<45 Male marriage premium =C-A	0.22553
Row E	Female and over 45	-0.15041	Male and over 45	0.26824
Row F	Female, over 45, and married	0.37132	Male, over 45, and married	-0.24559
Row G = A +B + E+F	Full effect of female over 45 and married	0.72449	Full effect of male over 45 and married	0.24818
Row H = A + E	Full effect of female and single, and over 45	0.13301	Full effect of male and single and over 45	0.26824
Row I = G – H	>45 female marriage premium	0.59148	>45 male marriage premium	-0.02006
Row J = Row A	Female	0.28342	Male (excluded dummy)	0
Row K	Female Divorced	-0.42862	Male Divorced	-0.68916
Row L= J+K	Full effect of female and divorced <45	-0.1452	Full effect of male and divorced <45	-0.68916
Row M= L-C	Divorce Discount from Marriage for female < 45	-0.64878	Divorce Discount from Marriage for male < 45	-0.91469
Row N	Female Divorced & Over 45	0.22278	Male Divorced & >45	0.48645
Row O =J+K+N	Full effect of female over 45 and Divorced	0.07758	Full effect of male over 45 and divorced	-0.20271
Row P =Row G	Full effect of female over 45 and married	0.72449	Full effect of male over 45 and married	0.24818
Row Q =O-P	Divorce Discount from Marriage for female>45	-0.64691	Divorce Discount from Marriage for male >45	-0.45089

Notes: Non-shaded rows show coefficients from the regression on the listed dummy variables in Table 7.4. Shaded rows represent calculations. Row B shows coefficients from the regressions that can also directly reflect marriage premiums. Higher numbers than other sex underlined.

in some states in America. Unchained At Last, an organization dedicated to ending forced and child marriages in the US, estimates that 7,876 minors in Virginia, some as young as 12 years old, were entered into marriage between 2000 and 2021. More than 80% of those marriages were between girls and adult men and almost all of those marriages involved a minor who was not old enough to consent to sex with their spouse.[4] Today, with the rise of LGBTQ+ rights, there are also marriages between people of the same sex. The bottom line for our purposes, however, is that for marriages to enhance people's well-being, mutual respect between the marriage partners and a growth mindset are prerequisites.

What makes a marriage successful?

We know that love is often not the reason for a marriage. But marriages need love in order to be successful in the sense of contributing to the well-being of the marriage partners. In this context, love strictly refers to a genuine respect or reverence for life and a genuine concern for the well-being of others and that of oneself. This is defined as true love. But even true love is not sufficient. Wisdom or Insight in the sense of seeing the big picture and having a sense of proportion is critical. As explained before, Love and Insight are the primary constituents of the "growth mindset." Keeping this growth mindset alive without fail, and applying this growth mindset in our daily life are Fortitude and Engagement, respectively.

It should be noted that many marriages are almost doomed to fail from the first day. These are typically marriages involving one or more who have a lot of negative mental capital and very little positive mental capital. People should be forewarned that believing that marriage and love will change someone who is very attractive in appearance but who has a lot of negative mental capital is normally wishful thinking.

If each person in a marriage does not see the other as a person deserving respect, then the marriage is likely doomed to fail. This is because, in an unequal marriage, one partner is seen to be subservient to the other partner, whose ego and power overshadows those of the first partner. Projection of that ego and power would leave little room for true love to emerge.

If one is attracted to marrying a partner who is short in LIFE mental capital and long in negative mental capital, hoping that he will change, the prognosis is grim. Since mental habits are hard to change, and since there is little incentive for someone strong in ego and short in humility to change, loving acts and words may not be appreciated, and pleas for a change in attitude and behavior may be interpreted as an incursion into one's natural rights. Clashes are likely to rise. The marriage is likely to break up and may even end in tragedy.

On the other hand, couples with a growth mindset will use any possible clash to their advantage, try to learn from any the mishap, and eventually turn an otherwise unhappy event into an opportunity for personal growth. Love will grow. Insight will grow. The bond will become stronger. The couple will then take each day they spend together as a great blessing.

Romantic affinity and love

It is important to distinguish between "romantic affinity" and "love." Although the term "romantic love" is used in the literature (Rubin, 1970) romantic affinity is *not* love. When a young man meets a young woman for the first time and suddenly "falls in love with her," he really only has a strong romantic affinity for the woman. Since it is the first meeting, how can there be a love for the woman that is different from love for other people? Does he really care for the well-being of the woman? There are stories of young men and women "loving each other" so much that they commit suicide together when something got in the way of their tying the knot together. Can this be love? There are also stories in which a "lover" kills his "beloved" when his love for him is rejected. Can this be love?

Zick Rubin did explicitly specify caring for each other as one of the elements of "romantic love." But love and romantic affinity are altogether two different things. Two lovers can, of course, genuinely love and care for each other, and they can also share a strong affinity for each other. They may express their love for each other in ways different from how parents express their love for their children, particularly but not exclusively through an intimate sexual relationship. But even though the ways of *expressing love* may vary depending on the relationship, the nature of love is really the same. It remains a genuine care for the feeling and well-being of the beloved person and reflects a reverence for life.

The romantic affinity between a couple can of course develop into true love. When true love takes hold, however, it must have transcended the relationship. Romantic love is just romantic affinity combined with love. Quite apart from the romantic affinity though, if you really love someone you would like him to make decisions that are good for him over the long term. Suppose she decides to leave you for another man, and you know that that man also truly loves her and is likely to bring her happiness, you would give her your blessing. Suppose she fell seriously ill: you would take good care of her just as a mother would take good care of her child if the child became seriously ill. Romantic love is not rare, but romantic affinity in real life is often mingled with a feeling of possessiveness and excessive attachment that is anything but love. Sadly, this sometimes leads to tragic consequences.

There are many literary works that glorify a lover committing suicide upon the death of one's beloved. I have yet to come across a literary work that glorifies a lover who willingly gives up his beloved to his competitor because this would make her happier.

Division of labor within the household

Recent data in the United States indicate that the traditional female premium over male in happiness has narrowed so much that it has virtually disappeared (Stevenson and Wolfers, 2009). These authors, citing Kahneman (1999), suggested that this might have to do with more honest reporting, as women enjoying better economic well-being and social status became more ready to deflate their previously inflated responses. Moreover, "increased opportunities available to women may have increased what women require to declare themselves happy" (p.223).

"Finally, the changes brought about through the women's movement may have decreased women's happiness. The increased opportunity to succeed in many dimensions may have led to an increased likelihood of believing that one's life is not measuring up" (p.223). None of these explanations is convincing. It appears to me that the rise in women's participation in the labor force plus the generally greater responsibilities of married women in taking up household chores than men is a key reason behind the decline in women's happiness relative to men. As was pointed out by a University of Michigan study in 2005, before having children married women did 17 hours of housework a week as compared with seven hours for men. After they had children, married women with more than three kids recorded an average of about 28 hours of housework a week, while married men with more than three kids logged only about 10 hours of housework a week, a difference of 18 hours per week. "This study shows with men and women working, men still lag women in housework."[5] More recent data from the Pew Research Center from 2003 to 2015 shows that while fathers are spending a lot more time doing housework and childcare, mothers are still doing almost double the amount.[6]

While excessive housework hours for women could be a key reason why women's premium over men's on happiness has fallen markedly, the solution is not necessarily "Let's divide up the work equally and rotate." As Paula Szuchman and Jenny Anderson (2011) advised in *Spousonomics: Using Economics to Master Love, Marriage, and Dirty Dishes*, husbands and wives should divide up the work along principles of comparative advantage and should not focus so much on equality as such. This is not to suggest that equality is unimportant. Equality is very important, but only in the sense of giving full respect for the other person as a person, as we do ourselves, and not in the sense of being very calculating to make sure that equality in some measure is achieved. In interpersonal relations, equality is an attitude and should not be measured quantitatively in terms of household work sharing. That indeed is one of the essentials of Love and Insight.

I am surprised that Daniel Carlson, Amanda Miller, and Stephanie Rudd (2020) concluded in their study, which used instrumental variables models and Actor-Partner Interdependence Models in their analysis of 487 couples from the 2006 Marital and Relationship Survey, that "strong communication skills help couples improve the long-term, global health of the relationship in a positive and constructive fashion that leads to mutual satisfaction" (p.15). What matters is not communication skills but the substance of what is communicated. If there is Love and Insight, what is communicated is "What can I do to help?" and "Can you do this for me?" If there is little concern for the partner's well-being, and if the partner does not care about one's well-being, then even if one has top communication skills, the marriage is not going to work.

To the credit of Carlson et al. the finding that the actual division of housework between husband and wife may be less important than "communication" is remarkable. The authors found that "male partner's communication quality … accounts for much of the association between women's perceived equity and their relationship satisfaction." (p.12)

It is important to note that "communication" in this context reflects a sense of the couple feeling connected and enjoying mutual respect. Jumping from "quality of communication" to "communication skills" is probably misguided.

Thus it is not just the hours of housework on top of a full-time job that affect women's happiness. More often there is the supposition that women should take up more of the household chores that gives rise to a feeling of unfairness or alienation. Putting down such supposition and letting the one with the comparative advantage do housework that furthers the best interest of the family is the best strategy and a sign of wisdom and mastery of the economics of love. Better still, treat the household "chore" not as a "chore," but as something that each happily takes up for the benefit of the family. This would nurture the "mental good" of love or loving kindness.

Conclusions

Married people statistically are more likely to be happier than unmarried people, but marriage does not always bring greater happiness. A successful marriage depends on the mental capital of the couple. Being married to someone who has more mental capital than oneself is likely to bring increased happiness. Being married to someone who has very little mental capital, or worse still, who has a lot of negative mental capital, could be the beginning of a nightmare. What matters most to the success of a marriage is mental capital. Children of parents with strong mental capital will likely develop strong mental capital.[7] Similarly, children of parents with weak mental capital

APPENDIX TABLE Online survey 2011 full model results

Ordinary least squares	*Observations = 7111* *F(18,7092) = 327.13* *Probability > F = 0.0000* *R-squared = 0.5135*	
	Coefficient	*t-statistic*
Love	0.16133	10.84
Insight	0.24630	12.43
Fortitude	0.16178	7.75
Engagement	0.33885	17.05
Household income over 40K*	-0.10952	-3.24
Household income below 10K*	-0.06201	-1.11
Financial stress	-0.44449	-16.95
Female	0.28342	5.84
Female and married	0.22016	5.26
Female and over 45	-0.15041	-1.34
Female and over 45 and married	0.37132	0.3
Male and married	0.22553	3.81
Male and over 45	0.26824	2.25
Male and over 45 and married	-0.24559	-1.8
Female and divorced	-0.42862	-2.72
Female and over 45 and divorced	0.22278	0.97
Male and divorced	-0.68916	-2.07
Male and over 45 and divorced	0.48645	1.17
Constant term	0.71691	5.94

* Monthly household incomes in HK$; HK$7.8 roughly translates to US$1. Because of missing values, out of a total of 8523 respondents, we only have 7111 observations for this regression.

will likely inherit the weak mental capital. Understanding the importance and the nature of mental capital will save many marriages, and perhaps avoid many unsuccessful marriages, and will help foster a generation of happier, healthier individuals, and may even revive the declining fertility rate common to many countries.

Notes

1 These include a 2024 released Gallup Poll report. See https://edition.cnn.com/2024/02/09/health/marriage-happiness-wellness/index.html

2 This appears to be untrue for adolescents. Moreover, while there is a tendency for men's mental capital to catch up with women, we cannot generalize to say that older males always have larger mental capital than females. Results in my telephone surveys through the years reported in Chapter 6 show older females may continue to have more LIFE mental capital than men.

3 Although it seems dated, the very large sample (over 8500 subjects responded) and the invariance of human nature makes the survey still highly relevant and useful for our purposes.
4 See "Map Shows 12 States That Allow Child Marriage After Virginia Passes Law", *Newsweek*, Published Apr 09, 2024. www.newsweek.com/child-marriage-ban-state-map-virginia-law-1888471
5 National Science Foundation: "Chore Wars: Men, Women and Housework," See www.nsf.gov/discoveries/disc_summ.jsp?cntn_id=111458.
6 See "Modern Marriage: Till Chores Do Us Part," available at www.todaysparent.com/modern-marriage-till-chores-do-us-part/. Accessed June 4, 2025.
7 See Ho and Ip (2018), where evidence was that children of parents who enjoy good spousal relations appear to be more loving.

Key points to note

- The key to a successful marriage—a marriage that enhances the well-being of the married couple and their offspring—lies in a growth mindset. Such a growth mindset is possible only when the couple have enough LIFE mental capital.
- To marry someone with a lot of negative mental capital, in the hope of changing him or her with one's love is a big gamble that is quite risky.
- The large scale online survey from Hong Kong provided evidence that the marriage premium in happiness as well as the often-observed female premium over male in happiness is related to LIFE mental capital. Females appear to have an early start, especially in Love mental capital. Males appear to catch up with age.
- Successful marriages are predicated on equality and mental capital. Equality in interpersonal relations should not be measured quantitatively but is a matter of attitude or mutual respect for each other as an autonomous person.

Some questions to ponder

- Read "From Best Friends to Platonic Spouses" in *The New York Times.* Why would people get married without sex?
- Read "Friendship Marriage: A new relationship trend gaining popularity" in *Times of India* at: https://timesofindia.indiatimes.com/life-style/relationships/love-sex/friendship-marriage-a-new-relationship-trend-gaining-popularity-in-japan/articleshow/110014064.cms dated May 10, 2024 accessed June 20, 2025

  The couples thus married would consciously decide to not have any physical or romantic intimacy with each other. If they have children, they generally choose other medical ways to have children together. Do you think this is good or bad for society? What do you think these people fear about intimacy?

- Why is a growth mindset important for successful marriages?
- Should we deliberately avoid "love at first sight"?
- Some people suffer from cherophobia. They have an aversion to "being happy." Are marriages without sex a reflection of cherophobia? What is the fear?

8

INSIGHT AND FORTITUDE

Love gives impetus and meaning to living. Insight shows us how to Love. Love and Insight, plus our learning through mistakes and reflections, adds to Fortitude. Motivated by Love and equipped with the know-how about living positively, we go about our lives in an Engaged way, gaining strength and reinforcing Fortitude through thick and thin, generating values in action.

Introduction

Economists understand that reaching the maximum value of an "objective function"—whether it is a profit function or a utility function—means climbing up the hill as long as the next step is up and stopping when the next step is down. "Never overdo and never fall short" is a dictum to be followed. Marginal thinking, interestingly, can also be excessive. Excessive marginal thinking happens when we are too calculating and lose sight of the big picture. This is not good advice for one who wants to live a fulfilling life.

Wisdom is certainly much more than marginal thinking and more than merely finding the maximum value of something that is at most an instrumental and not a final goal. Marginal analysis is a strong tool in economic analysis, but marginal thinking in daily life could degrade into "too calculating." To live happily we cannot be too calculating all the time. There are important things for which we need to be calculating. But there are many trivial things that would cost our energy too much if we are calculating at the margins all the time. To avoid excessive marginal thinking, we need to see the big picture and have a sense of proportion.

DOI: 10.4324/9781003507093-8

The term "big picture view" implies that Insight requires an ability to distinguish between ends and means. In the context of living, the big picture must be seeing the entirety of our life and making the most out of it. Only when we see the big picture can we appreciate the benefits of disappointments and sorrow. To make the most out of our lives, we must have the future in mind, and we must make the most out of our past experiences, and we must do what is best for us over the long term. Making the most out of our lives must be the most important objective. In comparison, making money, as well as building a career, must be considered only instrumental: we make money or build a career only as long as doing so helps enrich our lives.

Wisdom must be about taking command, rather than allowing our fate to be arbitrarily dictated by circumstances or by our impulsive responses to a situation. These impulsive responses are like reflexes. While some may be inherited, many impulsive responses are acquired and they become our "second nature." Chapter 5 emphasized the importance of habits, which are built up over time as we repeat the manner we respond to circumstances. If these mental habits are useful to us (such as reflecting on our experience to learn how we can do better), we call these mental habits positive mental capital. If these mental habits are harmful (such as procrastination and arrogance) to us over the long term, we call these mental habits negative mental capital. Only with the long view would we make the sacrifice and the effort to invest in mental capital.

Insight or Wisdom is such mental capital. If we have acquired a habit of seeing the big picture we will have a sense of proportion and know the difference between means and ends. We would know the importance of disciplining the mind and overcoming our own weaknesses and thus taking command of ourselves. Because of inertia, however, the mind keeps wandering around and is extremely difficult to control. This is the rationale for "mindfulness training," which Seligman also mentioned in his book *Authentic Happiness*.

Wisdom is also about knowing what you can control and what you cannot, then focusing on doing the best within what you can control, and not worrying about the factors that are totally beyond your control. We have already discussed the subject of real versus false constraints in Chapter 6, but need to reiterate the importance of not worrying about what we cannot control. Such worries only undermine our happiness and our ability to realize the best that is within our reach based on what we can control.

Wisdom is about being truthful and honest about our feelings. Reflecting truthfully on our experience and trying to do better next time while remaining truthful about ourselves is living truthfully. "A day truly lived is a day truly gained," as the saying goes. Learning from mistakes builds Fortitude. Going through ups and downs builds Fortitude. A big picture view builds Fortitude. Thus Insight and Fortitude are twins and obviously related.

Insight: Wisdom is …

Wisdom is to know the grand purpose.
The grand purpose is to realize Life's potential.
That requires taming our ancient weaknesses.
To be wise is to overcome mind's sicknesses.

Wisdom is a sense of proportion.
A sense of proportion is to abandon excesses:
Giving up the urge to keep seeking more;
To be wise is to be free from this scourge.

Wisdom is being able to tell means from ends.
That requires knowing what you really want.
You certainly want to achieve your goal.
But a goal does not mean much unless it serves your soul.

Wisdom is to see the transient nature of things,
To realize everything is but the result of transient causes and conditions;
The self as we know it should only be an instrument
To serve the master, like a servant.

Wisdom is never to worry,
When worrying doesn't do you any good.
Most worrying is really nonsense.
Why not simply do your best, and live in good conscience?

Wisdom is to live fully.
To live fully is to find value in every moment of your life
Even when it brings sorrow and pain.
A day truly lived is a day truly gained.

(Ho, 2020)

There is one facet of Insight that needs further elaboration. This is the subject of obsession, which is the exact opposite of seeing the big picture. Obsession means an excessive focus on something to the detriment of one's overall long-term good. We will first discuss the nature of obsession in greater detail, and then go on to the subject of how to free ourselves from obsessions.

Obsessions

Obsession refers to the enslavement of the mind as it is dominated by a persistent object of desire or fear, which can be physical or mental. Obsessions may vary in intensity, and the object of an obsession may also vary, from the mundane to the lofty. But desire-related obsessions share the commonality of stubbornly focusing and insisting on the pursuance of something, some experience, or some episode, and in doing so making a huge sacrifice in terms of the person's overall long-term welfare. Obsessions can result in obsessive-compulsive disorders. This insistence also makes it difficult to let go even when letting go is good for us. Obsessions significantly compromise a person's mental health because they linger in our subconscious mind, emerging every now and then, affecting sleep, concentration, and creating restlessness, sometimes without a break. Trying to suppress the thoughts or refocus on something else simply doesn't work.

One mild form of obsession is the idea that since certain things belong to us, losing them is unacceptable. A sense of loss is a "mental bad." This explains the so-called endowment effect in behavioral economics, which refers to the often-found result that people tend to require more compensation to part with something they already have than the price they are willing to pay to acquire the same thing.[1] Because the endowment effect is so commonly observed, we may say that human beings tend to be obsessed with objects owned to the extent that giving them up engenders a mental bad. This explains why many people keep accumulating things that are of little use in practice and that reduce living space.

A far more common form of obsession is "romantic love." Zick Rubin (1970) thinks that romantic love must involve a strong and even obsessive sense of attachment. This obsession is the subject of many great literary works. Here are a few passages from *Romeo and Juliet* to illustrate the strong affinity.

> One fairer than my love? The all-seeing sun
> Ne'er saw her match since first the world begun.
> (Act I Scene II)

> 'Tis torture, and not mercy. Heaven is here
> Where Juliet lives, and every cat and dog
> And little mouse, every unworthy thing,
> Live here in heaven and may look on her, But Romeo may not.
> (Act III Scene III)

In desperation, when Romeo mistook Juliet's fake death for real, Romeo sought to kill himself, saying:

> Well, Juliet, I will lie with thee to-night.
> Let's see for means:
> O mischief, thou art swift
> To enter in the thoughts of desperate men!
> (Act V Scene I)

Then, upon discovering that Romeo was dead, Juliet could not find the courage to live by herself. Before stabbing herself, and hearing that someone was coming, she said:

> Yea, noise? then I'll be brief. O happy dagger!
>
> This is thy sheath; (stabs herself) there rust, and let me die. (falls on Romeo's body, and dies)
>
> (Act V Scene III)

Stories like *Romeo and Juliet* in the West and the *Butterfly Lovers* in the East really share the same theme: in each case the young man would rather die than live without the woman he loves so deeply. But Romeo, as well as Liang Shanbo, the hero in *Butterfly Lovers*, should know that the woman who truly loved him would certainly like to see him live with courage and be able to cheer up even when she was not around. And similarly, Juliet should know that Romeo, if he truly loved her, would not have wanted to see her die.

But literature being what it is, the greater the attachment, the greater is deemed the love. Sadly, while making a great sacrifice, including laying down one's life, to better the life of someone else reflects a greater love, these stories are rarely heralded. Literary works on romantic love may be said to accurately reflect the obsessiveness of uncultivated human nature, but glorifying this kind of love as great has distorted the meaning of greatness and has indirectly encouraged many young people to do silly things, if for some reason they could not wed or keep their loved ones to themselves.

Sunk costs and past glory as obsessions

In economics there is a very useful concept called "sunk costs." Sunk costs are spent and cannot be recovered. Economists advise that sunk costs should not be considered at all in decision-making. Decision-making should be based on the costs and benefits *arising from* a decision. There is a lot of wisdom in this concept, because it advises us that, rather than being bogged down by the past, we should focus on the here and now. In so far as we make the best decision possible now, we will still realize the best that is possible. Being obsessed by sunk costs would affect our ability to make the best decision now.

Going back to romantic love, which by definition includes a strong sense of attachment, many couples when they have to break up cannot totally leave the episode behind. This obsession very much reflects a mental inertia. Because we are so used to something, we are psychologically not prepared for any change. But this is really silly, because there is nothing you can do to help if it is truly a *sunk cost*. Once the nature of a sunk cost has been recognized, therefore, the best strategy is always to leave it totally behind. There is truth in The Beatles' famous song which says the words "Let it Be" are "Words of Wisdom."

Another example of a sunk cost is years spent in acquiring a skill. Suppose that skill has now become obsolete, or, alternatively, suppose some opportunity arises that offers you new possibilities that are very attractive and that are entirely within reach. The wise person would forget about the sunk cost altogether. After all, it is the future that counts. Being bogged down by things in the past limits self-actualization.

Related to "sunk costs" is "past glory." Some very successful enterprises are bogged down by past glories and complacency, and are not able to evolve with the times. The stories of Wang Computers and Kodak are prime examples. One key and fatal decision was founder Dr. Wang's insistence that his son, Fred Wang, should succeed him. Fred Wang was not able to retain the key staff in charge of research and development and was too immersed in Wang Computers' past glory to understand the challenges that faced the company.[2] The story of Eastman Kodak is even more striking as an example of a company basking in past glory and failing to meet the challenges of new times. Kodak had long prospered on the "razor-blade" business model by selling cameras cheaply while making huge profits on films. The time-tested model, unfortunately, rendered the company totally unprepared for new times, to the extent that it actually lost its core business to its own invention—the digital camera. But "instead of marketing the new technology, the company held back for fear of hurting its lucrative film business, even after digital products were reshaping the market."[3] Thus Kodak's demise is a classic case of hanging on to the past and losing the future.

To think positively is not to dismiss misfortunes nor to discount the challenges that we face. What we need, instead, is not to be bogged down by the misfortunes or bad decisions in the past. Instead, we need to acknowledge the misfortunes, the setbacks, the challenges, and the negative emotions that may come with these things. So being aggrieved is not a problem at all. But instead of being bogged down by misfortunes and setbacks, we need to limit losses and focus on what we can do to make the most out of a difficult situation.

If we acknowledge the negative emotions but disallow the negative emotions to become destructive, we will grow out of them and become stronger. Limiting the losses means that, while expressing sadness, grief and anger is fine, we do not dwell on the foregone losses and never allow our sense of loss to overwhelm and shatter our lives. For example, suppose we are caught in an accident and have to face the fact that a leg has to be amputated. This is a physical loss that we have to recognize. The best strategy is accepting what has happened and learning to cope with it rather than being upset over it for an extended period of time. It is perfectly fine to cry for a day or two, but it's rather silly to keep crying for a year instead of learning to cope with the situation.

Similarly, if we have been robbed or have lost money on the stock market, losing sleep over it will not help. Allowing the sense of loss to damage our life further is adding another loss on top of the loss that has already taken place. Let bygones be bygones. Sunk losses cannot be reversed.

Obsessing over the disappointing results of a particular incident is why many people lack resilience. Instead of learning from the incident and looking forward to doing better next time, they tend to blame themselves, someone else, or bad luck, and cannot control their emotions. They cannot forgive themselves, nor can they forgive others, for the incident. They fail to understand that what has happened has happened. They fail to understand that if there was a cost to pay, it was a sunk cost, and nothing can be done to salvage it. The longer they let their emotions rule "over" them, the more difficult it will be for them to be on the way again. So instead of salvaging what has already been lost, they are losing even more.

Resilient people will limit their losses by preventing their emotions from blocking their way to future success. They also reflect on the incident and thus try to learn as much as possible from the experience. In this way they grow stronger and stand ready to meet the next challenge.

Fortitude appears to be the least important factor from regressions using the LIFE formula. The coefficient ranges from one-third to one-half of the size for Engagement, but Fortitude is really important at crucial times. Before one meets a setback, Fortitude does not play any role. This is why Fortitude appears not to be as important as the other LIFE variables. But when there is a setback, the resilient person survives and becomes stronger, while the one who does not pass the test collapses.

Those who "forgive and forget" are not bogged down by a painful experience and can move on to take advantage of other opportunities that life offers. Those who have an unforgiving mind will, on the other hand, miss out what life can offer. This is a key reason why happier people tend to be more successful.

Fortitude thus is not only driven by a strong sense of purpose but is also helped by the wisdom to limit losses and the growth mindset so one will emerge wiser and stronger. The growth mindset is a readiness to take every life experience as a nutrient to feed personal growth, so that one will benefit from both pleasant and unpleasant experiences.

The seven deadly sins all stem from obsessions

Mortal as we are, we all have to tackle the so-called "seven deadly sins": wrath, greed, sloth, pride, lust, envy and gluttony, not because they are immoral, but because they will erode our well-being. Overcoming them frees our mind from their toxicity and brings back our mental health.

Wrath is a more violent form of anger. It is generally a result of frustration.

Frustration occurs when what is intended fails to materialize. Wrathful people put an excessive focus on a disappointment and the goal that was missed. The frustration of not achieving an identified goal produces wrath. When anger takes over, a person might do destructive things, and could hurt himself and others.

Greed is a strong desire to possess more. The excessive focus is on the objects of the cravings. When greed takes over, again the person could ignore other people's welfare altogether, while the burning desire for more makes him restless and unhappy. Behavior motivated by greed could lead to a loss of welfare for others as well as for himself.

Sloth is failing to garner what lies within a person's ability to improve his own well-being or that of others. The person is a slave to his own inertia, and too focused on the difficulties that may beset him so will not make the effort to break from the path he is used to.

Pride in this context is arrogance.[4] It is an excessively strong sense of the ego, which blinds a person to his own inadequacies. The opposite of pride is humility. With humility, one can gradually develop one's latent strengths. With pride, weaknesses are preserved while the latent abilities continue to be undeveloped.

Lust is an excessive pursuit of the pleasures of sex, which blinds a person from seeing and developing other possibilities.

Envy is a negative emotion of discontent and resentment generated by desire for the possessions, attributes, qualities, or achievements of some other person (the target of the envy). It implies an excessive focus on oneself, never accepting the fact that another person appears to have a better life.[5]

Gluttony is simply excessive indulgence in the pleasures from material goods and services, which again blinds one to the many other good things that life can offer.

Evidence abounds that people under the grip of these "deadly sins" are unhappy. They are unhappy because they are no longer masters of themselves.

Pseudo mental goods

It may appear strange to us that some people appear to enjoy the very opposite of the mental goods that most people cherish. If human nature is universal, how do we explain some people's taking pleasure at seeing others suffer and be humiliated? A possible explanation is that when individuals fail to get or are denied a mental good they may develop an instinct to pursue the very opposite of what they have been denied, so that sadism is actually loving kindness transmuted into its very opposite. Loving kindness is a mental good that every person would aspire to by nature. When denied or deprived of it, an individual desperately needs something to take its place, and that something is the very opposite of loving kindness. A person denied autonomy or unable to realize autonomy may turn his natural desire for autonomy into a desire to control others. These transmutations of the original mental goods can be called "pseudo mental goods" and are potentially very dangerous because once the "pseudo mental capital" takes hold it is very difficult to eradicate it, and it can then become very destructive. Erich Fromm (1964, p.37) called an extreme form of this behavior *malignant narcissism* and referred to it as a severe mental sickness representing "the quintessence of evil." He characterized the condition as "the most severe pathology and the root of the most vicious destructiveness and inhumanity," leading to a descent into *necrophilia*, literally a love of death as a result of a failure to come to terms with life.

I call these transmutations of mental goods "pseudo mental goods" because, although people do derive a momentary pleasure or satisfaction from them, their minds are not really at peace. With an impulsive urge to hurt and manipulate others, they end up making a mess of their own lives and those of others.

Those who lose faith and collapse in adversity are often too focused on the difficulties of the moment to remember that life makes sense only when looked at in its entirety, and not in segments. If they are able to take a longer-term view, they will realize the importance of patience. If times are rough and fighting does not stand much chance of success, the best strategy may be patience, i.e., conserve your energy and wait, meanwhile remembering your longer-term goal. Trying to fight a big storm recklessly is not the spirit of Fortitude, and it may even constitute a misuse of the precious energy that we still have. The spirit of Fortitude is to survive and to stage a fight only when there is a fighting chance.

Seeing the big picture will tell us that there is value in what you are doing even when you are conserving your energy. Doing the best you can within the constraints is the spirit of economics, and that coincides with the spirit of Fortitude.

Building fortitude requires going through adversities

Fortitude is predicated on a strong sense of purpose, and Love, being the drive to nurture life to fruition, is that sense of purpose. Fortitude, however, does not come automatically once one has a strong sense of purpose. It has to be built up. One gains strength by first overcoming smaller adversities and then learning to overcome bigger ones. "Faith in life" is therefore a mental capital that needs to be accumulated through thick and thin. Being disappointed and frustrated from time to time in smaller ways is often a blessing in disguise, because only in this way can we develop our inner strength, so we can face bigger adversities. Fortitude is associated with a strong "faith" in life and a belief that after the winter there will be spring. You keep telling yourself that you will tough it out no matter what. You keep telling yourself that you need to always be ready for the opportunity to rebound when it comes. You keep telling yourself that you will not be beaten. Because the goal is so much valued, it is worth the fight and the patience and the hard work.

Building resilience is a great investment because it brings great returns in terms of happiness and a more fulfilling life, which is the return that really matters. This faith is moreover not at all an empty faith. It is based, in part, on the observation of the laws of nature that even the worst storm will pass, and that in the darkness of the night dawn always awaits, and in part, on the life skills that one has accumulated over the years. Equipped with those life skills, one just feels much more confident and naturally has the courage to face adversities.

Real stories

The rise of American basketball player Jeremy Lin to fame is a case in point. He had suffered many bad turns before, having been undrafted and then cut by two different National Basketball Association teams. He was about to be cut by a third team, when his chance came. With major players suffering from injuries and unable to play, the Knicks had to play him, and Lin seized the opportunity to put up a stunning show.

Lin's rise to stardom is not based on good luck. If he had not kept his skills at the top level through hard work, the chance would have just been a non-event. Instead of complaining about his bad luck, he used his precious energy to prepare himself for the golden chance. When the chance eventually came, he made the best use of it.

Lin cited the Bible: "suffering produces character, and character produces hope, and hope does not disappoint us." When the hard work bears fruit, the fruit is that much sweeter.

Eric Jackson, writing in *Forbes*, summarized the lessons to be learnt from the Lin story in ten points:[6]

1 Believe in yourself when no one else does. This belief has to be based on hard work and a strong dedication to your goal. Without the hard work it is not possible to build up the self-confidence. Thus during the time of patiently waiting we still need to work hard to prepare for the moment of truth.
2 Seize the opportunity when it comes up. Opportunities come and go. We need to watch out for opportunities as they come. Some opportunities may appear once in a lifetime. Thus always being well prepared is important.
3 Your family will always be there for you, so be there for them. The knowledge that your family members are behind you is often a strong boost to morale.

4 Find the system that works for your style. This is simply: 'Be yourself; do the best you are at.' This corresponds to comparative advantage in economics. Everybody has some comparative advantage.
5 Don't overlook talent that might exist around you today on your team. Too many people dismiss the talent that is available and within their easy reach.
6 People will love you for being an original, not trying to be someone else. Again, this is 'Be yourself.' We are all unique and valuable in special ways. We need to discover the potential within ourselves.
7 Stay humble. Humility is the precondition for improvement and particularly for personal growth. Only with humility can we learn and accumulate mental capital.
8 When you make others around you look good, they will love you forever. Offer others support when they need it, and you will be offered support when you need it.
9 Never forget about the importance of luck or fate in life. Gratitude attracts support from others and makes you strong.
10 Work your butt off. Hard work is indispensable.

When times are tough the one who sees the big picture and has the long view will persevere and will emerge from the difficulties stronger, wiser and happier, whereas the one who gives up and can't muster the courage to bounce back rarely recovers.

Another inspiring story, and one that we first encountered in Chapter 6, is that of Hirotada Ototake in Japan. He was born in 1976 with a congenital condition that left him with almost no arms or legs. Many parents would have abandoned him, and most people would not expect much of a future for him. But he nevertheless learnt to overcome many of the obstacles that he was born with, to participate actively in sports and in academic pursuits, and got into the prestigious Waseda University. His autobiography, *No One's Perfect* (2003), described his personal struggle and sold over 4,500,000 copies. He admitted that disabilities were of course not an asset, and that he was not always accepted by others, but rather than shying away from challenges, he mustered all the strength and ability he could, and managed to convince the world that a strong will and the spirit of never giving up will make a big difference. After publishing his bestselling autobiography, Ototake became a successful sports journalist. In 2007, he took a job as a primary school teacher in Tokyo.

Did the disability become an asset to Ototake? In one sense. Without his almost crushing disability, he would not have been able to demonstrate to the world that the human will can be very strong and that a strong will can make such a difference.

The story, as told in *No One's Perfect*, left one blogger "decidedly on edge" for the apparent lack of agony. "Are we to believe in all his twenty-five years he has never had even one dark night of the soul—wondering, 'Why me?' … if Oto is completely happy, then he is either one in a million, or he is a saint."[7]

There is no doubt that Ototake had many agonizing moments, but the important thing is that he did not let those moments bog him down. He would not let his mind keep dwelling on what he could not do but instead he kept looking for opportunities to make the best of what he could do.

Randy Pausch is yet another example of a truly resilient man. He was a Carnegie Mellon University (CMU) professor before he died of pancreatic cancer. His "Last Lecture" inspired people around the world as much as Ototake's writing did. The stories of Ototake and Pausch tell us that life is worth living after all, despite all the adversity.

Pausch delivered his "Last Lecture," titled "Really Achieving Your Childhood Dreams," at CMU on September 18, 2007. Like Ototake, Pausch showed his humanity and an unfailing faith in, and deep respect for, life. He was loving, humorous and upbeat, even though an earlier attempt to arrest his cancerous cells had failed. He capitalized on his otherwise tragic illness in the prime of his life to teach his students and the world that a passion for life and treasuring the valuable time that we have when we are alive are what it takes to live a fulfilling life. A book expanding on the theme of the Last Lecture and carrying the same title has been translated into 46 languages. The book sold more than 4.5 million copies in print in the United States alone (Pausch and Zaslow, 2008).

Finally, I would like readers to discover the story of Mike Wallace, the celebrated CBS News journalist who hosted the *60 Minutes* program. He had suffered depression for a number of years without letting others know about it. The depression became much more pronounced in 1984 after General William Westmoreland filed a $120 million libel suit against him and CBS over statements that were made in the documentary *The Uncounted Enemy: A Vietnam Deception* (1982). His wife Mary loved him and forced him to go to a doctor, who diagnosed him with clinical depression and treated him with an antidepressant and psychotherapy. These treatments helped pull Wallace through the severe bout of depression in the mid-1980s, which was so tough that at his lowest, he attempted suicide with an overdose of pills.

Attempting suicide is not, of course, an example of fortitude. However, his story is informative about how much difference love and a bit of luck can make. Suicide is almost always a grave and silly mistake. Surviving that attempted suicide, Wallace lived up to 2012 and died at the age of 93. Importantly, he expressed how much he owed his beloved wife Mary and said that the time since his attempted suicide 20 years previously turned out to be "the best in his life."[8] It was lucky of him that his wife found him unconscious at 3 am, in time for him to be revived. He could easily have died.

Adversity often implies loss and difficulties. But fortitude would have us focus not on what we have lost nor on what the future might have in store, but instead on what we can do today. Fortitude would also have us see beyond the present difficulties. Dawn is near in the darkest of the night. Moreover, there is usually something to be gained for every loss. Adversity often offers lessons to learn and makes us stronger and thus better prepared for the next adversity. If we value what we still have and learn to do the best with what we still have, we have fulfilled our duties. On the other hand, if we keep regretting what we have already lost—a bygone and a sunk cost or worrying about the future—and fail to make the best use of what is still within our control, we could ruin our only window of opportunity, which is today! Each day gone is gone forever.

Conclusions: transcendence versus obsessions

Life has to be viewed in its entirety in order to be understood. Seeing life in its entirety is transcendence. We would be groping in the dark if we did not see the big picture. We would never get the fulfilment that is possible. Making the most out of our lives, we must not allow obsessions of any kind to hold us up. Life is like a big picture with bright spots and shadows that would not make much sense when viewed in isolation. Only when we succeed in transcending the here and now, and take life in its entirety, can we achieve equanimity and avoid being overjoyed at success and losing heart at frustration or failure. Failing to do so, however, will inevitably lead to greater suffering under the laws of life.

Professor Yew-kwang Ng used to ask the audience in public lectures and in class if they thought it was better to be severely disabled (for example losing both legs) or to be killed in an accident. He found that shows of hands indicated that those who were in favor of being killed typically outnumbered those in favor of being severely handicapped by about 2–3 to 1. Professor Ng would then tell them, "Your preferences are incorrect!" Citing Brickman et al. (1978), he pointed out that studies show that quadriplegics are only slightly less happy than healthy people. "After a period of adjustment, the happiness levels of seriously disabled accident victims are [typically] restored to levels close to the pre-accident levels" (Ng and Ng, 2000). The resilience of people, if they give themselves the chance to test it, often goes beyond what they believe! How sad it is, then, to see people committing suicide in the face of some adversity that they thought was grave but that actually would not hurt that much over the long run.

Like Love and Insight, Fortitude can be cultivated. It is through learning to overcome smaller adversities that we gradually learn to overcome bigger adversities. But the courage to face and overcome adversities is always driven by a strong sense of purpose, particularly Love. When such a strong sense of purpose has been identified, achieving the purpose becomes much bigger than serving one's ego (the "false self"). When the obsessive ego itself is forgotten, Fortitude grows into a gigantic force, because, then, the "true self" gains the upper hand.

People who are really strong have their minds set on higher things and on longer-term goals than most people ever dream of. Through the eyes of the "true self" or the "soul," they see success as realizing the best that is possible within the constraints that they face. So they will not be defeated by short-term reversals. They could lose a battle, but they would never admit defeat. They are ready to change course when an instrumental goal is beyond reach. As long as they keep their eyes on their longer-term goals and keep fighting, they will indeed never lose the war. Rather than losing the war, because they make sure that each day of their lives brings them closer to their goals, their lives are truly successful. Their perseverance, truthfulness and passionate endeavors testify to the most valuable qualities known to humanity. Whichever day their life journeys end, they will have lived a meaningful, fulfilling life (Paul T.P.Wong et al. 2023).

Notes

1 Thaler (1980) coined the term "endowment effect." Tversky and Kahneman (1991) attributed this result to "loss aversion." By explaining the endowment effect by loss aversion they implicitly agree that having to give something up already owned produces a mental bad. To the extent that the mental bad is real, the claim that the endowment effect reflects that people are not rational is invalid. Acquiring the LIFE culture and hence giving up obsession, however, is rational and wise.

2 Wang Laboratories filed for bankruptcy protection in August 1992. After emerging from bankruptcy, the company changed its name to Wang Global. After being sold to Getronics of the Netherlands in 1999, it had ceased to exist as an independent company.

3 See E.D. Gibson (2024) "Kodak's Missed Opportunity: A Cautionary Tale of Corporate Myopia," published October 14, available at https://deconch30.medium.com/kodaks-missed-opportunity-a-cautionary-tale-of-corporate-myopia-fde4232ebd75. Accessed June 4, 2025.

4 The word "pride" may also mean a sense of dignity based on virtues. But in the context of the seven deadly sins it means arrogance.

5 According to the American Psychological Association, a related term, jealousy, always requires "a triangle of social relationships between three individuals: the one who is jealous, the partner with whom the jealous individual has or desires a relationship, and the rival who represents a preemptive threat to that relationship."

6 Available online at www.forbes.com/sites/ericjackson/2012/02/11/9-lessons-jeremy-lin-can-teach-us-before-we-go-to-work-monday-morning/. Accessed July 10, 2024.

7 L. W. Milam, "No One's Perfect Hirotada Ototake," available at www.krabarchive.com/ralphmag/AG/ototake.html. Accessed June 4, 2025.

8 See Mikaela Conley (2012) "Mike Wallace's Battle With Depression and Suicide," April 9, ABC News, available at https://abcnews.go.com/blogs/health/2012/04/09/mike-wallaces-battle-with-depression-and-suicide. Accessed June 4, 2025.

Key points to note

- Insight and Fortitude are twin brothers in that they reinforce each other, and they are both strengthened by Love.
- Seeing the big picture with an open mind breeds a sense of proportion, the ability to distinguish between means and ends, and the habit of reflecting on and learning from mistakes.
- Obsessions are self-inflicted obstacles to learning and growing up.
- The growth mindset, based on the LIFE culture, allows one to take pleasant and unpleasant episodes of life with a sense of equanimity so we will have a good understanding of our humanity and be on top of ourselves.

Some questions to ponder

- Why is the growth mindset so difficult to nurture?
- Is indifference equivalent to equanimity? If not, what is the difference between them?
- Are hedonism and eudaimonic happiness incompatible? Why does nature give us all the sensory pleasures if they do not mean much to enduring happiness?
- What role does Love play in a person's lack or fullness of Fortitude? Can you give real life examples to illustrate?

9

ENGAGEMENT AND SELF-ACTUALIZATION

Vanity versus achievement and self-worth

Engagement is being in the driver's seat in daily living: fully engaged with a sense of purpose and of taking control. It gives meaning to living and builds a sense of self-worth. When the self transcends to a bigger self so love extends to all humanity and even other life forms, self-actualization sublimes to spirituality, and self-worth will be accompanied by equanimity and inner peace and a strong sense of accomplishment. Vanity is a sense of self-esteem based on other people's recognition or envy. Pursuing vanity *per se* is driven by a culture that may be self-defeating. On the other hand, truthfully living and fully engaged people self-actualize and gain a sense of self-worth. They will not feel lonely because they know they are in the company of other true achievers.

Introduction

Abraham Maslow in his discussion on the hierarchy of needs put self-actualization as the highest aspiration of humankind. Self-actualization is realizing the potential within and following one's heart. For anyone who has experienced it, self-actualization is a wonderful experience in and of itself. Incidental to self-actualization, however, is the mental good called "sense of achievement/accomplishment." When people develop a strong passion for something and take self-actualization to be an end in itself, the degree of satisfaction achieved is very high and gives one a strong sense of self-worth. Still, while some people seek self-actualization as a natural yearning, others may seek achievement in order to win acceptance or recognition by others. For them the sense of achievement is built on recognition by others or their envy. Some people would call this vanity. Vanity carries the connotation that such

DOI: 10.4324/9781003507093-9

pursuit is morally wrong. While there is nothing wrong with desiring mental goods, the "vanity culture" is highly competitive because one's gain may be at the expense of others' loss.

Vanity-prone people may honestly compete for the recognition or may not. If they fail, they will be unhappy, but even if they succeed they are still likely to be under a lot of stress for fear of losing the crown. Because performing better than others through honest effort is so hard, many people take the easy way out. Some do this through cheating or through conspicuous consumption. This undermines sustainable development.

Today, many people try to gain recognition through social media. Those who are able to attract a lot of followers are not only rewarded financially but also gain the mental good of other people's admiration or envy. However, they are also highly susceptible to depression when they are disliked or when they attract cyberbullying. Those who perform dangerous acts, which includes taking "selfies" dangerously in order to attract attention, also risk killing themselves.

On the other hand, honest self-actualizers gain happiness without regard to what others think and do. In comparison to those who seek recognition by others, self-actualization is an easier and surer way to achieve happiness. They are happy without even thinking about happiness!

Nature of engagement

Traditionally, economists assume that individuals carry out their day-to-day activities to maximize "utility." Rational decision-makers are assumed to maximize the "discounted value" of utility over the rest of their lifetime. This perspective prompts the question: does this mean maximizing utility is the purpose of living? To answer this question we need to know that "utility" is just a term referring to the value associated with anything that is considered desirable. If helping others is deemed desirable, then altruism brings utility. Similarly we may also refer to the utility of making peace. Whenever someone truthfully and earnestly does something that one believes in, that someone is self-actualizing and deriving utility. Economists assume people are rational and seek utility in the sense that everything done is done for a purpose. Any judgment about the worthiness of the pursuits is entirely personal but must be authentic. When one pursues a goal earnestly because that goal is authentically taken to be valuable, one is engaged. Engagement, therefore, must be grounded on identifying a worthy purpose and then engaging in various tasks passionately in pursuit of the identified purpose.

Seeking utility or happiness may sound alien to Kant's (1964) characterization of the purpose of living, even though he does not exactly deny the human aspiration for happiness. To him, there is a "categorical imperative" for us to "act only according to that maxim whereby [we] can, at the same time, will that it should become a universal law" (p.31). This is the call of duty: doing something that is worthy entirely for its own sake and not as a means to something desired.[1]

The "call of duty" sounds antithetical to liberalism. However, taking the accumulation of mental capital and personal growth as the call of duty and the categorical imperative is compatible with liberalism, because mental capital is merely an asset to be used in one's own way. Blessed with LIFE mental capital, one stands a better chance to find one's dream!

It may be surprising to note that even following the call of duty can be reconciled with utility maximization! Following the call of duty does not free us from having to make choices. Choices are unavoidable in real life, and whenever we make a choice, we have to weigh one choice against another one according to some value metrics in order to make the best choice. Doctors following their call of duty in saving lives sometimes have to decide whether to save A's life or B's life. Any decision-making involves choice and implies maximization of "utility" which merely reflects some kind of value metrics for decision-making.

Ends, instrumental goals, and means

It is natural that our value metrics change in the course of our lifecycle. As a child, the key value metrics could be having fun and satisfying the urge of curiosity. For a student facing examinations, the key value metrics would likely be high grades. For a job seeker it could be a high-paying job or a job that offers a good career path. For a company executive it could be a promotion. For the CEO of a listed company, it could be profit maximization and enhancing the stock price of the firm. For a competitive athlete it could be winning a gold medal. For a parent, the key value metrics are likely to be bringing up a happy and "successful" child who will excel in studies and then in a career. More enlightened parents may just want to bring up children with self-discipline and a strong love for himself and for others.

Whatever we pursue, having some target makes our lives much more interesting and meaningful. Interestingly, however, over the long run, it does not really matter that much what we choose to pursue so long as we follow our heart with a growth mindset. Even in pursuing a career, different careers may offer totally different material rewards and opportunities. There is always so much uncertainty that one can never know if one has made the best decision. But choosing a career that does not fit with your personality and for which you do not feel much excitement is most probably a mistake.

Whatever goals we choose, as we work toward them, we will develop certain skills, some of which will prove useful for us later in life. Yet all these goals are really just intermediate targets. In a sense they are all a means to an end rather than the ends themselves. They are all means to an end because as we pursue these intermediate, instrumental goals we become more focused and then can perform better, with the result that we stand a far better chance of realizing our potential.

None of these intermediate goals should be considered as the ends themselves, because the final goal must be realizing the best within our reach, i.e., our full potential for happiness.[2] When we understand this, and when we have accumulated sufficient LIFE mental capital, we will have developed a strong sense of self-worth, to the extent that we can withstand the ridicule of cyberbullies and the influence of toxic cultures. We become independent and will not drift with the currents that are driving society into infighting and polarization.

Accumulating LIFE mental capital and achieving personal growth, then, is the "categorical imperative" for all of us. Making money is important, but only in so far as it allows us to survive, and to procure the means for having a fulfilling life. If we pursue greater wealth at the expense of a more fulfilling life, we become slaves to the money that we pursue. Similarly, if we pursue a career at the expense of a more fulfilling life, we become slaves to the career that we pursue. And we can substitute any of the intermediate goals in this sentence to underscore the fact that, after all, it is achieving a more fulfilling life that should be the final goal.

Whatever we pursue, having some target makes our lives much more interesting and meaningful. Whatever instrumental goals we have chosen, as we work toward them, we develop certain skills, some of which will prove useful for us later on in life. As explained above, instrumental goals give us a better chance at realizing our potential.

None of these intermediate goals should be considered as ends in themselves because the final goal must be realising the best within our reach. This is the "categorical imperative" for all of us. Making money is important, but only in so far as it allows us to survive, and to procure the means for having a truly fulfilling life.[3] If we pursue greater wealth at the expense of a fulfilling life, we become slaves to the money that we pursue. Similarly, if we pursue a career at the expense of a fulfilling life, we become slaves to the career that we pursue. And we can substitute any of the intermediate goals in this sentence, to underscore the fact that, after all, it is achieving a truly fulfilling life that should be the final goal. When we have a large store of mental capital, we can take on the world and "self-actualize" and find our dreams our own way.

That is why it is heart-breaking to see students kill themselves for not being able to meet the demands from their school or from the education system, whether imaginary or otherwise. After all, education is supposed to be for their benefit. When instead of benefiting from their education students feel helpless or worthless under its weight, the education must have gone wrong. Education is only a means towards achieving a better life. When, instead of helping students discover a more worthy life, education drives them to suicide, education must have failed its mission.

Helping students to see the distinction between means and ends and to know that life is more important than anything else must be central to the mission of education. It is instructive for us to ask why people confuse means with ends, and this brings us back to the discussion about mental goods and bads. It is no use telling a student that passing an examination is not the most important thing on earth, when all the signals from around them are that passing an examination and getting good grades is super-important. You can see them in the principal's speeches; you can see them in the special sessions that teachers arrange for students after class; you can see the extent to which the timetable is structured; you can see them in conversations among students. When high performers are honored and poor performers are shamed or ignored, students will feel the pressure. All this forms a toxic culture that cannot be easily dismissed. Students need to learn that doing badly in examinations is not such a big deal, although doing the best they can while maintaining a good work–life balance and always reflecting. We all need to learn that practising the happiness formula—Love, Insight, Fortitude and Engagement—by living a truly engaged life with these guiding principles is the key to living a truly fulfilling life.

Loving parents or vain parents

Most parents derive a lot of satisfaction from seeing their children make notable achievements. This may reflect two kinds of emotions, which can coexist. First is a genuine relief and joy that their beloved children could do so well. Second is the thought that the children's achievements reflect their own achievements as parents. Vain parents are those who push their children in directions consistent with what they think constitutes success—which is generally what their peers consider to be success—against the best interests of their children.

Whether vanity is involved or not, however, as humans, all parents cherish a sense of achievement. Wise and loving parents differ from vain parents in that they see achievement differently. Parents blessed with Love and Insight derive a sense of achievement when they see their children independently discover and live a fulfilling life. Vain parents derive a sense of achievement when they see their children accomplish what the parents' peers consider to be remarkable achievements. So they have different "production functions" for the mental good called "sense of achievement." As discussed before, these differences in production functions reflect differences in culture.

Parents with "different household production functions" based on different cultures produce different effects on the children. With wise and loving parents devoted to bringing out the potential of their offspring, children pursue their own goals and enjoy a sense of autonomy. Parents who do not impose their will on their children but instead just focus on nurturing their LIFE mental capital will succeed in conveying their love to their children. In response to this Love, children will grow up and develop their talents with courage and self-discipline. With vain parents obsessed with seeing their children "successful" in illustrious career paths, children are compelled to pursue the goals identified by their parents and suffer a loss of autonomy. They may sense that their parents are selfish and will not sense the love from their parents. Using the jargon of economists, as vain parents strive to acquire their sense of achievement, they impose an external cost on their children making them suffer a loss of autonomy. Their children lose the opportunity to self-actualize and may not find life worth living.

Let me share with readers a sad and true story. It is about a talented and kind-hearted man by the name of Wang Shang-yi, who was born in Henan in mainland China. At the age of 12, he came to Hong Kong and later moved to Taiwan with his parents. He was particularly fond of literature and creative writing and regularly contributed to school publications. He also had talents in art and music. The violin was his favorite instrument. His excellent academic performance allowed him to be admitted to the best medical school in Taiwan, which was what his parents wanted. Discovering that he lacked interest, he wanted to change to philosophy. Facing strong objection from his father, he unwillingly completed his medical studies. His humanitarian instinct drove him to follow the footsteps of Albert Schweitzer, serving the poor and the needy. Unfortunately, he soon died of liver cancer at the tender age of 26. His book *A Wild Pigeon at Dusk* (野鴿子的黃昏) was published after his death. Even more sadly, two girls were so depressed after reading the book that they killed themselves.[4]

Self-Actualization, a sense of achievement, and the nature of achievement

It must be pointed out that self-actualization, although at the top of Maslow's hierarchy of needs, is not at all something limited to talented people or even adults. Small children, even toddlers, self-actualize in their own ways. Self-actualization simply means following one's heart with regular honest reflections. As people learn to know themselves better, they self-actualize in their preferred ways. When they are not allowed to do what they really want, they suffer a loss of autonomy, which can drive them into depression. Wang Shang-yi had already suffered such a loss of autonomy at school when he not allowed to act in a play that did not follow the political lines of then-ruling Chinese Nationalist Party (Kuomintang). He suffered another loss of autonomy because his father did not allow him to change his studies from medicine to philosophy.

Self-actualization brings joy. Loss of autonomy brings pain. This is as true for small children as it is true for adults. Even mentally handicapped people can self-actualize and find their share of joy. People are not born equal. But all people deserve equal respect as a person entitled to achieve their own dreams as long as they do not adversely affect the freedom or the well-being of others.

While it is commonly believed that competition helps push standards higher and forges progress, excessive emphasis on outperforming others may give rise to serious social, economic and psychological problems. The social cost is just too big. In a society that equates success with outperforming others, few can stand tall and stay aloof from the toxic atmosphere. This phenomenon, which arises from excessive competition, is called neijuan in China.

Two of the most striking ills from excessive emphasis on competition are doping and excessive inhumane training for the Olympic Games. While the spirit of the Olympic Games has always been held to be friendly and fair competition, doping has a long history. Winning a medal, particularly a gold medal, is a big deal. Many countries give gold medalists huge financial rewards. Since first place and second place translate into vastly different rewards, it is not surprising that some athletes resort to unfair competition. With all the eyes focused on whether one wins the gold medal, winning the gold medal is taken to be a big achievement. But honestly, if the gold medal is won through cheating, is that an achievement? How much satisfaction does such "achievement" offer?

In contrast to winning a gold medal, some people quietly achieve what they can with hard work without people taking notice. There are some lone rock climbers who tackle very difficult cliffs and their success is known only to themselves. In 1984, a Frenchman, Patrick Bauer, decided to embark on a self-sufficient 350-km journey across the Algerian Desert on foot. It took him over 12 days. Having completed the journey, he figured that other people could share his passion. So, in 1986 he began to organize an ultramarathon, which then attracted 23 participants. Since then, it has become an annual event, and in the course of 28 years has attracted more than 12,000 participants. Today, the Marathon des Sables (MdS) is a major endurance event that offers people the opportunity to choose different lengths in different destinations. MdS has now transformed itself and aims to be accessible to everyone so many more people can have a taste of the challenge.

When it was still in its earlier form, finishing the ultramarathon was extremely hard, billed as "the toughest race on earth." A CNN report began the feature article asking readers: "Would you pay thousands of dollars to spend seven days running under the scorching sun of the Sahara Desert, traversing shifting sand dunes and punishing rocky plateaus for more than 220 kilometers, with all your food and kit affixed to your back?"

Since participants did pay the required cost and attempted the tough challenge, economists would logically conclude that, for them, the utility of taking up the challenge and that of the prospect of completing the challenge must be greater than the sum of the disutility of the stressful training and the tough run itself and the financial cost needed to participate in the race. But what is the nature of that utility? My answer is that it is the utility of the mental good that comes with tackling a big challenge and the prospect of success in overcoming the discomfort and making to the finish line. Thus, "achievement" to Patrick Bauer and to those who participate in the race must involve a kind of satisfaction "that money can't buy." These people would certainly not cheat to "achieve." Cheating cannot be achievement. These people find satisfaction in overcoming challenges, and this may have little to do with getting others' recognition.

Nature of self-worth

Obviously, cheating will never give one a sense of self-worth. Self-worth must be based on integrity and honesty as a person. Consider the following verse in my poem cited in Chapter 3 (Box 3.4) on "LIFE as the Happiness Formula":

> Insight is Wise Living.
> Considerate, congruent, and contemplative:
> Keep an eye on the big picture.
> For what you see is all relative.

To be considerate means that a person must not be self-centred and must put himself in other people's positions and consider their feelings and well-being. To be congruent means that a person must have integrity. He must not say one thing and do another thing. He must not cheat. To be contemplative means that one should think deeply about life. Self-worth must be grounded in truthfulness and honesty to oneself. This is far more rewarding than self-esteem. Many people make huge sacrifice, sometimes even giving up their own lives for a cause that they believe in.

The "household production" of self-worth, like those of other mental goods, is affected by culture. Under one culture, honestly making an effort for something considered worthy, even without tangible results, is enough to generate a sense of self-worth. Under an alternative culture, honestly doing one's best is not enough. Only tangible results count. If one cannot generate the desired result, "that proves one is not worthy"! "Success" is understood as achieving the desired objectives and must be recognized by others as success. I strongly detest this kind of culture. This culture creates a lot of needless and pointless suffering. Whether things turn out the way we want depends on many factors, some of which are beyond our control. We need to acknowledge this. So parents should find comfort in seeing their children make an honest effort in everything that they do and give them sincere applause. Recognizing their effort and appreciating their courage will encourage them to continue to always make an honest effort. If parents do this, their children will keep trying their best in everything they do. I would call this a great success in its own right.

Learning through thick and thin

The key to purposive living is not only to live with a purpose on some days, but to live fully and passionately with a purpose every day. After all, each day in our life is equally precious. Each day deserves to be used to serve our final purpose, which must be discovering and realizing the potential within ourselves. "A day truly lived is a day truly gained." Whether the day appears to go in one's favor or against one's favor, with the right attitude, in the end it will be a good day, because it tests out your sense of equanimity, which if underdeveloped, points to more spiritual work. It takes seeing the totality of life, with favorable and unfavorable days combined, to enrich and feed one's spiritual life. Zen ("Zen" is the Japanese pronunciation of the original Chinese character read "Chan") Master Sengcan's Xinxin Ming or "Song of the Truthful Mind," begins with:

> The Way of the supreme is not difficult,
> If only people will give up preferences.
> Like not, dislike not.
> Be illuminated.[5]

He maintains that giving up the idea of favorable and unfavorable leads one naturally to the highest level of understanding. Another Zen Master, Weixin of the Song Dynasty who lived more than four centuries later, wrote:

> Before I began my spiritual enterprise
> I saw mountains as mountains, and rivers as rivers.
> When I began my spiritual practice,
> Mountains were no longer mountains,
> And rivers no longer rivers.
> When I fulfilled my spiritual endeavor,
> Mountains were mountains again, and rivers again rivers.[6]

> It is always attitudes that erred,
> Never the external world ('mountains and rivers')
> The uninitiated never notice the erring.

> The to-be-initiated notice the erring, but try to find reality from the outside. The wise dispel their own biased views, and see reality for what it is.
>
> (Ho, 2020)

It is inevitable that some of the days in our lives appear to be favorable while some other days appear to be unfavorable, in terms of the intermediate goals that we have chosen for ourselves, or simply in terms of our day-to-day functions. You could make a serious mistake at work, flunk a test, break up with your partner, or fall sick. Rather than simply dismissing these as bad days, seeing the big picture and swallowing it without complaint could allow us to learn from our experiences. Someone who has so disciplined his mind that he can focus his mind easily can do much more than others who cannot. Someone whose mind is out of focus most of the time will let opportunities pass and will have decisions made by default rather than deliberately when the chance to deliberate on one's own terms is gone.

Mindfulness is particularly important to help us guard against silly, momentary decisions and behavior that we could regret for life. Sometimes, just a flash of the mind could lead us to misbehave, and the consequences can be very serious. Not being mindful means that we may just not be aware of the dangers of the acts that we may do. There was a case in Hong Kong involving a young doctor who had worked hard and achieved excellent academic results but lost his mind and sexually assaulted a patient. With the criminal conviction, his loss was huge. In hindsight, the sexual assault reflects a lack of control and a lack of mindfulness. The young doctor was momentarily "out of his mind." Only when we are mindful and alert can we stop the mind's unbridled adventures from playing havoc with our lives.

To get a glimpse into the mind's unbridled adventures, we may do a very simple exercise called Breathing Attention Exercise, which is detailed in Chapter 11. This training helps improve self-awareness so it will be easier to maintain your temper and to maintain your focus.

Conclusions

Life is a journey. A journey with a purpose is usually a more interesting journey. You will never be bored. Making a journey with curiosity and zeal is always a more fruitful journey than making one in which you merely follow what others do. Different people have different goals in life, and that is just fine. It takes work and effort to achieve any goal. But most goals in life are intermediate goals and are more in the nature of an instrument than a final goal. Yet intermediate goals are still very useful, for they give us drive, help us focus our minds, and provide us with meaning. Which intermediate goal we choose is not nearly as important as simply following our heart or being truthful with ourselves: for living against our nature is very depressing. Because the world is uncertain, we may never know if a particular choice was the best choice at the time. Interestingly, however, we will learn that it does not matter that much over the long run. What is more important is making sense of our experience. Interestingly, with the right attitude—an open and humble attitude—every day of our lives can be just as inspiring and meaningful, regardless of the careers that we choose, unless we somehow have chosen a career that goes counter to our inner nature.

Notes

1 Taking an untraditional perspective, Wike (1994) argued that Kant's key propositions are not inimical to happiness having a positive role to play in Kant's ethic.
2 See the introductory chapter in Ng and Ho (2006), where there is a discussion on happiness as a final goal.
3 As to what is a truly fulfilling life, each person must be truthful and honestly reflect and find out.
4 It is not possible to prove any connections. But it is known that unhappiness and especially chronic depression undermine health, and that there is such a thing as the emotional contagion. The two girls who committed suicide may have their own problems, but any negative emotion may be amplified when they felt connected with a distressed, kind-hearted young man unable to realize his dreams.
5 My translation of the Xinxin Ming or "Song of the Truthful Mind" is provided in Human Spirituality and Happiness (Ho, 2020) and is also available from www2.buddhistdoor.net/features/xin-xin-ming-song-of-the-truthful-mind.
6 This is the translation of another Zen master's writing. The source is 指月錄 (literally, "Records of Finger Pointing at the Moon") and attributed to Master Weixin from the Tang dynasty.

Key points to note

- Self-actualization is doing what one's inner nature calls one to do.
- Self-actualization ranges from toddlers exploring the surroundings and playing with whatever comes its way to artists' creative activities and scientists' scientific inquiry and inventions.
- Self-actualization in its sublime form gives one a strong sense of satisfaction and self-worth.
- Vanity is based on other people's recognition. Because it requires other people's recognition and comparative performance, it is also a source of anxiety and stress.

Some questions to ponder

- What is "immoral"? Is vanity immoral?
- Is self-worth important to everybody? If there is a difference from person to person, why?

- "What you do should be congruent with what you know (to be right)" (知行合一) is a philosophy preached and popularized by Wang Yangming, a Song dynasty philosopher. What emotions will follow if one practices this philosophy?
- Is equality worth pursuing? Why? How should we understand equality?

10

THREE HAPPINESSES AND HOLISTIC PERSONAL GROWTH AS SUCCESS

As we grow old, our outlook on life changes. But whether we experience personal growth is uncertain. Growing up requires a growth mindset, which requires the humility to admit our inadequacies and the desire to change for the better. One's well-being at any moment is not just related to what one is doing at the time but is also conditioned by one's past as well as one's expectations or apprehensions about the future. Only the present, however, represents the window of opportunity for us to make a positive difference in the rest of our lives. This is why "a day truly lived is a day truly gained." Personal growth represents broadening our view on life, learning to see life in its entirety, and accepting that life consists of both pleasant and unpleasant experiences, both of which are required to understand humanity. Accumulation of LIFE mental capitals enables personal growth, which enhances our emotional health and well-being.

Introduction

Many people talk about the benefits of "living in the present."[1] However, this is very difficult to do because, on the one hand, regrets about the past or unhappy memories may prove difficult to ignore or dismiss, while on the other, worries about the future may distract our attention from the present. As a result, we may not be fully engaged with the task at hand. Our performance may decline, and we may fail to get as much out of an otherwise enjoyable experience as we could. Since the present is really the only time when we can make a difference, failing to do the best we can in the present translates to wasting the precious window of opportunity that we have today.

DOI: 10.4324/9781003507093-10

A team of researchers from Princeton University developed a systematic account of "evaluated time use." The study, based on a nationwide telephone survey of nearly 4,000 people in the spring and summer of 2006, with the help of the Gallup Organization, tried to collect information on individuals' reported emotional experiences, such as the intensity of pain, happiness, stress and so forth[2] (Krueger et al. 2009). Based on this Princeton Affect and Time Survey (PATS), the research team compiled a "U-index" that measures the proportion of time an individual spends in an unpleasant state. The unpleasant state is defined as an episode in which the maximum rating on any of the negative affect dimensions, such as "depressed," "angry," and "frustrated," is strictly greater than the maximum rating of the positive affect dimensions, such as "happy," "enjoy myself," and "friendly."

This approach does offer some advantages and it complements national income accounting[3] in that it offers additional information about well-being that national income accounting ignores. Yet it is not educational and may even be counter-educational. It conveys the erroneous implicit message that that the effects of an activity, whether positive or negative, on emotions are intrinsically associated with that activity. The truth is that the extent to which an activity is pleasant or unpleasant often depends on the attitude of the person undertaking it and may not be intrinsic to the activity. For example, you may take a taxi to cover a one-mile journey to save energy. But then people may walk or jog an even longer distance for exercise. There is the story of an official in the Jin period in ancient China by the name of Tao Kan (259–334), who was demoted and exiled to the then remote city of Guangzhou in the south as a result of envy by a powerful official. With nothing much to do, he decided to keep busy by moving a hundred bricks from his study to his courtyard in the morning and moving them back to his study in the evening. Certainly, moving the bricks is physically very strenuous, as is rock climbing, or even doing a work-out in the gym. Understanding the importance of attitude to the quality of life and gradually forming an attitude or mindset that dissociates unpleasantness from a task that we do is an important part of personal growth. This is not only good for mental health, but also will enhance fortitude and performance. Given his strong ability as a military commander, Tao Kan was summoned by the emperor to fight rebels. He repeatedly defeated them and was honored as the Duke of Changsha. His story has been handed down for centuries as a model to emulate.

Moreover, as David Cutler points out,[4] while the U-index and the evaluated time use approach can measure the utility or disutility derived from an activity, "they are less good at measuring the value of what comes out." From a more holistic perspective, an activity that may not be pleasant at the moment—often requiring effort and sacrifice—may make the achievement of a goal possible and meaningful. The satisfaction thus derived is for that reason much greater.

Past, present and future

Jeremy Bentham is well known as the father of utilitarianism, and his "felicific calculus" would have us subtract all the pains and add all the pleasures to get the net gains in terms of utility. But life is really an integral whole and is much more than the sum of its parts. In particular, the past is linked to the present, and the present is linked to the future. In a sense, although what's done is done, in the sense that you cannot go back to the past and remake a decision, what was done in the past is reflected in the present, while what we do today will certainly be reflected in our life tomorrow. How we live, the choices we make, the way we think, *at all the phases of our lives*, are part of us and cannot be wiped out. If we keep learning from all the "good" and the "bad," the "pleasant" and the "unpleasant," and learn to see life in its entirety, we become enlightened and feel a strong sense of accomplishment. We are on the road to personal growth!

I agree with Maurer et al. (2023, p.6) that "personal growth is 1) *holistic*, in that it is fundamentally embedded within the entire system into which the individual fits—including the physiological, biological, cognitive, emotional, social, and cultural realms, 2) *dynamic*, in that the process is not sequential or linear, but chaotic and iterative, 3) *gradual*, in that it is often arduous and occurs over a long period; and 4) *well-being enhancing*, in that it a process of increasing one's capacities and skills for well-being."

The past is affecting our life conditions today in three ways. First, we are likely to accumulate both positive and negative mental capitals. Some people may like to call this "karma," but whatever you call it, the habits we have built up will significantly impact our lives. Some of these habits have become so much a part of ourselves that they have become our personal traits or our "second nature" and are very difficult to change. Second, pleasant experiences with other people in the past tend to make us more optimistic and trusting of others, while unpleasant experiences in the past may make us more pessimistic and distrustful of others. Third, regrets about something we did wrong in the past often haunt us, while past generosity and kindly acts tend to give us peace of mind, so we are better able to enjoy the pleasures and delights of the here and now.

Because the past can affect our life conditions so much, and because the here and now will become the past, we need to be mindful of what we think and do today, so we will accumulate positive mental capital today. Today is our only window of opportunity to make a difference. There is of course another today tomorrow. But a "today" that is gone will be gone forever, while "a day truly lived (thus contributing to growth) is a day truly gained."

The future is also affecting our life conditions in several ways. First, we may worry about uncertainty. We are generally more comfortable with what we are familiar with but are apprehensive about whether we can cope when something that we are not familiar with happens to us. Second, we may worry about something terrible that may or may not happen to us. For example, during the episode of severe acute respiratory syndrome (SARS) that struck China and the Hong Kong Special Administrative Region in 2002–2003 and then spread to the rest of the world, many people were terrified, and were afraid of meeting people and of travelling. The airlines had a very difficult time because there were hardly any passengers on most flights. Third, instead of worrying we should focus on doing the best we can to secure a brighter future. This way we can cherish hope even during times of difficulties and great hardship.

In short, happiness *today* is not determined just by what we experience today, but also by past events and experiences, and by the future that has not yet arrived, and, above all, our mindset or our attitude today.

We tried to test the "three happinesses hypothesis," which is the hypothesis that the past and the future, as much as the present, all have an important bearing on our happiness.

We designed three groups of questions to gauge the effects of past, present and future on the happiness of people. Respondents were asked if they agreed or disagreed with the statements below, on a scale of 0 to 10, with 0 being "most disagree" and 10 being "most agree."

Prospective happiness

- I meet each day with excitement and joy.
- I do not usually worry about the future.
- I expect to continue to learn more things in the rest of my life.

Happiness in process

- I enjoy my work/housework.
- I enjoy my time with my family.

Retrospective happiness

- I am pleased with how I have conducted my life.
- I have grown wiser because I am able to learn from my mistakes.

The average scores of each of these three categories were then used as regressors to explain the overall happiness index, also on an 11-point scale (0–10). The sample is subdivided into three age groups and the regression separately run. The results are listed in Table 10.1.

TABLE 10.1 Changes in the three happinesses at different phases of the life cycle (2008 Hong Kong Happiness Randomized Telephone Survey)

Age (years) (observations)	*21–29 (163)*	*30–60 (502)*	*60 or above (94)*
Constant	1.322 (2.751)***	1.442 (4.383)***	1.259 (1.582)
Prospective happiness	**0.419** **(4.666)*****	0. 279 (6.389)***	0.228 (2.005)***
Happiness in process	0.37 (4.562)***	0.233 (4.942)***	0.262 (2.365)**
Retrospective happiness	0.036 (0.461)***	**0.293** **(5.808)*****	**0.353** **(3.316)*****
R bar square (*F*-statistic)	0.476 (50.416)***	0.396 (110.794)***	0.393 (21.276)***

Notes
Figures in bold indicate the highest of the "three happinesses" for the age group.
*** Significant at 1%; ** significant at 5%.

It is interesting to note that the coefficients or weights pertaining to prospective happiness and happiness in process tend to decline with age. This seems to make sense, because as one gains in age, life expectancy declines, and health conditions tend to deteriorate.

The tenfold rise in the coefficient on retrospective happiness from youth to old age is worth noting. It means that the past continues to have tremendous effects on the well-being of a person. While prospective happiness is very important when one is in one's twenties, its weight keeps shrinking while that of retrospective happiness keeps rising. While the weight of retrospective happiness keeps rising with age, there is no guarantee that personal growth will happen for everybody. Those with little personal growth will accumulate anger and obsession; those with a lot of personal growth will grow out of obsessions and become freer and happier.

Personal development and successful living

Successful living is all about personal development or "whole-person development," which is a somewhat overused term often found in university missions. To say that it is overused is not to say that whole personal development should not be central to university missions. The term is overused because universities may be saying this so often that their management might not really think seriously about what this means, ending up merely paying lip service to whole-person development.

Personal development is about bringing out the potential that lies within. It is generally accompanied by an accumulation of positive mental capital and decumulation of negative mental capital. It is also about ridding us of our obsessions, and getting to know how we can best procure our mental goods. What Maurer et al. (2023, p.2) refer to as "well-being capacities" we call "mental capitals." Like Maurer et al., we stress the authenticity of the personal growth process. Authentic means that one's experience of personal development and growth is entirely personal. No one can accomplish the growth process on behalf of someone else.

Maurer et al. (2023, p.3) see personal growth and personal development as distinct concepts. While personal development may refer to the developmental changes in physical, cognitive, and socio-emotional spheres as one ages, "whole person development" is growth and requires a "growth mindset." This growth mindset is my desire to be a better me today than the me I was yesterday. This requires an admission of inadequacy and a desire for change. This admission requires humility and an open mind. Humility and an open mind are twins: one cannot really have an open mind if one thinks that one is always right.

Personal growth must be accompanied by an accumulation of mental capital. With the growth mindset, one deliberately chooses to invest in LIFE mental capitals. As LIFE mental capitals accumulate and negative mental capitals dissipate, our sense of self-worth grows, and happiness grows. What used to bother you suddenly bothers you no more, while what used to elude your attention suddenly is rediscovered and becomes a source of delight. This is successful living.

Some may argue that success should be defined by the individual, so imposing one interpretation of successful living as the correct one would be illiberal. But personal development as realizing one's potential is very broad and very liberal. People have different strengths and weaknesses and it is up to them to develop their potential in their unique ways. The bottom line is that we are all human beings, and that we can and should do the best with our lives. Learning to do the best with our lives is personal development. Personal development is entirely personal or authentic. Successful whole person development is personal growth.

Scientifically, there is a lot of evidence that people who love more, people who have a sense of proportion and self-control and who see success more as doing the best they can rather than in terms of doing better than others, people who can "tough it out" no matter what, and people who live an active life with a clear purpose, will be happy. Ultimately, we need to be honest with ourselves and reflect on what we do and how we see things and if what we do and how we see things make us happy. Personal development requires honest reflection and living truthfully.

Happiness at the moment versus enduring happiness

As we accumulate more mental capital, we respond to different situations in wiser ways. Instead of frowning or panicking over an adverse situation, we have the composure to deal with every situation using all the assets at our command. We will find our ability to cope with pressures and frustrations and losses grow with time. We do not care so much about whether things have turned out the way we would like. We face each day with a passion: to enjoy it if it is enjoyable, to learn from it if there is a lesson to be learnt, to test our strength and to train to be stronger if the day is rough and tough. We do not worry so much about whether an experience or an activity is enjoyable, boring, hard, or a struggle. Daily or hourly happiness gradually will not count as much, as we have our eyes on a broader and farther horizon. In this way, we gradually acquire an attitude that fosters enduring happiness, and rejoice in discovering that we keep gaining something each day, no matter what.

This is why I have some problems with the "National Time Accounting" (NTA) work pioneered by Alan B. Krueger, Daniel Kahneman, David Schkade, Norbert Schwarz, and Arthur A. Stone (KKSSS) (Krueger et al. 2009). They have described their approach thus:

> Our project is distinguished from past efforts in that we approach NTA from more of a psychological well-being and Experience Sampling Method (ESM) perspective. For example, our measure of emotional experience is multidimensional, reflecting different core affective dimensions. And like ESM, we try to measure the feelings that were experienced during different uses of time as closely as possible. We also developed an easily interpretable and defensible metric of subjective well-being, which combines the data on affective experience and time use to measure the proportion of time spent in an unpleasant state.

They cited Gregory Dow and Thomas Juster (1985) and Juster et al. (1985), who emphasized the notion of "process benefits," or the flow of utility that accrues during particular activities, such as work and consumption. With the assumption that process benefits from activities (in our example, preparing and consuming a meal) are separable, utility can be written as:

$$\text{Total utility} = \text{Utility from work} + \text{Utility from cooking} + \text{Utility from eating}$$

Utility from work is dependent on the time spent on work and the exertion required; utility from cooking is dependent on the time spent on cooking and the quantity of food; utility from eating is dependent on the time spent eating and the quality and quantity of the food. This notion of process benefits is related to the concept of experienced utility proposed by Kahneman. KKSSS defines an individual's experienced happiness on a given day by the average value of this dimension of affective experience for that day. Experienced happiness, so defined, is influenced by the individual's allocation of time: a longer lunch and a shorter commute make for a better day.

However, the amount of enjoyment or displeasure from an activity is not intrinsic to that activity. Often it depends on the individual's state of mind. Cooking can be fun, but it can also be a chore. Attending a concert can be very pleasurable, but it could also be a pain, if a person, while attending the concert, keeps thinking about the work that he has yet to do or the work that he is having difficulty completing, or the grudge that he has against someone who had treated him unfairly. I proposed that happiness may comprise three components, and they may not be additive. These are "prospective happiness," "process happiness," and "retrospective happiness." Prospective happiness refers to the happiness or unhappiness that one experiences as one faces a welcomed or feared prospect. We can be very happy looking forward to a wedding, or a new job, or meeting someone we have missed for many years. We can be very unhappy regretting something that we had done before, or very happy cherishing the sweet moments that we had in the past spending time with our loved ones. Such prospective and retrospective emotions will affect the enjoyment from an ongoing activity. *Someone with a growth mindset will have high retrospective happiness, high process happiness, and high prospective happiness, because he is pleased with how he/she has grown wiser and realizes that whatever that had happened in the past have contributed to his/her personal growth while looking forward to even more growth to come.*

Many mental goods one experiences may depend on apparently unpleasant activities such as arduous training. The way the questions are asked means that the enjoyment of mental goods enabled by such unpleasant activities is not reflected in the time accounting surveys. Without the arduous training, there can be no sense of achievement for an athlete who wins in a game or a musician who thoroughly enjoys his own music playing. What is more, without going through pain and suffering, it will be impossible to understand other people's pain and suffering, and there can be no empathy, no love and no appreciation.

In a chapter written by Cutler and collected in the KKSSS volume, these points are recognized. "Pleasures of wealth, skill, amity, a good name, piety, and benevolence are generally missing" from the U-index. KKSSS would not dismiss these criticisms but noted that NTA nevertheless offers a dimension of well-being that is not captured in conventional economic statistics.

Holistic living

So personal development is a process of gradually accepting life as it is, in its entirety, and unleashing the potential within us. The interesting thing is that we do not really need to wait till we have finally unleashed all the potential within us to become happy. The growth process itself is already quite fulfilling. Like a chick breaking the eggshell breathing the first breath of air from the outside, the joy is immense. I have seen many handicapped people—blind people, deaf people, people who have lost limbs, people who have lost their speech—find fulfilment in their lives. I have seen people who have shown a sea change in their outlook after having recovered from a near-death experience. They start treasuring the days that are left and finding meaning in their lives.

This readily brings to mind one blogger's skepticism over Ototake (see Chapter 8): "Are we to believe in all his twenty-five years he has never had even one dark night of the soul—wondering, 'Why me?' … if Oto is completely happy, then he is either one in a million, or he is a saint." There is no doubt that the severe handicaps faced by Ototake and others certainly are sources of tremendous hardship and suffering. The fact that Ototake finds his life fulfilling and is "perfectly happy" does not mean the handicap did not matter. This is exactly why "perfectly happy" is not the same as "perfectly satisfied." It would be nice if the handicaps could be removed, so the blind could see and the deaf could hear again, and the limbless could walk and could handle things. It is also true that some people really live miserably because of these handicaps. But from a holistic viewpoint, all the suffering that humanity has endured allows us to know love, empathy, support, courage, endurance and kindness (Wong, Paul T.P. 2023; Wong, Paul T.P. et al. 2023). Complaining is of no use at all. If a person is already handicapped, that means he should work harder to put into good use what functionality he still has. While Ototake would certainly be better off if his handicaps were removed, his handicaps with which he was born have, in a sense, become an asset to him as he was then able to preach his message of engaged and courageous living more convincingly. Adrian Anantawan is yet another example of fruitful, courageous and earnest living. He is a world-class violinist, but incredibly, he was born without a right hand! With loving parents who wanted to give their then nine-year-old child a musical instrument despite his handicap, and thanks to inventive technicians, the young boy was given a custom-made prosthetic to hold the bow. This device, made of plaster, aluminum, and Velcro straps, allowed Adrian to play and to achieve his dreams.

The following excerpt of what Anantawan said in an interview with a CNN reporter is truly remarkable and instructive. After reviewing some stories about handicapped people overcoming their handicaps and started learning to play an instrument the reporter cited Anantawan:

> In most of these stories, it's never about the technique or technology that is important, but the desire to live life authentically and creatively. We often forget even 'traditional' musical instruments are technological adaptations in their own right—they are tools to manipulate sound in a way that we couldn't do with our bodies alone.[5]

To be able to grow up despite challenges gives us a great sense of accomplishment, and a great sense of joy. Think about the trophy that an athlete wins because he really trains hard and does his very best. Would a trophy mean much if it was within easy reach without effort?

Holistic living is looking beyond our handicaps and looking beyond the pain or the joy of the moment. Our lives will be much more meaningful and our potential will be much more likely to be realized when life is viewed in its entirety. With a broader view and a longer view, we will never give up. We may lose many battles, but we will never allow ourselves to lose the war: the war against our own fears, our anxiety, our narrow-mindedness and other mental weaknesses. A lack of the will to grow our strengths is the single truly inhibiting factor that prevents us from playing out the strengths that we have.

Spiritual living

The goal of all personal development is "spiritual living." Spiritual living, however, is nothing mystical. Nor does it mean anything "otherworldly." Spiritual living is simply living with deep respect for life, and living with the realization that every human life deserves growth and happiness. The spiritual person has given up egotism, and with this has developed the ability to be passionate but not attached. Since he does not distinguish between himself and others, he will never hurt others to advance himself. Although he is passionate about life and goes about his day-to-day affairs not much differently from others, he is not too attached to material things or personal relationships. His mind is free, so that he is always at ease, and able to avoid being biased by prejudices. He has gradually overcome his weaknesses.

Spiritual living is not beyond the ability of most people. Rather, it is entirely within the ability of every person. All that is required is a genuine respect for life and humility. With humility, it is possible to make progress on the spiritual front, and only then can we make the best use of our time, because such progress allows us to enjoy life truly. In contrast, hedonism at best will give us a momentary sense of ecstasy. This is *not* to say that material gains are of no use. The spiritual person will simply take things easy. He will not overly indulge himself, and he will neither be overjoyed with material gains nor overly saddened by material losses.

It does not matter if our progress is a bit slow at first. But it is important to make an honest and earnest start. Spiritual living is about living humbly and honestly. It is useful to start by making some promises to oneself:

- I promise that I shall respect life and start doing so by treasuring my own life and never harming anybody.
- I promise to do my best to make full use of the potential that life has given me.
- I promise to exercise prudence in everything I do.
- I promise to abstain from harmful substances.
- I promise not to be bogged down by obsessions of any kind.
- I promise to reflect honestly to keep refining myself.

Traditional economics shies away from values and culture and often takes them as given. As David Throsby (2001) observed:

> The fact that economic agents live, breathe, and make decisions within a cultural environment is easily observable. So, too, is the fact that this environment has some influence on shaping their preferences and regulating their behaviour ... Yet in its formal analytics, mainstream economics has tended to disregard these influences, treating human behaviour as a manifestation of universal characteristics which can be fully captured within the individualistic, rational choice, utility maximizing model, and seeing market equilibria as being relevant to all circumstances regardless of the historical, social or cultural context (p. 11).

But, as we have argued, because culture determines the household production function it determines the efficiency of the transformation of material inputs and time into mental goods that people need as human beings. Instead of taking culture as given, we should see culture as a choice. *Humanity needs to choose a culture that is compatible with sustainable development* or humanity will be doomed. A spiritual life helps generate self-worth, inner peace and a sense of achievement without excessively depleting our scarce resources. This is achieved because the individual can seek value and dignity in self-affirmation: there is no need to have others approve, affirm or recognize our status or self-worth. We free ourselves from the treadmill.

From individual to society to the world

Although this book was intended as an aid to individuals as they go about their life journeys, we should spend a moment looking around ourselves and pondering what we can do in our world of conflict. Through human history, regrettably, religious conflicts have left a horrifying number of casualties and broken families, and the tragedy has yet to stop. Religious conflicts historically have probably been even worse than tribal conflicts. Ironically, all religions preach peace and ask their followers not to kill. Religions can help foster peace if and only if we focus on the spiritual teachings of religions instead of the theologies. The spiritual capital of a country has nothing to do with how many temples, churches or mosques it has. Rather, spiritual capital refers to:

> the interconnectedness of the human existence that awakens each individual to the common roots of humanity. It consists of a deep respect for life that is entrenched in the institutions of the country and in the minds of the people. Interestingly, when social spiritual capital is high, individuals are much more likely to be spiritually inclined. The spiritually awakened person will then begin to transcend the kind of maximizing behavior that economists talk about.
>
> *(Ho, 2011, p. 47)*

In order to promote spiritual capital, the following Charter for Inter-Religious Understanding and Spiritual Development was proposed at the end of a conference held at Lingnan University back in 2007.[6]

- All religions shall take as their mission the promotion of peace, including inner peace and peace between nations, races, and different cultures.
- All religious leaders shall accept that the different theologies of the different religions owe their origins to their different historical and cultural backgrounds. Such different theologies do not affect the commonality of their teachings in terms of spiritual practice.
- Spiritual practice requires an abstention from killing and other violent acts and a respect for life.
- The world's great religions offer different routes[7] to the same destination, which may be considered as adaptations to suit different peoples in different cultures.
- Substance is important, not labels. Regardless of the label, all religious practices that liberate the mind from the enslavement of greed, lust, anger, hatred, ill will, and unforgivingness are true and laudable spiritual practices.
- Spiritual practice constitutes the essential teachings of great religions, not theology. The theologies of religions may differ and may conflict with science as we know it today, but theologies are like the parables that Jesus and the Buddha used to guide people to spiritual practice. It is the spiritual messages behind the parables that really matter, not the literal meanings.[8]

Conclusions

Seligman, in his book *Authentic Happiness*, had chapters on the past, the present and the future. He recognized the fact that happiness in general is not just based on the "here and now." Some people feel miserable because they cannot forget traumatic events in the past or they have some misgivings about how they have been treated unfairly, or because they feel they made a grave mistake in the past. Their "here and now" is haunted by their past. At the same time, although the future has not yet arrived, the future may be taking its toll on happiness now if people are worried about it. Alternatively, people may look forward to the future so much that they feel excited and joyful right now.

Among past, present, and future, what distinguishes present from the other two is that it represents a window of opportunity to act on. The past is behind us; the future has not come yet. Living in the moment means grabbing the opportunity today to make wise choices. Investing in LIFE mental capitals must be the wisest choice. All that it takes is an effort to change our attitude and start looking at life as a gift that we must treasure, and keep reminding ourselves of the importance of having the right mindset and forming a habit of reflecting on how well we have spent our day. Then we can anticipate a better tomorrow.

The competition for relative supremacy (whether by wealth, by intelligence, by military power, by influence, by being in the limelight) is a treadmill and is very inefficient. Keeping up with the Joneses is self-defeating and is unsustainable. Since economists are interested in efficiency, it is strange that they appear to be so indifferent to this inefficiency that arises from a "wrong" culture. The only reason they have ignored this inefficiency for so long is that they have failed to see the human need for mental goods. Even Gary Becker, widely recognized as a giant in modern economics, in the paper he wrote with Kevin Murphy (1988) on "rational addiction," recognized only the utility derived from consuming the addictive substance, and totally ignored the disutility from the "mental bad" in the form of a sense of being "hooked," i.e. losing the sense of autonomy, which is much valued by all humans; they also ignored the disutility associated with social disapproval or stigma due to substance abuse, which a World Health Organization study confirmed to be at or near the top among various disabilities (Newcomb et al. 1993).

One nice thing about spiritual living is that it is a non-rival personal "good." Economists distinguish between private goods and public goods. Private goods are "rival" in the sense that, when it is consumed by someone, it is no longer available for another one. Others can buy what is still available in the market, but with more people buying the price goes up and what is available is effectively rationed off to people through "price rationing." That is, those who do not want to pay the going market price will go without it. Public goods are "non-rival" in the sense that one's consumption does not reduce the good's availability to others. Spiritual living is a personal "good" because it must be individually and authentically experienced. Yet it is non-rival, and it also produces "external economies" on others. As one adopts spiritual living, one spreads the message of Love and Insight and Fortitude and Engagement.

A culture of respect for life develops and spreads, as more and more people become spiritual, and this, in turn, benefits sustainable development.

Notes

1 Two handy example are: "The Art of Now: Six Steps to Living in the Moment," *Psychology Today*, and "Live In the Moment: 10 Ways to Live In the Present." (declutterthemind.com)

2 See Alan Krueger, Daniel Kahneman, David Schkade, Norbert Schwarz, and Arthur Stone, Chapter 1, in Alan B. Krueger (ed.) (2009) "Measuring the Subjective Well-being of Nations: National Accounts of Time Use and Well-Being, National Bureau of Economic Research and NBER Working Paper" (2009) "National Time Accounting: The Currency of Life," downloadable from: www.nber.org/chapters/c5053.pdf.

3 National income accounting is the traditional way of compiling data to show the overall economic performance of the macroeconomy. National income is considered to be a good measure of economic well-being.

4 The conference volume was published as Kruegar, Alan B. (ed.) (2009)

5 See the report by Brandon Griggs in CNN, available at https://edition.cnn.com/2013/03/15/tech/innovation/adrian-anantawan-violinist/index.html. Accessed June 4, 2025.

6 The conference title was "Spirituality, Value, and Culture," and it was held on June 22, 2007 at Lingnan University in Hong Kong.

7 Today I would say "different labels of the same route" instead of different routes, because spiritual practice requires overcoming our ancient weaknesses and that is to give up the obsessive mind.

8 Ho (2024) presented statistical results using the World Value Survey wave 5 data that supported "George Bernard Shaw's transcendental interpretation of religion as an understanding of life more than as faith to a theology (Pathak, 1985, p.18). In addition, they corroborate with a recent finding by Holder et al. (2010) and another recent paper by Ford et al. (2023) which maintain that spirituality enhances happiness and human flourishing and that this is not necessarily related to formal religions" (p.1681).

Key points to note

- The advice to live in the present is to grab the window of opportunity that the present provides to realize personal growth.
- Personal growth is not automatic. With some luck we all grow old, but only the initiated will grow up.
- Transitioning from a segmented view of life, which sees life as a mixed bag of undesirable experiences of pain and desirable experiences of joy, to a holistic view of life enables personal growth.
- The growth mindset can turn "unpleasant" experiences and challenges around so they can enrich our lives.

- Spirituality is transcendence, which allows us to see the common roots of humanity and connect with the rest of humanity.

Some questions to ponder

- Why do some people never "grow up"?
- If humanity has common roots, why have there been so many conflicts throughout history?
- We all die in the end. Why then is indulging in worldly pleasures not advisable?
- Do spiritual people not enjoy worldly pleasures?
- What is meant by holistic living?

11

REGRETS AND WORRIES, STRESSES, TOO MANY CHOICES, AND OTHER NEGATIVE EMOTIONS

Negative emotions are part of life and need to be accepted as such. However, the accumulation of LIFE mental capital will help reduce the emergence of negative emotions and enable us to manage them so they will not turn disastrous. Given the prevalence of uncertainty and a lack of information, all humans will make wrong decisions from time to time. We should learn from our mistakes and face the results from our decisions with courage. Similarly, we should exercise reasonable precautions to avoid big mistakes, avert possible risks and stop worrying. LIFE mental capital boosts our self-efficacy, resilience, optimism, and hope, and builds a sense of self-worth that can beat loneliness, bullying, and bewilderment in the face of too many choices.

Introduction

We live in an uncertain world, and there are always many unknowns in the future. We can never be sure whether and where dangers are lurking. Here is one report of an accident that led to the death of 16 people in Arkansas in June 2010[1].

> Tragedy struck Arkansas when flash floods hit the Caddo and Little Missouri rivers that rose by 20 feet overnight. The result was the hikers and campers who were spending the night in tents along the rivers in the isolated Ouachita Mountains were unsuspectingly swept away. It was reported that 16 people had died in flash floods and dozens are missing in Arkansas after flood waters swept through a campground. Sadly, many of the dead reported are children and there are still as many as 20 people missing after the flash flood.

DOI: 10.4324/9781003507093-11

In 2010 a tourist group was about to leave a parking lot in Manila when a gunman suddenly got onto the bus and held them hostage. The incident ended up with eight Hong Kong tourists killed and many others wounded.

The fact is that, while we can and should avoid obvious dangers, we can never be sure if some unforeseen mishaps are awaiting us as we conduct our day-to-day lives.

But worries are of absolutely no use. Worries only undermine our welfare and make us less happy. While playing safe may be wise, those who play safe could still worry. During the episode of severe acute respiratory syndrome (SARS) attacks in 2002–2003 some 300-plus people died in Hong Kong and globally some 810 deaths were reported from 29 countries. The scare this generated, however, was debilitating and not commensurate at all with the small number of infections and deaths. In contrast, the World Health Organization states that approximately 1.19 million people die each year as a result of road traffic crashes.[2] People were so scared of SARS that airlines saw their passenger numbers plunge to a tiny fraction of normal. Worries disrupt our plans and undermine self-actualization, inflict big costs, but give us little benefit. What, then, is the point of worrying?

This chapter argues that, while taking precautions to protect oneself and one's loved ones is advisable, worries are unwarranted. Uncertainties are a fact of life. We may never know if a decision we took was wise. But for good or ill, decisions must be made and we have to face the consequences. That is life. Regardless of what happens, let us enjoy peace of mind knowing that we have done the best we could, given the constraints.

Worries about how people think about us

Many people are worried about how other people think about them. Many people are stressed because people misunderstand them and might have a bad impression of them. Many people are stressed out facing unreasonable people who hurt them with their words, or even abuse them physically. Unfortunately, these things do happen sometimes in real life.

The fact is: there is not much we can do about what other people think and do. So we should just focus on doing what is reasonable to protect ourselves. If we have conducted our own affairs in good conscience, but somehow people continue with their misunderstanding and even become unreasonable, then the problem is theirs and not ours. I would not get upset and pile additional losses on what these people have caused us.

In general, we should never worry about how people look at us. Instead, we should just focus on what we can do. Moreover, it is always good advice not to reason or engage with unreasonable people.[3]

Coming to terms with uncertainties

Worrying is not the same as recognizing a possible risk. We all need to recognize possible risks, and then try to avert the dangers or to minimize the losses in the event a mishap occurs. But worrying is counterproductive. Rather than goading us into action where action is due, worrying, particularly panicking, prevents us from taking proper action.

There are always things within our control and things beyond our control. Doing what is necessary and appropriate within our control and not worrying about things that are beyond our control (how other people think and what other people do, in particular) is always the best strategy. This, unfortunately for many, is easier said than done. In real life, even though we tell ourselves not to worry, worry often creeps in, often even without our being aware of it.

Here is a simple exercize that can help us ignore the worry or wild thoughts that keep coming back to us. The method is adapted from a Buddhist meditation exercise, but it has nothing to do with worship.

A breathing attention exercise

Find a position that you feel comfortable so you can relax fully. Relax the muscles in your face to your neck and shoulders, and then to your hands, and down to your abdomen and your legs. Be fully relaxed and breathe naturally at its own pace.

Inhale. Know that you are inhaling. Focus on the air coming in. As you exhale, count the number 5.

Inhale a second time. Watch the air inflow. As you exhale, count 4.

Inhale a third time. Watch the air inflow. As you exhale, count 3.

Continue till you count to 1, then go back to 5 and start all over again.

Whenever you notice a random thought arise, ignore it, and count number 5, which is your anchor, your refuge from random thoughts. And start all over again.

The idea is not to suppress the random thoughts but to bring your attention back to number 5, your anchor, once you notice a random thought emerging.

We use this method as an instrument so our mind will not be carried away. The reason why we count backwards is because we are used to counting in natural order. We are better able to be attentive when we count backwards. The reason why instead of counting from one to ten we only count from five to one, is because we can be better "anchored." We will be more effective in avoiding drift without our notice so we will not be carried away by wild thoughts.

Notice that in this exercise, there is never a conscious thought to suppress the wild thoughts, particularly worries. By the way, during bedtime, this method can also help to put you to sleep readily.

Apart from this training we can tell ourselves positively: *Worrying is of no use. My duty and responsibility now are to do whatever is within my control to avert the possibilities of danger and to minimize possible losses. Once I have done this I shall have done my job. I shall leave it to [my Father in heaven, my fate, whatever]. Whatever comes, I shall take it as it comes.*

After doing this again and again, being aware of random thoughts becomes a habit, and not easily carried away becomes a habit. Then we shall have accumulated a *mental capital* against worries and *panic attacks.* This is *investing in mental capital.*

Here is a poem that might help in mindfulness training to avert worries and panics. Read it slowly, and imagine that it is a friend talking to you. Tell yourself: no matter how difficult the situation is, give yourself a break.

FIGURE 11.1 "Blessed." Courtesy S.K. Chan.

Blessed
(26 May 2006, Villa Serbelloni, Bellagio, 6 am)

Blessed are those who can put down the day's worries and concerns ...
Never mind if it rains or shines tomorrow.
Never mind if it is right or wrong.
Never mind if someone is honest or dishonest.
Never mind if someone understands me or not.
Never mind if someone means ill or well.
Never mind.

Forget gains and losses.
Let it be.
Only know that
You are blessed.
Let sleep come naturally.
Let the new day come naturally.

Smile a natural smile.
Let blessings come Nature's way.
For you are always at home,
wherever you go.

Avoiding big mistakes that cause too much distress

Humans are naturally "out of their minds" at times. If we are out of our minds, that means we are not aware of what we are doing. We are then prone to making huge silly mistakes that can cause us such distress that it is very difficult to handle. One example is borrowing from a loan shark. Another is committing a mindless crime. Years ago, there was one young medical doctor who committed indecent assault against his patient while working in a hospital in Hong Kong. The young doctor had done very well academically and was at the beginning of a very promising medical career. Yet he lost his mind one day and committed an indecent assault on his patient. He was convicted. Another example of a silly mistake is responding to a hoax call or email that leads to a big financial loss. Fraudsters often take advantage of people's vulnerability to greed or fear. So to tempt and to scare are their key strategies. Another example of a mistake is a brawl with a stranger over something that you consider to be unfair or unreasonable. Any of these could lead to disaster. You would never want to encounter any of these situations. But life being what it is, people can be out of their minds sometimes. This is why self-awareness is so important. The breathing attention exercise will help us avoid going out of our minds and making big mistakes.

Coming to terms with difficulties and misfortunes

There are times when the situation is very difficult. Sometimes one can encounter bad luck. And there are times when the consequences of our past mistakes catch up with us. Coming to terms with difficulties and misfortunes is recognizing them for what they are. It is always better to face the reality than to try to run away from it. If the bad consequences are a result of our mistakes we should learn from the mistakes, and we should pick up the courage to face the consequences. If the difficulties are just a result of bad luck, we should accept that bad luck is part of life. Under such circumstances we will still need, perhaps even more so, to focus on what we can do to minimize the damage and to do our best to get out of the situation.

Over the longer run, the difficulties will pass, and even though the circumstances are hard, toughing it out will usually bring rewards down the road. The difficulties often have a silver lining, and difficulties do build character.

Coming to terms with negative emotions

Negative emotions are part of life, and we have to live with them. This is true of everyone, Overcoming them in the sense of not being ruined by them is a challenge, and is not going to be easy, but overcoming them paradoxically enhances our sense of self-worth. From this perspective, negative emotions make our lives meaningful.

Negative emotions are difficult to overcome, because it may be difficult to identify the reason for their emergence, and it may reflect the presence of a "negative mental capital stock," which is not going to disappear overnight. The negative mental capital stock has been accumulated over a long time in the past. Given the negative capital stock, we may hate someone, we may feel jealous and we may be easily irritated. Two households living next door to each other may accumulate so much hate and anger toward each other that a minor incident could trigger a real fight. I know of a true story of someone killing his neighbor in great fury because of the noise he produced.

As is sometimes pointed out, hatred is often manipulated for political purposes by artful politicians. The most well-known example in history is, of course, Adolf Hitler's manipulation of the Germans' hatred of the Jews. Hitler blamed Jews for Germany's defeat in WWI and created a common enemy to unite the German people.

To come to terms with negative emotions is not to suppress them. Coming to terms with negative emotions begins with recognizing their potentially ruinous effects and deciding to contain them. Instead of attempting to suppress them, we can let out these emotions in the least harmful, or preferably even totally harmless way, by reasoning ourselves out of these emotions over the longer run, and by turning our attention away from the negative thoughts when they emerge. The breathing attention exercise discussed earlier will help.

Seligman (2002) has this to say about negative emotions: "Expressed and dwelt upon … emotions multiply and imprison you in a vicious cycle of dealing fruitlessly with past wrongs." It is a pity that a person, thus "imprisoned," often loses control of himself, and could in some circumstances let out her emotions in horrific, destructive ways.

One example of such horrific, destructive ways of letting out one's negative emotions is the Oakland, California campus shooting in 2012. A former student gunned down and killed seven people and wounded three others at an Oakland nursing college. He had held a grudge against the school for expelling him, was deeply in debt with tens of thousands of dollars in federal tax liens against him, and two of his immediate family had died the previous year.

"We've learned that the suspect was upset with the administration at the school. He was also upset that students in the past, when he attended the school, mistreated him, disrespected him, and things of that nature," Oakland Police Chief Howard Jordan said on *Good Morning America*.[4] The world has never been short of tragedies involving angry people killing and hurting innocent people.

Understandably, for some people "reasoning oneself out of the negative emotions" is very difficult, as the anger may be explosive and spontaneous. The reason why it is so difficult is that the habit of storing (instead of letting go of) negative emotions has been formed. The negative mental capital is there. Recognizing the nature of the problem is the beginning of the solution.

Instead of recognizing that the negative emotions are potentially harmful, some people have chosen to identify themselves with those emotions, and "reason" that they are well justified to avenge their grievances, or to create chaos and thus call upon society to "correct" itself.

The Norway massacre of July 22, 2011, involving a car bomb exploding in Oslo and a shooting spree shortly after on the island of Utøya, by a 32-year-old Norwegian, Anders Behring Breivik, is a classic example of terrible acts being self-justified by a self-professed worthy cause. At his trial for the killing of 77 people and injuring others, Breivik declared: "I acknowledge the acts, but not criminal guilt, and I claim legitimate defence." There was no trace of remorse, only self-congratulation on his success of capturing national and international attention for his cause, which was summarized in a manifesto titled "2083: A European Declaration of Independence," bearing the name "Andrew Berwick"—the English version of his name. He was angry with the flood of Muslims into his country and into Europe and with the politicians who allowed this to happen.

It is clear that Breivik had felt threatened. He saw Muslims as alien to his culture and acted to "defend" what he believed was his entitlement—a Norway and a Europe free of Muslims. But what was the cause of the "mental bad" associated with the immigration of Muslims to Europe? Was it just because they were different, or was it because they were associated with some undesirable behavior? What can be done to alleviate the mental bad? Can people be educated to become more tolerant of people who are different from them? Should Muslims work harder to win others' trust and to avoid producing the negative impressions people may have of them? Rather than simply putting the blame on one person we need to understand how the mental bads "threat" and "anxiety" were produced.[5]

Breivik certainly needs to be punished for his acts, regardless of how he justified his actions. But more important is that we need to know that many violent acts have their seeds in mental bads, and that their perpetrators also routinely justify their antisocial behavior just as Breivik did. Much family violence can be seen in this light. In each case, innocent people are hurt, but the perpetrator may have no remorse at all and may think that he is doing nothing wrong.

Norway, the home of Breivik, along with other Scandinavian countries, is well known for its adherence to the cause of democracy and tolerance. Yet tolerance for people who are just different implies inequality:

> When a group of individuals, whether it is a group bound by a common religion or a shared ideology, boasts that they are tolerant of another group which coexists within society, they are in no way equating themselves with the tolerated group; rather, they are pronouncing themselves as superior to the tolerated group, for when we tolerate something aren't we inadvertently saying that we do not agree with it, that we do not approve of it, but nevertheless, we will let it coexist alongside of us?[6]

This observation comes from an article on the website of the International Raoul Wallenberg Foundation, which is devoted to promoting "the values of solidarity and civic courage, ethical cornerstones of the Saviors of the Holocaust."

So, we have discovered that the root of some of the most dangerous negative emotions that haunt humankind include the failure to see the solidarity of mankind and a disrespect toward life. Coming to terms with our negative emotions requires promoting the values of respect for all human life. Any group—religious, political or otherwise—that preaches the contrary, should not be tolerated in a civilized society because it is socially destructive. Such groups are subversive of the common values that bond humankind together, destroy mental goods, create mental bads and form what may be called *negative social capital.* Humankind in the twenty-first century must not tolerate a religion or a creed that preaches superiority of one race over another.

Loneliness

Buecker et al. (2021) reported in a meta-analysis of 345 studies that loneliness levels linearly increased between 1976 and 2019, suggesting loneliness may be of rising concern in emerging adulthood. Another, more recent, Meta-Gallup survey of more than 140 countries, indicates that almost one in four of the global population report being fairly or very lonely (Maese, 2023). According to Hawkley and Cacioppo (2010), a growing body of longitudinal research indicates that loneliness predicts increased morbidity and mortality. That the US Surgeon General issued a report in 2023 with the title "Our Epidemic of Loneliness and Isolation" underscores the psychological and physical harm loneliness may cause to people. All this shows that loneliness has not abated even though the internet and social media have presumably better connected people.

Unfortunately, the knee-jerk conclusion that social contact will relieve loneliness is not warranted. Hawkley and Cacioppo noted the surprising phenomenon that "People can live relatively solitary lives and not feel lonely, and conversely, they can live an ostensibly rich social life and feel lonely nevertheless." It is possible for someone to feel "alone in a crowd." Indeed, being in a crowd can amplify the feeling of loneliness, because the mental good of feeling connected with someone that one trusts cannot be acquired by simply being in a crowd or by superficial exchanges of words without touching a person's soul.

To Hawkley and Cacioppo (2020, p.2), "loneliness is the social equivalent of physical pain, hunger, and thirst; the pain of social disconnection and the hunger and thirst for social connection motivate the maintenance and formation of social connections necessary for the survival of our genes." To me, loneliness is so damaging for one of two possible reasons. One is the pain arising from the departure or separation from some people to whom a person feels very much attached. The other is that loneliness may result from a feeling of being deserted by others and sensing a loss of self-worth. When this sense is very strong, the social contact whereby people try to help them could be perceived as pity, further aggravating the sense of self-unworthiness. When this happens, a lonely person may refuse to see people in the midst of loneliness.

Accumulating LIFE mental capital will help "immunize" a person against loneliness that may arise from the departure of close family members or a close friend, because LIFE suggests no excessive attachment and only healthy attachment to people we love. LIFE mental capital also equips a person with a growth mindset and such psychological capital as self-efficacy, resilience, hope, and optimism and a strong sense of self-worth that is not dependent on other people's recognition. People with strong LIFE mental capital will not feel lonely because they sense that they are in the company of people who engage themselves in living out values in action.

Perceptions and decisions

Economist and Nobel Laureate Paul A. Samuelson proposed the theory of revealed preference, which assumed that "to choose is to prefer," which at the time upended the survey-based Contingent Valuation Method for cost-benefit analysis. His idea seems appealing and more scientific: what people say they prefer may not be what they prefer; they reveal their true preference through their actual choices. Much cost-benefit analysis is still built on that principle. Unfortunately, in reality people's choices are all based on their perceptions—perceived risks and opportunities and perceived constraints, and human perceptions are flawed. That is why the results of cost-benefit analysis based on observed decisions and choices, like those based on the Contingent Valuation Method, still need to be taken with a grain of salt. Drunk drivers choose to drive after drinking because they are sure that they can harness their cars' power without any problem. People do not choose to be addicted to drugs, gambling, alcohol, or social media, but they end up becoming addicts. Sometimes people know what they actually prefer, yet they just cannot follow through with their decisions.

This is not to say that people are irrational. They are rational in the sense that they have a purpose in their behavior and do not act randomly. But human weaknesses have caused them to choose a lifestyle or to do things that over the long term go against their own interest. Many parents genuinely love their children and want them to live well and flourish, but they "choose" misguided parenting methods to help their children. Shoppers sometimes make impulsive decisions to buy things that they end up never using because at the moment they just don't want to miss the chance to, for example, get something on sale.

Exactly because humans have so many weaknesses, the most important choice in life is to decide early to commit to overcoming these weaknesses. This is investing in life. Deciding and committing to overcoming our weaknesses through thick and thin is the growth mindset.

Too many choices

Psychologist Barry Schwartz's 2004 book, *The Paradox of Choice—Why More is Less,* is a blow to one of the central assumptions of traditional economics. Economists traditionally assume that more is better, and more choice is always better than less choice. This stems from a misguided understanding of rationality. The notion of rationality in economics is simply based on the observation that human behavior typically is motivated by some purpose. To the extent that people want to achieve their purpose, but there are dilemmas involving trade-offs, people would *want* to make the choice that best furthers their purpose. This is "maximization" or "optimization." But wanting to make the best choice does not mean that people are always *capable* of making the best choice. This is because choices must be based on perceived options and perceived payoffs from the options. But perceptions are *always* flawed. One serious and common flaw in perception is mistaking means for ends, for example mistaking making money to be a life goal while hurting the quality of life. When the perceptions do not deviate too far from reality, people can still achieve a high level of utility, where utility is just another word for the intended purpose. But when the perceptions deviate from the reality significantly, or when people are confused, they are likely to fail badly in achieving their purpose.

Schwartz's book shows that when there are too many choices, people may get confused. They know that they lack the information about the payoffs from all the choices to make the best choice, and they worry about making the wrong choice and missing out on a much better one. This worry, unfortunately, is a mental bad, which undermines the welfare of the person independently of a possible decision over an inferior choice.

If people have an unlimited capacity to process information, *a priori*, having more choices will always be better than having fewer choices, because there will be greater chances of coming across a better option than hitherto available. However, our lives are finite, and our capacity to process information within a short space of time is limited. Processing information requires an effort and is taxing on our scarce resources, and may not be worthwhile. When an employer wants to recruit staff, he would not let his advertisement run for many days, and he would normally set a deadline. Although not being able to wait much longer may be one reason for setting a deadline, the cost of having to screen many candidates may also be a reason. In an attempt to process too much information in too short a time, people may get confused. Some people may even show anxiety at being confronted with too many choices.

Having more choices does not always cause more anxiety. If the decision is over some relatively trivial matter, it is generally not a problem at all. A diner offered a lot of choices on the menu generally will not panic. He may simply pick from the meals with which he is familiar, and, from time to time, may try some of the other meals for the first time, and enjoy being delighted by an occasional pleasant surprise. Picking something that he thinks "tastes terrible" is, after all, not the end of the world and is easily dismissed and will not lead to a noticeable fall in happiness.

On the other hand, some choices will prove difficult. Having the choice of a marriage partner among several, each of whom is attractive in his or her own way, may seem a good thing, but could present difficulties. Here's what John is thinking: *Mary is very beautiful, but so is Pauline. Marilyn may not look as attractive, but she has a very pleasant character, and has a very nice and gentle voice, and she gives me support and encouragement each time I am down. But I really do enjoy being with Mary, and Pauline has that sense of humor and is always well organized, and loves music, which I love too.*

Consider the dilemma that a young man or a young woman is looking for a soulmate, and it is not difficult to see that having multiple choices could be very difficult for some people.

This difficulty in part has to do with the fact that the choices in real life involve trade-offs, and also with the fact that, especially in personal relationships, emotions are involved. When, in the end, you have to choose among several possible mates, having to sever previous relationships may be emotionally very difficult. The fact that most major choices in our lives are discrete—you may choose *A* or *B* or *C*, but never some of each—may make people confused. Some people simply cannot make up their minds. This is further complicated by the fact that the future is uncertain. In a sense, every choice is a gamble.

Thus when confronted with many choices, instead of being confused by them, recognizing the few key criteria for making the choice and sticking to them will allow us to make decisions that benefit us over the longer run. With the key criteria determined, it will be much easier to discard all the irrelevant choices, so you can focus on the few "short-listed" candidates and make your final choice.

Simple is beautiful

In the 1970s, E.F. Schumacher wrote a very influential book, *Small is Beautiful* (1973). Schumacher was a respected economist who had served as the Chief Economic Advisor to the UK National Coal Board. His thesis is related to our subject in this chapter. He believes that enough is enough, and asks us to be contented with a simple life and to think more about sustainable development than about economic growth *per se*. He argues that "the aim of human endeavor" ought to be "to obtain the maximum amount of well-being with the minimum amount of consumption, since consumption is merely a means to human well-being":

> Thus, if the purpose of clothing is a certain amount of temperature comfort and an attractive appearance, the task is to attain this purpose with the smallest possible effort, that is, with the smallest annual destruction of cloth and with the help of designs that involve the smallest possible input of toil. The less toil there is, the more time and strength is left for artistic creativity.[7]

He goes on to argue for local production to fill local needs, as "dependence on imports from afar and the consequent need to produce for export to unknown and distant peoples is highly uneconomic and justifiable only in exceptional cases and on a small scale."

This indeed appears alien to a basic tenet in economics: free trade and free markets work like an invisible hand to further the common good. Adam Smith (1759) taught that division of labor is limited by the extent of the market. With globalization, the extent of the market has grown to a size never known before, and the production of goods has never been as "fragmented" as it is today. All this has given rise to a counter-movement, and author and filmmaker Helena Norberg-Hodge took up the mission first raised by Schumacher: a return to the *localization* of production using local resources, rather than the relentless expansion of world trade, and a renewed emphasis on simplicity, ecological awareness and the spirit of the local community. Norberg-Hodge rightly noted that the attainment of happiness has much to do with culture, and she founded the International Society for Ecology and Culture, and made two films, each of which was translated to over 50 languages: *Ancient Futures* (1991) and *The Economics of Happiness* (2011).

Notwithstanding the efforts of many people joining hands to fight globalization, globalization as a phenomenon is likely to continue. But the key message of the activists involved in this issue is really for us not to confuse means with ends. After all, life is for us to enjoy, and simplicity is beautiful. A good understanding of what we really want will help us avoid *excessive globalization*, *excessive sophistication* and *excessive division of labor*. Economics tells us there is often too much of a good thing. Excessive globalization happens when local cultures are drowned out by the dominant cultures that dominate because the key players that matter are driven by huge financial incentives. Excessive sophistication happens when the sophistication no longer serves us. Excessive division of labor happens when workers lose a sense of purpose. When globalization is creating mental bads, such as a sense of loss and anxiety that more than offset all the good that it brings about, globalization will have become excessive. A world without excesses is a simpler, more beautiful world.

Conclusions

Life can be simple, but the mind often tends to make life complicated. Oftentimes we struggle over what choices to make, because we simply do not know the best choice. In the end, we still have to make a decision, or the decision will be made by default. What we should do is not to worry if a wrong choice has been made. Once a decision has been made, there is no point looking back, since looking back is not going to help at all. After making the choice, you will have to make your best subsequent choices in the face of new opportunities and new risks.

There are indeed important decisions for which we must make the right choices. But many other choices may not really matter that much in the long run. I would argue that the most important decision in life is to invest early in LIFE mental capital. You will never regret investing in Love, Insight, Fortitude, and Engagement. As we've discussed, for those who want to get married, choosing the right mate is very important, because living with someone full of negative mental capital may be very tough and costly in a myriad of ways. Career choice is yet another choice that truly matters, because some people may be the wrong fit for certain careers.[8]

Often, making a choice may not really be that difficult "if we know what we want." Here, "what we want" refers to our values and priorities. Of course, it is up to each person to decide his own values and priorities, and it is not for anyone else to tell him what they should be. But people should be aware that humans are liable as has been made clear over and over, to mistake means for ends. In particular, any political system is just a means to good governance. Whether a particular political system is effective in improving governance is an empirical question that needs to be examined scientifically. Asserting that a particular political system is one's value is confusing means for ends.

The purpose of this chapter is to suggest that human beings are subject to distractions. Here again mindfulness can make a big difference. The mindful person is not easily distracted and knows what he wants. When we say simple is beautiful, it is because most of our needs are really simple. When we know our needs and dismiss the distractions, life becomes that much simpler and that much more enjoyable. We will avoid over-thinking.

Negative emotions are part of life. But they are only a part of life. They could bode ill or well, depending on how we take them. Because of this, "negative" emotions may not be negative at all. If we let them take over our speech and our acts, they could feed other people's negative emotions, and mutually reinforce them in the process. They "multiply and imprison you in a vicious cycle." They could bring catastrophic consequences. On the other hand, if we confront our negative emotions positively, their influences subside and the energy that feeds those negative emotions may be transformed into positive emotions that produce positive influences. We grow stronger and gain happiness in the understanding that we have overcome the negative emotions. Having gone through them ourselves, we gain an insight into how they may inflict damage on others and how we may cope with them. We develop a better sense of the common roots that we share.

Notes

1 The link to this particular report is no longer accessible. But reports on the event are still available. One is an ABC News report: "At Least 16 Campers Killed in Arkansas Flash Flood Campers at the remote Albert Pike campground were swept away by rising rivers," dated June 11, 2010, availale at https://abcnews.go.com/WN/Media/campers-killed-arkansas-flash-flood-albert-pike-campground/story?id=10889327. Accessed June 4, 2025.

2 See undated World Health Organization report titled "Road Traffic Injuries," available at www.who.int/health-topics/road-safety#tab=tab_1. Accessed June 4, 2025.

3 Parents should nurture this mentality in their kids. Not engaging with bullies will discourage bullying.

4 See Reuters report (2012) "Suspected shooter at California college targeted administrator, classmates," April 4, available at www.reuters.com/article/world/suspected-shooter-at-california-college-targeted-administrator-classmates-idUSBRE8310XO/. Accessed June 4, 2025.

5 Much of Islamophobia can be reduced if true religious freedom is practiced, which implies that kids should retain their freedom to choose their religion (or to not have any religion) when they attain adulthood instead of being dictated by their parents at birth or when they are young.

6 See Baruch Tenembaum (2004). "Tolerance," The International Raoul Wallenberg Foundation, available at www.raoulwallenberg.net/articles/tolerance.

7 This resonates with our discussion on the relationship between culture and the efficiency of household production.

8 Career choice should make reference to the person's personality, which is important. Considerations about financial returns, social standing, or glamor are far less important.

Key points to note

- Life is short. Investing in LIFE mental capital early will help us deal with the uncertainties in life, overcome worry and anxiety, and achieve a sense of self-worth.
- We should focus on what we can do, instead of worrying about what other people think, which is beyond us.
- Mindfulness training using the breath attention exercise is a great aid to help us avoid being "out of our mind" and doing something counter to our long-term interests.
- Our needs are simple. If we know the beauty of simplicity our life will be full of wonders.
- We don't need more choices. We need to know what we really need.

Some questions to ponder

- "The mind often tends to make life complicated." Can you find examples of such "overthinking"?
- Why do people often mistake means for ends?
- Do people in the West and people in the East have different values? Are there Asian values that are distinct from "Western values"?
- Some people advise: "Avoid discussing politics or religion" because that would hurt feelings. Does this advice make sense? Why?
- What is the difference between loneliness and solitude?

12

CORPORATE LIFE AND HAPPINESS AT WORK

The LIFE framework can be easily adapted to the corporate environment. Corporate Love makes employees feel at home and cared for in the family of the company. Corporate Insight reflects a corporate culture that sees the big picture and supports a reasonable and effective management style. Corporate Fortitude is fostered by a team spirit and strong morale built on a vision that draws minds and hearts together. Corporate Engagement is enabled by an open-minded management style that respects and values worker input. Workers cannot fully engage without a sense of identifying with the mission and vision of the company.

Introduction

The title of a 2023 article in *Harvard Business Review* tells it all: "Creating a Happier Workplace Is Possible—and Worth It." This happens to be the same findings I got in one of the first studies on happiness-at-work in Hong Kong. That study was commissioned by the Hong Kong Productivity Council and took place in 2011. I applied my LIFE framework and adapted it to the business world, introducing the concepts of **Corporate Love**, **Corporate Insight**, **Corporate Fortitude**, and **Corporate Engagement**, and found that these factors boost happiness at work and improve corporate performance. Table 12.1 presents the descriptive statistics in that survey.

Jennifer Moss, author of the *HBR* article, at the end of the article made this proposal to employers. In her words: "Start by asking your employees: What is one thing I can do for you to make next week easier, and go from there." This resonates with my concept of **Corporate Love**.

DOI: 10.4324/9781003507093-12

TABLE 12.1 Descriptive statistics

Variable	*Obs*	*Mean*	*Std. Dev.*	*Min*	*Max*
Happiness at Work	1297	6.64	2.02	0	10
Overall Happiness	1291	6.94	1.85	0	10
Age Group	1279	4.41	2.04	1	10
Level of Education	1275	2.89	0.98	1	5
Marital Status (Married)	1271	0.46	0.50	0	1
Number of Children	1254	1.57	0.86	1	5
Work Hours (scale)	1290	3.14	0.78	1	5
Income Group	1246	1.28	0.51	1	3

Notes: Work Hours on a scale from 1 to 5 ranging from 30 hours or below to 61 hours or above. 3 is 41 to 50 hours. Income (per month) Group: (01) $19,999 or below (02) $20,000 to $50,000 (03) $50,001 or above.

Engagement is defined as acting proactively and autonomously with a strong sense of purpose. In the *HBR* article, again in the words of Moss: "A culture of autonomy, belonging, and purpose comes from a shared vision, and right now, it's fair to say that many companies and their employees are simply not seeing eye-to-eye." She lamented the erosion of value and vision in the corporate world. An answer to a question on Quora about loyalty to the company one works for that was posted in 2023 attracted seven upvotes. It read:

> Company loyalty was once valued (by both employees and employers), but it is not anymore. It's all about the bottom line. Companies will terminate you without a second's thought if it benefits them financially. So why should you view your company as anything more than a paycheck?

Prevalence of such perception leads to a lack of engagement. Workers tend to "do what you are paid for and go home." This will only lead to a lose-lose result.

A lack of engagement is reflected in a sense of losing control. Srikumar Rao, author of *Happiness at Work* (2010) says a loss of control is "the most common complaint" among employees. This is as true today as when Rao's book was published back in 2010.[1] This happens when one feels someone else is in charge, not oneself. So giving some room for employees' decision-making is a good start. But a lack of engagement may also be a result of a lack of the motivation to engage. This happens when the company does not take employees' suggestions and concerns seriously and when the company culture does not foster a team spirit. Gallup found that businesses with engaged workers see higher profits and significantly less turnover and absenteeism than businesses with unhappy workers. This echoes a result we found in the 2011 study. Corporate engagement is important because it gives meaning to work. Gallup estimated that a lack of employee engagement costs the world $8.8 trillion in lost productivity, amounting to 9% of global GDP.[2]

Interestingly, team spirit, corporate culture, and a shared vision are all important for resilience. **Corporate Fortitude** will not be possible without employees and the management standing together to face adversity and to fight for a better future. But this is possible only when employees have a strong sense of engagement. Moreover, a strong sense of engagement is possible only when the management have the insight to be open-minded and give employees sufficient room to make some decisions on their own and the insight to respect those suggestions and views, while holding onto a vision that employees can identify with. Only when the management is enlightened, able to self-correct, decentralize decisions where and when it is appropriate, and taking proactive steps when necessary, and always seeing the big picture with a good sense of the market and the economy and the changes going on in technology and consumer needs and wants, will workers hold the management in high esteem and feel motivated to fully engage in their work. This is **Corporate Insight**.

Just as Love, Insight, Fortitude, and Engagement contribute to personal happiness and growth, Corporate Love, Corporate Insight, Corporate Fortitude, and Corporate Engagement contribute to happiness at work, better performance, and corporate growth.

Corporate LIFE

Moss, citing the 2023 Global Culture Report by O.C. Tanner, noted that organizations that score high on the Community Index—where employees feel like they belong and contribute to shared goals in meaningful ways—have a 62% increase in employee-estimated tenure at their current workplaces. A sense of belonging to an organization reflects a congenial atmosphere in the workplace. Our study on happiness at work in 2011 tells pretty much the same story. Happiness at work was measured on a scale based on the response from employee respondents to the question: "Considering all factors relevant to my job, I rate my overall Happiness at Work on a scale 0 to 10 at … (your answer)." Happy workers want to stay.

We gauged **Corporate Love** with two questions which asked the worker-respondent to what extent he agrees with the statements: "My company is concerned about the well-being of its staff," and "My company gives me a feeling of a big family." The 2024 Global Culture Report found evidence supporting the result that organizations that are perceived to be aware of, understand, and attempt to address employee needs will increase employees' sense of belonging and connection and will improve business outcomes, like attracting and retaining talent. The Global Culture Report has been conducting a similar survey every year since 2019. Their study examines the current state of the workplace with data collected from more than 42,000 employees, leaders, HR practitioners, and executives from 27 countries worldwide.

One main finding of the 2024 Global Culture Report is that "people-centric solutions are the ones that win and endure, every employee wants to feel seen and valued, and resilience must exceed surviving the next challenge." Employers who are perceived to be out of touch with workers will not have loyal workers, leading to high absenteeism and low productivity. Our main findings back in 2011 are confirmed in the Global Culture Report. As indicated in **Table 12.2**, Corporate Love, Corporate Insight, Corporate Fortitude, and Corporate Engagement are all positively and significantly related to happiness at work. We used ordered probit estimation[3], controlled for the different sectors of the industry, and had a total of 957 employees responding from 5 industries, including manufacturing, trade and logistics, finance insurance and professional services, restaurants and hotels, and retail and wholesale. Additional control variables include Senior, Middle, Junior Management (dummies, excl. non-management), education, and marital status.

One might wonder why the coefficient on Corporate Love is far smaller and less significant than Corporate Insight, Corporate Fortitude and Corporate Engagement. The key reason is that the question on employers' attention on Work-Life Balance, which reflects Corporate Love, is included in the computation of the **Corporate Insight** index, which is compiled using responses on "The policy and system in this company is reasonable all the time"; "My company takes work-life balance as important" and "The management style is characterized by a good balance of control and decentralization/delegation."[4]

As we have explained in the earlier chapters, to a large extent Insight is the "how" of love and the "why" of Fortitude, while Engagement is the practice of love on a day-to-day basis. In the corporate setting, Fortitude is very much determined by culture. In our questionnaire, the **Corporate Fortitude** questions include: "The leadership in my company inspires confidence even under difficulties"; "My company helps or encourages me to learn from my mistakes"; "My company makes me feel that we stand together' when faced with challenges"; and "Morale for workers in my company is very high," and "Team spirit in my company is very high."

Generally, it is only when the company has a vision that is shared by employees and the management will morale stay high even when facing huge challenges. Moss stated it well: "Happiness at work has to come from a deeper, more intrinsic connection to why we're there. A culture of autonomy, belonging, and purpose comes from a shared vision."

Table 12.2 shows the Corporate Engagement not only carries the biggest coefficient among all the Corporate LIFE variables, but it is also the most statistically significant. This is for a good reason. Workers who feel that they are just paid to perform assigned duties can never build a sense of engagement. Only when they are both motivated from within (i.e., they see a purpose that

TABLE 12.2 Ordered probit regression of Happiness at Work (scale 0 to 10) focusing on corporate LIFE

Explanatory Variable	*Coefficient*	*z- statistic*	*Prob >|z|*
Corporate Love (1 to 5)	0.065722	1.90	0.057
Corporate Insight (1 to 5)	0.220813	3.87	0.000
Corporate Fortitude (1 to 5)	0.1755022	2.88	0.004
Corporate Engagement (1 to 5)	0.2966034	5.19	0.000
Income Group (1 to 3)	0.320315	0.36	0.715
Work Hours	-0.350922	-.64	0.521
Married	0.0943035	1.25	0.213
Number of Observations	957	**Pseudo R2**	0.2560
Prob > Chi Sq	0.0000		

Note: Coefficients on dummies representing sectors and some other control variables not presented. *** indicates significance at 1%.

is higher than just their pay) and from without (i.e., their contributions are welcomed, recognized, appreciated, and taken seriously) will they enjoy their work and find it rewarding beyond their take-home pay. An interesting finding from **Table 12.2** is that while income (high, middle and low) carries a positive coefficient, the coefficient is not statistically significant. The coefficient on work hours is negative, but again it is not that significant. Some people work long hours but a strong sense of purpose would give them drive so the work can bring satisfaction that may more than offset the disutility of weariness.

To gauge Corporate Engagement, we used five questions, including: "My company takes staff development seriously."; "My company has clear goals for sustaining long-term business success"; "The management actively seeks ideas and suggestions"; "My company offers me opportunities to bring out my strengths and to realize my potential", and "My company offers me a promising career path."

This is not to say that workers do not mind long working hours. Jobs come in different varieties. Some jobs are repetitive and boring. Some jobs allow little room for innovation and judgment. Some jobs require brain power; others physical strength. Some jobs require teamwork; others require working without much interaction with others. Excessively long working hours deprives workers of rest and spending time with their families. Long working hours are unsustainable and have killed workers through greater incidence of accidents and health problems. When such unfortunate things happen, morale will be damaged, and the company may suffer serious setbacks.

Corporate social responsibility

Milton Friedman famously argued that the social responsibility of business is to increase its profits.[5] He thinks that businessmen who espouse corporate social responsibility (CSR) "are unwitting puppets of the intellectual forces that have been undermining the basis of a free society" and are "preaching pure and unadulterated socialism." He does not realize that businessmen are humans too, and many humans, businessmen and shareholders included, have eyes beyond profits. They feel good knowing that their businesses are concerned also about sustainable development and the social good. Profit is money and money is no more than an instrument to a good life, and certainly not a good life by itself.

As we have discovered, a good life needs both physical goods and mental goods. Money can buy physical goods and services. But although these are often inputs in household production to produce mental goods, money cannot directly buy all the mental goods that humans need. Vernon L. Smith's reading of Adam Smith's "Wealth of Nations" and "Theory of Moral Sentiments" reflects this understanding. He showed his understanding of mental goods when he wrote that when people trade or exchange one thing for another, what is traded "include not only goods, but also gifts, assistance, and favors out of sympathy," noting that "whether it is goods or favors that are exchanged, they bestow gains from trade that humans seek relentlessly in all social transactions" (Smith, 1998).

Exercising corporate social responsibility is a form of production. It produces goods and services that may not be traded in the market but that produce social benefits. It also produces a mental good, in the form of a sense of self-worth and love, for the executives who proactively espouse CSR, their workers, their shareholders, and their customers. There are many private equity funds that bill themselves as focusing on ESG. To wit, according to Eccles et al. (2022)

> A huge opportunity for private equity—and for society—now exists. PE (private equity) has moved far beyond its Wall Street niche to become a major player in the global economy. In 2021 the industry had $6.3 trillion in assets under management (compared with about $90 trillion for public equities) and close to $2 trillion in "dry powder" (funds raised but not yet invested). Those assets are projected to exceed $11 trillion by 2026. Roughly 10,000 PE firms worldwide oversee more than 20 million employees at about 40,000 portfolio companies.

The interesting thing is that private equity firms, and investors in general, are acting autonomously and according to their free will to support sustainable development, which is now universally identified as a CSR. Who is "undermining the basis of a free society"? By calling businessmen who espouse CSR "unwitting puppets of the intellectual forces that have been undermining the basis of a free society," Friedman hurt the feelings of CSR-minded businessmen and intellectuals who speak their minds and ask for corporate caring. Frankly I think this is illiberal and undermines the cause of sustainable development, to the detriment of humankind and other species on earth.

Trust as social capital

We asked participants to look at two key statements to measure Trust in the corporate setting. One was "My supervisors are honest." The other was "The management makes me feel I am respected and trusted in the company." The two statements reflect trust from both directions: trust of higher rank or the management by workers or lower rank staff, and trust of workers or lower rank staff by higher rank staff or the management. Trust is often regarded as an important part of social capital. As such, trust does not come about overnight and has to be built up over time. The importance of trust in the business world and in society at large has attracted a large literature. Our first study in 2011 on happiness at work commissioned by the Hong Kong Productivity Council confirmed the importance of trust in happiness at work. **Table 12.3** replaced the Corporate LIFE variables with a single variable—Trust—considered, as has been said, an important social capital and which would be fostered by Corporate Love, Corporate Insight, Corporate Fortitude and Corporate Engagement. The magnitude of the coefficient on Trust is huge. At 0.5547273, it is bigger than the coefficient of Corporate Insight and that of Corporate Engagement combined. The z-statistic is also a huge 17.64.

The Global Culture Report provided evidence that trust grows when the leaders in an organization would share information with the employees and consult them about changes that may affect them, and when the voices expressed by their employees are heard through focus group meetings or townhall meetings. Empathetic practices such as these, as well as context support and active support such as mental health services, family and career counseling, and childcare, and publicly recognizing the efforts of their teams will produce the greatest impact on trust for the leaders of the organization,

TABLE 12.3 Ordered probit regression of Happiness at Work (Scale 0 to 10) focussing on trust

Explanatory Variable	*Coefficient*	*z- statistic*	*Prob* >|*z*|
Trust (1 to 5)	0.5547273	17.64	0.000
Education (1 to 5)	-0.0054543	-0.14	0.888
Work Hours (1 to 5)	-0.1001732	-2.08	0.037
Income Group (1 to 3)	-0.0328763	-.039	0.698
Married (1 or 0)	0.1280452	1.37	0.172
Number of Observations	970	**Pseudo R2**	0.1997
Prob > Chi Sq	0.0000		

Note: Coefficients on dummies representing sectors and some other control variables not presented.

with progressively greater positive impact when the listed empathetic practices are added one by one on top of the others.

Interestingly, our 2011 study on Happiness at Work found that Corporate Engagement is significantly enhanced by Trust and an enlightened leadership that offers two-way effective communication. Here "Understanding" was measured with the following questions, which sought respondents' rating, with five being "fully agree" and one being "totally disagree: "The management knows what is going on in company and its challenges in the market place"; "The staff is well informed about the policy of the management"; "There is effective dialogue between management and staff"; and, lastly, "The management is open to ideas and suggestions." These questions closely resemble the Global Culture Report's emphasis on sharing of information, consultation through meetings, including townhall dialogues, and focus group discussions. **Table 12.4** shows that understanding through effective communication and sharing of information, fairness, perception of a good working environment, and trust are all conducive to a sense of engagement in the workplace, contributing to happiness at work.

Finally, let us look at what happens to the results if we drop all the Corporate LIFE variables and related concepts like Trust and Fairness as well as other aspects about the working environment. The results are presented in **Table 12.5**. With fewer explanatory variables, we had a bigger sample with a total of 1,218 observations. A congenial working environment that is rich in Corporate LIFE, Trust and Fairness would significantly ameliorate the negative effects of long working hours and reduce the positive effects of income on happiness at work. Marital status, interestingly, now carries a much more statistically significant coefficient. In a favorable working environment, the positive effect of the married status tends to be overshadowed by the benefits of engagement at work that the working environment fosters.

TABLE 12.4 Ordered probit regression of Engagement (scale 1 to 5) focusing on the roles of trust and understanding

Explanatory Variable	*Coefficient*	*z- statistic*	*Prob* >|*z*|
Trust (1 to 5)	0.0820483	1.87	0.061
Fairness (1 to 5)	0.1972606	4.72	0.000
Understanding (1 to 5)	0.2176902	3.98	0.000
Work Environment	0.0495264	1.71	0.087
Working Hours	-0.053512	-1.12	0.262
Number of Observations	964	**Pseudo R2**	0.1837
Prob > Chi Sq	0.0000		

Note: Coefficients on dummies representing sectors and some other control variables not presented. Coefficient on Income Group (not shown) was tiny and not significant at all.

TABLE 12.5 Ordered probit regression of happiness at work (scale 0 To 10) with all working environment variables dropped

Explanatory Variable	*Coefficient*	*z- statistic*	*Prob >|z|*
Work Hours	-.1194214	-2.82	0.005
Income Group	0.2127167	3.35	0.001
Married	0.163258	2.26	0.024
Age Group	0.0076732	0.40	0.687
Number of Observations	1218	**Pseudo R2**	0.0073
Prob > Chi Sq	0.0000		

Note: All explanatory variables are listed. No sectoral dummies.

The future of work: the universal basic job

Admittedly, for some jobs it is not easy for workers to have a strong sense of engagement. In the marketplace, moreover, given the competitiveness of the market and the pressures on the bottom line, many workers are put under tremendous pressures to be "productive," and to be "productive" for workers in food delivery, factory workers on the production line, truck drivers, etc., means there is not much room for career development, innovative ideas or even time to take a break. Happily or unhappily, many of these tasks will disappear with technological innovations and automation. Already there are factories with very few workers on the production line. With the increasing sophistication of technology, robotics can replace humans completely on the factory floor.

Human society is now on the eve of the Fourth Industrial Revolution. The Fourth Industrial Revolution will not only replace manual labour, but will also gradually replace workers who make their living with brain power. Artificial intelligence (AI) can now compose music, write novels according to specifications about style and themes, create art pieces that can earn the admiration of many, write poems, etc. It seems that even professionals and artists are now at risk of losing their jobs, because machines can do the same thing faster and at very low cost.

In the past industrial revolutions, changes merely reshuffle jobs. While there are adjustment costs, new jobs are created and the new jobs often offer better pay. In the Fourth Industrial Revolution there is very little place to hide at the onslaught of AI and market forces.

While we are concerned about happiness at work, we also need to be concerned about the unhappiness of being out of work. All the evidence shows that even though workers may not be very happy at their jobs, they almost always report higher happiness compared to the unemployed.

Scientific and technological advancement are supposed to make life easier and better for people, and scientific and technological progress is unstoppable.

According to the Future of Jobs Report 2023 of the World Economic Forum, "businesses predict the strongest net job-creation effect to be driven by investments that facilitate the green transition of businesses, the broader application of ESG standards and supply chains becoming more localized, albeit with job growth offset by partial job displacement in each case."[6] There is, however, no guarantee that the jobs available in the marketplace will be enough for all job seekers. The potential for productivity growth through AI and automation cannot be fathomed.

Luckily, the size of the labour force is shrinking in many countries, and this is especially true of economies where scientific and technological advancement is most pronounced. According to an article in *The Lancet* (2020)[7], the global Total Fertility Rate was forecast to fall to 1.66 by 2100. Global population is expected to peak in 2064 at 9.73 billion people and decline to 8.79 billion in 2100. The countries with the largest population in 2100 will include India (1.09 billion), Nigeria (791 million), China (732 million), the USA (336 million) and Pakistan (248 million). By 2050, 151 countries were forecast to have a Total Fertility Rate[8] or TFR lower than the replacement level (TFR <2.1), and 183 were forecast to have a TFR lower than replacement by 2100.

In principle, the surge in human productivity and technological advancement should be a great blessing for humanity. But when humans are so powerful they also threaten sustainable development and have already led to the extinction of many species. A declining human population may be what is needed to leave some living space for the other species.

The surge in human productivity means that humans can work less hard and still enjoy the goods and services that they used to enjoy. When firms' productivity explodes because they pay less in wages and salaries and because the incidence of faulty products have declined, their profits will also explode—as long as people have money to spend. This means that there is a need to recycle their profits to potential consumers who will then have the income to buy the needed products.

The logical arrangement then is to tax the profits and to set up a mechanism to recycle part of the increase in profits so consumers will have the income to spend. While some economists and some countries have proposed the Universal Basic Income, this approach would turn out undermining the well-being of many—those who want to work but who cannot find work, whose "basic income" handout would be perceived as "not deserved." A loss of self-worth is a serious mental bad.

Instead of Universal Basic Income, I therefore proposed the Universal Basic Job, which are designed to be truly productive jobs from the social point of view, even though the output may not carry a price tag and may not be traded in the market. People can engage themselves in visiting the sick, the elderly, and prisoners, to show their love and to entertain them with music, magic, dances, art, etc. They can help with public health work such as cleaning country parks, eliminating rats and mosquitoes, and cleaning garbage in the oceans. They can propose projects for community building. They can even propose artistic or other projects so they can self-actualize and leave a legacy that reinforces the LIFE culture. As former jobs are displaced by AI and robotics, many firms' profits would skyrocket—if and only if people have incomes to buy their output. Thus, recycling the profits through tax and transfers is required for sustainable development. Firms that produce goods cheaply but without buyers cannot survive! Governments can work with NGOs to create jobs or directly create jobs with revenues collected from businesses through higher taxes on profits and on the incomes of the well to do. The Basic Jobs would enable every able-bodied person to get a job that will pay at least a livable wage.

Under the Universal Basic Job initiative, a job would be available to anyone who needs one. However, performance should still be monitored. Salary increases should be given to good performers. Non-performers should be given smaller or even no raise. Persistence of non-performance and breaching basic standards of performance should elicit dismissal. Dismissed workers should, however, be given a chance to be rehired after a waiting period. These signals give performers a signal that their work is recognized and appreciated.

According to *The Global Sustainable Investment Review* 2022, Global Sustainable Investment Assets had breached $35 trillion in 2020 but dipped to $30.3 trillion in 2022. Another report from Morgan Stanley observed that sustainable funds outperformed their traditional peers across all major asset classes and regions in 2023 with sustainable funds outperforming traditional funds by almost 50% at 12.6%. These are encouraging figures and suggest that global awareness of the importance of sustainable development has risen, so that firms that hire a workforce to promote ESG not only create jobs to absorb displaced workers on the production line, but also attract greater demand and lower capital costs.

Conclusions: the management philosophy of Kyocera

Happiness at work is NOT the overall happiness of workers. To measure happiness at work, we asked workers to rate "overall happiness at work considering all factors relevant to my job." The factors that are relevant include not only the physical working environment, the hours of working, the degree of exertion at work, but also the management style and the corporate culture, the effectiveness of communication, among other things. We proposed to use the LIFE framework so that in our 2011 study on Happiness at Work we asked workers questions that allowed us to compile indicators of Corporate Love, Corporate Insight, Corporate Fortitude, and Corporate Engagement. We found that these contributed to happiness at work.

The founder of Kyocera, Kazuo Inamori, a Japanese philanthropist, was a very successful entrepreneur and business executive. He managed to save Japan Airline from the verge of bankruptcy by focusing on the quality of service to passengers. Formerly known as Kyoto Ceramic Co., Ltd., Kyocera started with a capital of 3 million yen and 28 staff members and was a producer of fine ceramics. Today, Kyocera has become a global corporation producing advanced products that help spearhead the application of science and technology for the betterment of humankind. It has adopted the motto: "Respect the Divine and Love People," and it implores members of the company to "preserve the spirit to work fairly and honorably, respecting people, our work, our company, and our global community."

Words, however, need not mean much. Enron also had high-sounding pledges. It pledged to preserve Respect, Integrity, Communication, and Excellence as the core values of the corporation. But it said one thing and did another thing. This is exactly the opposite of integrity. When a company is perceived to be dishonest, workers lose the trust of their employer, and will never get job satisfaction. Happiness at work becomes a joke.

Jeffrey Skilling joined Enron in 1990 and became Enron's president and chief operating officer in 1997. With a mindset bent on the single purpose of making money, he changed the culture of the company. He turned the company into one that focused on quick profit from derivative product trades. Atmosphere in the company became toxic. When profits turned south, the company turned to fraudulent accounting with the complicity of its consultant and auditor Arthur Anderson.

The stated core values of Enron sound great. If upheld earnestly, they would have earned the trust of the company's workers and customers and would have done well, because they are essential to Corporate Engagement and Corporate Fortitude. But the company had forgotten Love and Corporate Love. With no heart to serve, and with a heart focused on profit, any company is likely to fail.

Notes

1 "Employee happiness has hit a three-year low, new research shows." (cnbc.com) October 2, 2023. www.cnbc.com/2023/10/02/-employee-happiness-has-hit-a-3-year-low-new-research-shows.html?msockid=1b2bf02e34456e411442e4d0354d6f61

2 See Ryan Pendell (2022) "Employee Engagement Strategies: Fixing the World's $8.8 Trillion Problem." Gallup.com, September 11, 2023, available at www.gallup.com/workplace/393497/world-trillion-workplace-problem.aspx. Accessed June 4, 2025.

3 Ordered probit is less well known than OLS, and we used Ordered Probit regressions in that study because it is in principle preferred when the dependent variable is ordinal, such as on a Likert scale. See www.emerald.com/insight/content/doi/10.1108/eb047369/full/html

4 Recall that Insight or Wisdom is very much about the "how" of Love.
5 See Milton Friedman (1971) "A Friedman doctrine—The Social Responsibility of Business Is to Increase Its Profits," *New York Times*, Sept. 13, available at www.nytimes.com/1970/09/13/archives/a-friedman-doctrine-the-social-responsibility-of-business-is-to.html. Accessed June 4, 2025.
6 World Economic Forum (2023) "The Future of Jobs Report," available at www.weforum.org/publications/the-future-of-jobs-report-2023/digest/. Accessed June 4, 2025.
7 Stein Emil Vollset et.al.(2020) "Fertility, mortality, migration, and population scenarios for 195 countries and territories from 2017 to 2100: a forecasting analysis for the Global Burden of Disease Study," *Lancet*, 396(10258), 1285–1306, available at www.thelancet.com/action/showPdf?pii=S0140-6736%2820%2930677-2. Accessed June 4, 2025.
8 The total fertility rate (TFR) of a population is the average number of children that are born to women over their lifetime.

Key points to note

- Work is important for well-being, not just because it offers a source of income, but because engaged workers find meaning and a sense of self-worth.
- Corporate LIFE helps build trust and energizes a company so its workers become an important asset to the company and can survive difficulties and gain strength over time.
- Corporate culture is not just beautiful words, but a code of conduct that permeates the entire company from the leadership to front-line workers.
- AI and robotics will replace workers for production, but all firms need a market so the savings from wages need to be injected into the economy. Hiring workers for ESG is good for everybody.
- Basic Job trumps Basic Income in that it offers a sense of self-worth and contributes to realizing the potential of those who are employed. Governments should ensure that all job-seekers can find a job through hiring or through NGOs that work with the government.

Some questions to ponder

- Do socialism and capitalism represent different values?
- Why do many people think that socialism and capitalism represent different values?
- If companies all uphold CSR, and society seeks institutions that provide incentives for people to work productively, and the interface between the market and government is intelligently designed, is there still a distinction between socialism and capitalism?
- Why do people have hangups about ideology?

13

PSYCHOMETRIC PROPERTIES OF LIFE MENTAL CAPITAL SCALE ACROSS DIFFERENT POPULATIONS[1]

The LIFE mental capital scale demonstrated satisfactory reliability and validity when administered to the general public and students within the Chinese community across various social settings, including unrest in society, infectious disease outbreaks, and post-pandemic circumstances. Moreover, the scale's application was discussed, and early evidence indicated that its psychometric properties were satisfactory for both online and in-person data collection approaches.

Introduction

Chapter 6 explained the conceptualization of LIFE mental capitals and its role in Seligman's happiness formula. Briefly, the mental capitals Love, Insight, Fortitude, and Engagement represent a voluntary accumulation of mental habits that contribute to enduring happiness. They foster positive emotions, meaning, personal growth, and a sense of self-worth enabling one to overcome adversities and regardless of other people's perceptions of us. LIFE mental capitals contribute to the production of mental goods such as self-efficacy, autonomy, resilience and self-esteem.[2] Many studies have applied LIFE mental capital as a key component in the Hong Kong general since 2008 and the family happiness index survey from 2018 to 2024 (Ho, 2011; Ho and Ip, 2018; Chan et al. 2024; Ho et al. 2025; Lam et al. 2025a, 2025b; Odetayo et al. 2025). Furthermore, the different versions of LIFE mental capitals have been adopted in different types of happiness index, namely, family happiness index, workplace happiness index and children happiness index. However, empirical psychometric properties of these versions in respective target

DOI: 10.4324/9781003507093-13

populations have not yet been comprehensively reported. This chapter aims to report the psychometric properties of different versions of LIFE mental capital through three methodological studies below:

Study 1: Psychometric properties of 4-item LIFE Mental Capital Scale used in family happiness index among Chinese adults in Hong Kong under the situation of social unrest.
Study 2: Psychometric properties of 4-item LIFE Mental Capital Scale for the use in general happiness index among Chinese people in Hong Kong during the COVID-19 pandemic.
Study 3: Validation of 12-item LIFE Mental Capital Scale for Chinese Students in Higher Education

Methods

These three methodological studies employed a correlational and cross-sectional design. The approach complied with the "Recommendations for Studies of Instrument and Scale Development and Testing" guidelines released by the Enhancing the Quality and Transparency of Health Research (EQUATOR) Network (Streiner and Kottner, 2014).

Face validation before data collection

Before the data collection, an initial assessment called face validation was executed to ensure the comprehensibility and interpretability of the items (Lam et al. 2023). A group of 20 respondents with different demographic characteristics (e.g. age, gender and educational status) were invited to spell out their interpretations of the items. The participants were instructed to paraphrase the questions in their language while maintaining the meaning of the original question as closely as possible. A researcher grouped the responses into four categories: fully correct, generally correct (with slight modifications or omissions), partially correct (where the respondent understood the basic concept only), and wrong or incomprehensible (Lam et al. 2023). Items achieving 80% interpretability were deemed suitable for psychometric testing (Lam et al. 2023); those that did not were either altered or deleted.

Psychometric testing

Internal consistency (i.e. Cronbach's alpha analysis and corrected item-total correlation), and construct validity tests (such as Exploratory Factor Analysis, Confirmatory Factor Analysis, and hypothesis testing), were used to evaluate the psychometric properties of the 4-item and the 12-item LIFE mental capital scales across the three studies.

Study 1: Sample and sampling from the Family Happiness Index survey[3]

The participants were recruited from the general population under the situation of social unrest in 2019. Participants at various locations in Hong Kong Islands (Aberdeen, Central, Chai Wan, Sai Wan, and Siu Sai Wan), Kowloon (Lam Tin, Mong Kok, Po Lam, and Tsim Sha Tsui) and the New Territories (Sha Tin, Sheung Shui, Tin Shui Wai, Tseung Kwan O, Tsuen Wan and Yuen Long) were invited to respond to the survey through a face-to-face structured interview. Such data collection methods returned a better mix of individuals from different sociodemographic backgrounds, which enhances representation (Lam et al. 2018). The questionnaire included demographic data (e.g. age, gender, education attainment, relationship/marital status, and income), the 4-item LIFE mental capital scale, and the three items on happiness. According to a published systematic review on instrument validation, over 50% of methodological studies used a sample size of more than 300 (White, 2022). Coupled with the previous validation studies (Kwan et al. 2022; Liu et al. 2020), a sample size above 300 was considered adequate to perform psychometric testing of the 4-item LIFE mental capital scale. A total of 1,005 questionnaires were collected eventually. The dataset was accessible for retrieval via the Mendeley repository (Lam et al. 2025).

Study 2: Sample and sampling from the General Happiness Index survey

The participants were recruited from among the general public in 2021 during the COVID-19 pandemic. Both online and face-to-face methods were used for data collection. Participants were invited to complete the online questionnaires through online survey platforms (i.e. Facebook and Google Form). The face-to-face questionnaires were collected in the Kowloon district of Hong Kong. Two research assistants invited pedestrians in train stations to respond to the self-administered questionnaires using the paper-and-pencil method. The questionnaires included demographic data, the 4-item LIFE mental capital scale, external quality of living and the three items on happiness (refer to the data for the full description of variables; Chan et al. 2024; Lam et al. 2025a). The data were exported from the platforms and downloaded for analysis. For this 4-item LIFE scale, a sample size above 300 was considered adequate, which was estimated based on the same methodology as in previous validation studies (Kwan et al. 2022; Lam et al. 2018) and the recommendation from a recent systematic review (White, 2022). A total of 1,557 questionnaires were collected eventually. The dataset was accessible for retrieval via the Mendeley repository (Chan et al. 2024).

Study 3: Sample and sampling from the students in higher education

The participants were recruited from a higher education institution in 2024, post-COVID normalcy. Paper-and-pencil and online methods were used to collect the data. A research assistant invited some participants to complete self-administered questionnaires distributed during a lecture and a college seminar, and some participants were randomly invited to complete the questionnaires using the online survey platform (i.e. Google Form). The questionnaires included demographic data, the 12-item LIFE mental capital scale, and three items on happiness. Since confirmatory factor analysis (CFA) is needed to check the factorial validity of the 12-item LIFE mental capital scale, a minimal sample size of 300–500 is recommended (Liu et al. 2020; Lam et al. 2019; Tabachnick and Fidell, 2019). A total of 503 questionnaires were collected.

Measurement

The questionnaire used in the three studies consisted of two parts. Part one was demographic data, such as sex, age, relationship/marital status, education, and income. Part two comprised the 4-item LIFE mental capital (for Study 1 and 2) or the 12-item LIFE mental capital (for Study 3), and the three happiness indices (i.e., individual happiness, satisfaction with life, and meaning in life[4]).

The LIFE mental capital scale in Studies 1 to 3 has four dimensions (i.e. Love, Insight, Fortitude, and Engagement). In Studies 1 and 2, a single item was employed for each dimension Lam et al. 2025a; Study 3 utilized three items for each dimension. All LIFE mental capitals were measured on an 11-point Likert scale from "very much disagree" (0 points) to "very much agree" (10 points). A higher score indicates a higher level of mental capital.

Alternative measures of individuals' subjective well-being (SWB) were assessed by individual overall happiness, satisfaction with life, and meaning in life respectively. Participants were asked to self-rate their feelings on the single-item scale with the questions, (1) "Overall, how happy would you say you are?" (Raudenská, 2023). For this item, 0 means "very unhappy," while 10 is "extremely happy." This single-item scale used with three other assessment instruments by Abdel-Khalek (2006) demonstrated good temporal stability of 0.86 and satisfactory convergent and divergent validities. (2) "How satisfied are you with your life?" (Cheung and Lucas, 2014). For this item, 0 means "very dissatisfied," while 10 is "very satisfied." Cheung and Lucas (2014) used this single-item measure and four other groups of assessment instruments to examine criterion validity. The result showed good criterion validity of 0.64 (zero order) and 0.80 (unattenuated). (3) "I live a meaningful life" (which is a part of Seligman's PERMA model; Seligman, 2018). For this item, 0 means "strongly disagree," while 10 is "strongly agree." This model, recently validated by Nie et al. (2024), showed good convergent validity (r=0.85) and divergent validity.

Data analysis

SPSS version 28.0 for Windows (IBM SPSS, Inc.) was used for the analysis. Descriptive statistics (e.g. frequency, percentage, mean, and standard deviation) were used to describe and summarize the questionnaire data. Inferential statistics, including Cronbach's α and corrected item-total correlation coefficients, were used to assess internal consistency. Exploratory factor analysis (EFA) was used to explore the factor structure of the LIFE scale (Study 1 and 2). IBM SPSS AMOS 28 (IBM SPSS, Inc.) was used for the CFA (Study 3). The level of significance was set at ≤0.05. What follows describe the specific benchmarks for evaluating the psychometric properties of a scale.

Reliability

The internal consistency of the 4-item LIFE scale (Study 1 and 2) and 12-item LIFE scale (Study 3) was examined using Cronbach's alpha (α)statistics and the corrected item-total correlation (r). An $\alpha \geq 0.70$ indicates a satisfactory result, and $r \geq 0.30$ indicates a homogenous item, indicating satisfactory internal consistency (Huang et al., 2022; Li et al., 2023; Portney, 2020).

Construct validity

Since the 4-item LIFE mental capital scale can only be a single-factor scale, EFA (rather than CFA) would be appropriate to examine its factor structure (Study 1 and 2). The suitability of the data for factor analysis was assessed using Bartlett's test of sphericity and the Kaiser-Meyer-Olkin (KMO) measure of sampling adequacy (Tabachnick and Fidell, 2019). Bartlett's test of sphericity of statistical significance (i.e. $p<0.05$) and the KMO value of >0.60 were considered to support the factorability of the correlation matrix (Tabachnick and Fidell, 2019). Principal axis factoring was used for extraction, which was recommended and suitable for most studies in social and health sciences (Kwan et al. 2022; Lam et al. 2018; Costello and Osborne, 2005). The factor loading of each item to their latent factor should exceed 0.40 (Finch, 2020; Costello and Osborne, 2005).

CFA was performed to examine the degree of fitness of the 12-item LIFE scale (Study 3), allowing its internal structure to be determined. Goodness-of-fit measures, including the chi-square/degree of freedom ratio (χ^2/d.f.), comparative fit index (CFI), root mean square residual (RMR), normed fit index (NFI), root mean square error of approximation (RMSEA), and incremental fit index (IFI), were used to evaluate the model fitness. In this study, the measures yielded an acceptable fit if χ^2/d.f. < 5.00; RMR < 1; NFI, CFI, and IFI > 0.90, and RMSEA < 0.08 (Hair et al. 2018; Byrne, 2016). All the data in study 3 were used to compute the CFA model.

For hypothesis testing, based on the literature, mental capital is a consistent correlate of three SWB indices, namely individual happiness (Ho, 2011, 2014), satisfaction with life (Deci and Ryan, 2008; Peterson et al. 2005), and meaning in life (Vittersø, 2013, pp. 39–55; Deci and Ryan, 2008). It is hypothesized that the strength of the correlation coefficient between the LIFE mental capitals and happiness indices (i.e. individual happiness, satisfaction in life, and meaning in life) would be strong (range of 0.6 to 0.8) (Cohen, 1988), indicating an optimal relationship supporting the construct validation (Akoglu, 2018).

Ethical considerations

Ethical approval was obtained from the ethical committee of local institutions (ref: HSEARS20201002002; REC2022124) and the collaborator. The research team applied the LIFE mental capital scale with permission from the corresponding copyright holders (Ho, 2014). Appropriate methods were used to obtain consent from the participants, including implied consent from participants recruited among the general public in railway stations and written consent from bachelor students recruited on campuses.

Results

A total of 1,005, 1,557, and 503 participants were recruited for studies 1, 2, and 3, respectively. The majority of the participants in all three studies were female (60.1%, 60.9%, and 62.0%), single (38.4%, 42.5%, and 65.6%), and had tertiary degrees (54.5%, 57.6%, and 88.6%). Table 13.1 presents the demographic characteristics of the participants.

Psychometric testing results of Study 1

Table 13.2 shows the results of the internal consistency analysis. The Cronbach's alpha of the scale was 0.844. The corrected item-total correlation ranged from 0.611 to 0.745 and was considered homogenous, supporting the reliability of the 4-item LIFE mental capital scale in the family happiness index.

EFA and hypothesis testing were conducted with all 1,005 samples. For EFA, the statistical significance of Bartlett's test of sphericity (χ^2=1654.29, d.f.=6, $p<0.001$) and the KMO value at 0.802 indicate the dataset's factorability. The one-factor model of the 4-item LIFE mental capital scale had a factor loading ranging from 0.669 to 0.844, the total percentage of variance at 68.26%, and

TABLE 13.1 Characteristics of study participants in Study 1 (N=1005 samples in 2019), Study 2 (N=1557 samples in 2021) & Study 3 (N=503 samples in 2024)

Characteristics	*Study 1*	*Study 2*	*Study 3*
	n (%)	*n (%)*	*n (%)*
Age, years			
15-18	228 (22.7)	84 (5.4)	159 (33.8)
19-24	276 (27.5)	220 (14.2)	151 (32.1)
25-34	140 (13.9)	443 (28.5)	121 (25.7)
35-44	146 (14.5)	430 (27.7)	40 (8.5)
45-54	137 (13.6)	197 (12.7)	-
55 or above	78 (7.8)	180 (11.6)	-
Missing	-	3	32
Gender			
Female	604 (60.1)	948 (60.9)	300 (62.0)
Male	401 (39.9)	608 (39.1)	184 (38.0)
Missing	-	1	19
Relationship status			
Single	386 (38.4)	661 (42.5)	321 (65.6)
Dating	246 (24.5)	344 (22.1)	124 (25.4)
Married	349 (34.7)	479 (30.8)	44 (9.0)
Divorced/Widowed	24 (2.4)	72 (4.6)	-
Missing	-	1	14
Education			
Secondary or below	422 (42.1)	521 (33.5)	38 (7.6)
Tertiary	547 (54.5)	897 (57.6)	441 (88.6)
Postgraduate	34 (3.4)	138 (8.9)	19 (3.8)
Missing	-	1	5
Occupation			
Full-time students	445 (44.4)	182 (11.7)	424 (85.3)
Job seeking	33 (3.3)	239 (15.4)	10 (2.0)
Employed	418 (41.7)	1035 (66.6)	63 (12.7)
Homemaker	71 (7.1)	98 (6.3)	-
Retired	36 (3.6)	-	-
Missing	2	3	6
Monthly income, USD (HKD)			
<643 (<5,000)	525 (52.9)	342 (22.0)	-
643-1,929 (5,000-14,999)	125 (12.6)	395 (25.4)	-
1,929-5,143 (15,000-39,999)	281 (28.3)	625 (40.2)	-
5,143-9,001 (40,000-69,999)	48 (4.8)	151 (9.7)	-

(Continued)

TABLE 13.1 (Continued)

Characteristics	*Study 1*	*Study 2*	*Study 3*
	n (%)	*n (%)*	*n (%)*
9,001 or above (70,000 or above)	14 (1.4)	43 (2.8)	-
Missing	12	1	-
Self-rated financial status			
Very bad	-	41 (2.6)	3 (0.6)
Bad	-	177 (11.4)	53 (10.6)
Neutral	-	943 (60.6)	291 (58.0)
Good	-	337 (21.7)	105 (20.9)
Very good	-	58 (3.7)	50 (10.0)
Missing	-	1	1

TABLE 13.2 Psychometric testing of 4-item LIFE mental capital under the situation of social unrest in 2019 (Study 1, N=1005)

	Methods	*Statistical methods*	*Results*
Reliability			
Internal consistency	Cronbach's method	Cronbach's alpha statistic	0.844
	Corrected item-total correlation	Pearson moment-product correlation coefficient	0.611-0.745
Validity			
Construct validity	Hypothesis testing[a]	Pearson moment-product correlation coefficient	personal happiness (g1): r=0.667, $p<0.001$ life satisfaction (g2): r=0.700, $p<0.001$ meaning in life (g3): r=0.752, $p<0.001$
	Factor structure	Exploratory factor analysis[b]	KMO=0.802 Bartlett's test of sphericity: Chi-square= 1654.29, $p<0.001$ One-factor model with factor loading ranged from 0.669 to 0.844 Communalities=0.447 to 0.712 Total variance= 68.26%

[a] Correlation result based on 1005 datasets

[b] Result was calculated based on 1005 datasets.

communalities ranging from 0.447 to 0.712. These EFA results supported the one-factor model of the 4-item LIFE mental capital scale.

For hypothesis testing, the LIFE score significantly correlated with the single-item happiness score ($r=0.667$, $p<0.001$), single-item satisfaction with life score ($r=0.700$, $p<0.001$), and the single-item perceived meaning in life score ($r=0.752$, $p<0.001$). The strength of correlations matched with the required hypothesis as stated above, indicating the satisfactory construct validity of the scale.

Psychometric testing results of Study 2

Table 13.3 shows the results of the internal consistency analysis. The Cronbach's alpha of the scale was 0.853. The corrected item-total correlation ranged from 0.670 to 0.728 and was considered homogenous, supporting the reliability of the 4-item LIFE mental capital scale in the general happiness index.

TABLE 13.3 Psychometric testing of 4-item LIFE mental capital during the COVID-19 in 2021 (Study 2, N=1557)

	Methods	*Statistical methods*	*Results*
Reliability			
Internal consistency	Cronbach's method	Cronbach's alpha statistics	0.853
	Corrected item-total correlation	Pearson moment-product correlation coefficient	0.670 to 0.728
Validity			
Construct validity	Hypothesis testing[a]	Pearson moment-product correlation coefficient	personal happiness (g1): $r=0.667$, $p<0.001$ life satisfaction (g2): $r=0.718$, $p<0.001$ meaning in life (g3): $r=0.760$, $p<0.001$
	Factor structure	Exploratory factor analysis[b]	KMO=0.780 Bartlett's test of sphericity: Chi-square=2796.37, $p<0.001$ One-factor model with factor loading ranged from 0.737 to 0.810 Communalities=0.543 to 0.656 Total variance= 69.43%

[a] Correlation result based on 1557 datasets

[b] Result was calculated based on 1557 datasets.

EFA and hypothesis testing were computed with all 1,557 samples. For the results of EFA, the statistical significance of Bartlett's test of sphericity (χ^2= 2796.37, d.f.=6, *p<0.001*) and the KMO value was 0.780, indicating the dataset's factorability. The one-factor model of the 4-item LIFE mental capital scale had a factor loading ranging from 0.737 to 0.810, the total percentage of variance at 69.43%, and communalities ranging from 0.543 to 0.656. These EFA results supported the one-factor model of the 4-item LIFE mental capital scale.

For hypothesis testing, the LIFE score significantly correlated with the single-item happiness score (r=0.667, *p<0.001*), single-item satisfaction with life score (r=0.718, *p<0.001*), and the single-item perceived meaning in life score (r=0.760, *p<0.001*). The strength of correlations matched with the required hypothesis as stated above, indicating the satisfactory construct validity of the scale.

Psychometric testing results of Study 3

Of those 503 participants, only 403 students who completed all items were selected for analysis. Table 13.4 shows the results of the internal consistency analysis. The Cronbach's alpha was 0.917 for the overall scale and ranged from

TABLE 13.4 Psychometric testing of 4-item LIFE mental capital post-COVID normalcy in students in 2024 (Study 3, N=403)

	Methods	*Statistical methods*	*Results*
Reliability			
Internal consistency	Cronbach's method	Cronbach's alpha statistics	alpha of scale=0.917; alphas of scale=0.917 to 0.855
	Corrected item-total correlation	Pearson moment-product correlation coefficient	0.52-0.77
Validity			
Face validity	Review by target population[a]	Frequency and percentage	100%
Construct validity	Hypothesis testing[b]	Pearson moment-product correlation coefficient	personal happiness (g1): r=0.588, *p<0.001* satisfaction in life (g2): r=0.634, *p<0.001* meaning in life (g3): r=0.679, *p<0.001*
	Factorial structure	Confirmatory factor analysis`	Factor loadings=0.60-0.87 χ^2/d.f.=3.411, CFI=0.955, RMR=0.150, NFI= 0.939, RMSEA=0.078, IFI=0.956

a. Result was calculated based on 20 students.

b. Result was calculated based on 403 students.

0.693 to 0.855 for subscales (i.e. love subscale = 0.758, insight subscale = 0.693, fortitude subscale = 0.855, and engagement subscale = 0.846). The corrected item-total correlation ranged from 0.515 to 0.766 and was considered homogenous, supporting the reliability of the 12-item LIFE mental capital scale used in the students in higher education.

CFA was performed with 403 selected samples. Figure 13.1 shows the results of the 4-factor model of CFA. The 12-item LIFE mental capital scale yielded a satisfactory fit (χ^2/d.f.=3.411, GFI=0.938, CFI=0.955, NFI=0.939, IFI=0.956, RMR=0.150, and RMSEA=0.078). The standardized coefficient of all items was acceptable, with factor loadings ranging from 0.60 to 0.87. All paths were significantly loaded to their respective factors.

For hypothesis testing, the LIFE score significantly correlated with the single-item individual happiness score (r=0.588, $p<0.001$), single-item satisfaction with life score (r=0.634, $p<0.001$), and the single-item perceived meaning in life score (r=0.679, $p<0.001$). The strength of correlations matched with the required hypothesis as stated above, indicating the satisfactory construct validity of the scale.

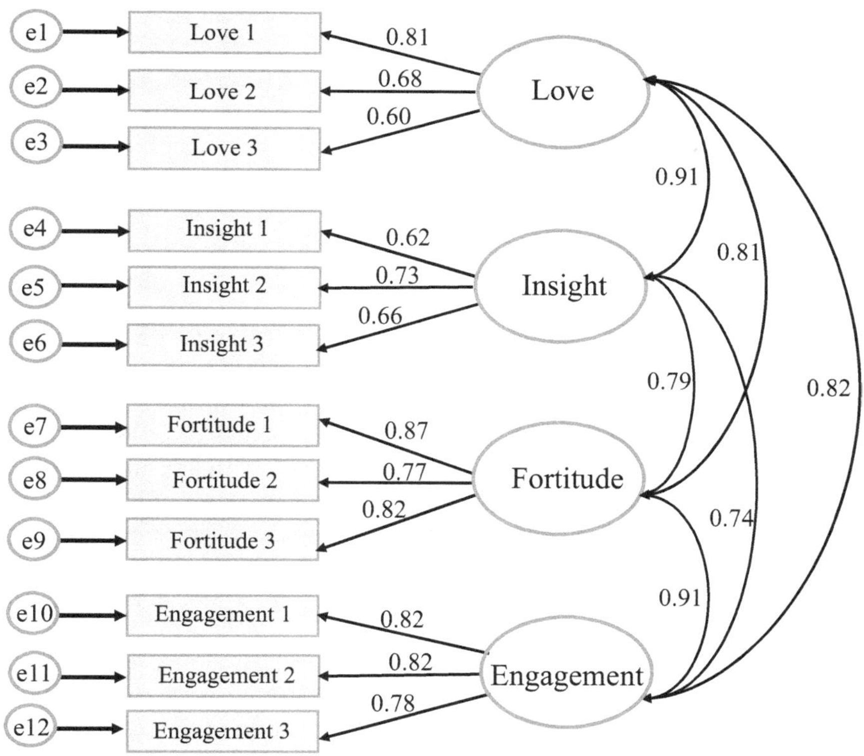

FIGURE 13.1 Confirmatory factor analysis model for 12-item LIFE mental capital scale in study 3 ($N = 403$).

Discussion

The validation of the LIFE mental capital scale, encompassing both the 4-item and 12-item versions, supports the scale as a practical and user-friendly instrument for assessing mental capital related to the prediction of happiness. A notable strength of these studies was the diverse demographic samples utilized across the three investigations. Additionally, data collection occurred during various life events: Study 1 took place amidst social unrest, Study 2 during the COVID-19 pandemic, and Study 3 in post-pandemic normalcy. The consistent results of psychometric properties underscore the applicability of the LIFE mental capital scale in different social and health circumstances. The results of this research hold significant implications for researchers, healthcare providers, social and mental health professionals, and policymakers, offering a reliable and valid instrument for evaluating mental capital across different populations within the Chinese community.

Reliability

The internal consistency across the three studies was similar. The 4-item (in Studies 1 and 2) and 12-item (in Study 3) scales showed satisfactory internal consistency, as reflected by good Cronbach's α of 0.84, 0.85, and 0.92, respectively. The homogeneity of the items was further assessed through the corrected item-total correlation. The correlation coefficient for each item across the three studies was above 0.3, demonstrating satisfactory homogeneity and supporting the reliability of both versions of LIFE mental capital scale in health and social sciences (Lam et al. 2018; Liu et al. 2020; Portney, 2020).

Validity

Hypothesis testing, EFA, and CFA are common and standard methods for evaluating the construct validity of instruments in psychometric studies. These tests confirm the validity of both the 4-item and the 12-item LIFE scale.

The significant relationship between the LIFE mental capital and three happiness indices (i.e. individual happiness, satisfaction with life, and meaning in life) supported the scale's construct validity, demonstrating that higher levels of mental capital are associated with increased happiness. More importantly, the strength of correlation coefficients was consistently regarded as strong, which matched the stated hypothesis (Deci and Ryan, 2008; Peterson et al. 2005; Ho, 2014; Vittersø, 2013).

EFA, another method for evaluating the construct validity, was used in Studies 1 and 2. Bartlett's test of sphericity of statistical significance and the KMO value showed good factorability of the correlation matrix (Tabachnick and Fidell, 2019). EFA is used to examine an item set associated with a construct (Goretzko et al. 2023) and to understand relationship patterns among observed variables (Finch, 2020). EFA (rather than CFA) was employed in Studies 1 and 2 due to the simplicity of the factor structure of the 4-item LIFE mental capital scale, which necessitated a one-factor model.

In Study 3, CFA showed a satisfactory goodness-of-fit index for the 4-factor model of 12-item LIFE mental capital scale. CFA is considered the most suitable approach for examining the hypothesized relationships among the underlying latent and observed variables that comprise the LIFE scale's internal structure (Portney, 2020). The results of the CFA of LIFE mental capital scale were comparable to that of most of the scales in health and social science (Huang et al. 2022; Kwan et al. 2022; Lam et al. 2018; Liu et al. 2020; Portney, 2020).

Applicability

As mentioned before, the LIFE mental capital scale, complemented with happiness indices, has been used to monitor the trend of happiness index for close to two decades (Chan et al. 2024; Ho et al. 2025), which influenced social and political decisions. The LIFE scale was found to be a consistent salient predictor for the happiness index even in different populations and social circumstances. The current results of consistent psychometric properties as reflected by the Study 1 to 3 enriched our understanding that LIFE mental capital was of enduring characteristics but not a temporary/state one. Such characteristics gave a good explanation to the consistent and significant association between LIFE mental capital and happiness indices.

Moreover, the reliable psychometric properties of the LIFE mental capital scale bolstered the researchers' confidence regarding its applicability across various social events and contexts. The abbreviated version of the LIFE mental capital scale consists of just four items. The simplicity and brevity of this scale significantly enhance its applicability, as it can be easily complemented or supplemented with additional concepts or instruments during a single survey period (Kwan et al. 2022).

The data collection methods, whether performed online or in person, did not influence the psychometric properties of the LIFE mental capital scale, as evidenced by the comparative results of Studies 1, 2 and 3. The results improved the applicability of the scale by refining the feasibility of data collection methods across various social situations encountered.

Limitations and recommendations

In general, the use of self-administered questionnaires can lead participants to give responses they believe are socially acceptable (Andrade, 2020). In principle, it will be desirable to minimize this bias. However, in contrast to certain medical studies that utilize biomarkers or blood tests, incorporating objective measurements for mental capital or a happiness index proves to be challenging and often unattainable. A sufficient sample size serves as a viable strategy to mitigate the influence of the social desirability bias. Secondly, our study does not cover test-retest reliability and concurrent validity. Consequently, the research cannot offer any evidence regarding the stability and criterion validity of the LIFE mental capital scale.

Acknowledgements: We would like to thank the funding bodies, and all those that voluntarily participated in this study. We would also like to thank Ms. Phoebe Wan, Ms. Vicky Kung, and Ms. Paula Chung for their assistance in the data collection, data input, and press conference. These studies were funded by the Lee Kum Kee Family Foundation, Wofoo Social Enterprises (ref: ZH3U), Wofoo Foundation Limited (ref: WOFOO21041) and Research Matching Grants Scheme, University Grants Committee, Hong Kong SAR. The funding bodies had no contribution or involvement in this study. All necessary ethical clearance has been obtained.

Data availability statement

The data and materials are partly available in Mendeley Data (doi:10.17632/czxznncsv2.2, Chan et al., 2024; doi:10.17632/wmh87245bj.1, Lam et al., 2025). All other data are available from the corresponding author upon reasonable request.

Notes

1 Authors include:
Simon Ching Lam (1, 2), Aderonke Odetayo (1), Shun Chan (1), Daphne Sze Ki Cheung (3), Ken Hok Man Ho (4), Summer Cho Ngan Siu (5), Elaine Hoi Yee Chow (1), Jasmine Cheung (1), Jenny Hiu Wai Tse (1), Jessie Kaur Dhaliwal (1), Vivian Ching Man Pang (1), Anson Chui Yan Tang (1, 2), Lorna Kwai Ping Suen (1, 2), and Lok Sang Ho (6)

1. School of Nursing, Tung Wah College, Hong Kong SAR, China.
2. Translational Research Centre for Digital Mental Health, Tung Wah College, Hong Kong SAR, China.
3. School of Nursing and Midwifery, Deakin University, Australia.
4. School of Nursing and Midwifery, La Trobe University, Australia.
5. School of Arts and Social Sciences, Hong Kong Metropolitan University, Hong Kong SAR, China.
6. STEAM Education and Research Centre, Lingnan University, Hong Kong SAR, China.

2 As explained in Chapter 6, Seligman's PERMA model (Seligman, 2011) is very much similar to LIFE while Diener and Seligman, 2002, stressed especially the importance of interpersonal relations and connections that are directly related to Love.

3 We use the individual happiness measures which are collected alongside the Family Happiness Index for this exercise for validation of the LIFE scale.

4 This corresponds with "How much do you agree that life is worth living" which appears in studies led by Ho.

APPENDIX 12-item LIFE mental capital scale (LIFE scale) 4-item LIFE mental capital scale indicated with asterisk (*)

No.	*Item*	*Response format* 非常不同意 *(Very much disagree)* 非常同意 *(Very much agree)*										
Q1	L1: I love and take good care of my health and my life 我熱愛並且很好地照顧我的健康和生活。	0	1	2	3	4	5	6	7	8	9	10
Q2	L2: I love and care for my family. 我愛護和關心我的家人。	0	1	2	3	4	5	6	7	8	9	10
Q3	L3: I am willing to help others.* 我樂意助人。	0	1	2	3	4	5	6	7	8	9	10
Q4	In1: Success to me is achieving my best within my ability. 我認為在自己能力範圍內做到最好已是成功。	0	1	2	3	4	5	6	7	8	9	10
Q5	In2: I seek for balance in life, with moderation in work, entertainment, food and drink.* 我力求生活平衡、工作娛樂飲食均能適度節制。	0	1	2	3	4	5	6	7	8	9	10
Q6	In3: I take the environment and sustainable development seriously. 我認真對待環境和可持續發展。	0	1	2	3	4	5	6	7	8	9	10
Q7	F1: I will not give up when facing difficulties.* 當我面臨逆境時，我不退縮不氣餒。	0	1	2	3	4	5	6	7	8	9	10
Q8	F2: When I face an adverse outcome, I reflect and learn from my mistakes. 當結果不如理想時，我會反思並從錯誤中學習。	0	1	2	3	4	5	6	7	8	9	10
Q9	F3: Regardless of what happens I always stay hopeful. 無論事情怎麼樣，我仍保持希望。	0	1	2	3	4	5	6	7	8	9	10

(*Continued*)

APPENDIX (Continued)

No.	*Item*	*Response format* 非常不同意 *(Very much disagree)* ←								非常同意 *(Very much agree)* →		
Q10	E1: I have clearly identified goals and purposes in life.* 我有清晰的人生目標和目的。	0	1	2	3	4	5	6	7	8	9	10
Q11	E2: I always look for opportunities to realize my potential. 我經常尋找機會發揮我的潛能。	0	1	2	3	4	5	6	7	8	9	10
Q12	E3: When I decide to do something, I will do my best to do it well. 當我決定做某事時，我會全力以赴。	0	1	2	3	4	5	6	7	8	9	10

Source of LIFE mental capital scale: Ho et al. (2025)

EPILOGUE

Pray humans will become truly civilized

The LIFE framework is not only applicable to personal development at the individual level, but also applicable to the business world and the country level. Businesses need Corporate Love, Corporate Insight, Corporate Fortitude, and Corporate Engagement. Governments need Love, Insight, Fortitude, and Engagement to bring health, peace, prosperity, and happiness to their peoples. Nurturing LIFE mental capitals from the individual level to the country level is building a pro-LIFE mental capitals culture in the country and beyond. Physician, theologist, and musicologist Albert Schweitzer's life mission and vision was to transcend national boundaries and ethnic differences to foster reverence for LIFE. There is no resource more valuable than life, and there is no value greater than LIFE. Only with the big picture in mind will humans achieve sustainable development.

Our planet has all the resources we need for a good life for everybody, but only if we have a culture that is consistent with sustainable development. The categorical imperative for us is to achieve personal growth and acquire the pro-LIFE mental capitals culture, so that we can more efficiently procure for all our needs, including our mental good needs. As we progress to this end, we become truly civilized. The alternative would be "forever scarcity" and forever wars.

Introduction

Although positive psychology has become increasingly popular, I have noticed there are quite a few sceptics. I have read at least a couple of articles that equate positive psychology with a cult that tries to convince people that things are

DOI: 10.4324/9781003507093-14

better than they really are. But positive psychology cannot be positive if it is escapist or if it ignores the challenges posed by the reality that life is often hard.

Christopher Peterson has this to say about positive psychology:

> Positive psychology is the scientific study of what makes life most worth living. It is a call for psychological science and practice to be as concerned with strength as with weakness; as interested in building the best things in life as in repairing the worst; and as concerned with making the lives of normal people fulfilling as with healing pathology.[1]

As an economist, I see positive psychology as "constrained maximization": taking the real constraints for what they are and doing the best one can to maximize one's long-term interest. This is "positive living." This would usually mean overcoming imagined or temporary constraints, not worrying about things beyond one's control, and not being bogged down by sunk costs and foregone losses. Positive psychology is not about dismissing the real constraints. Positive psychology is about the will to do one's very best and to achieve one's very best, given the real constraints.

Unfortunately, in real life too many people fail to achieve the happiness that lies within their reach, often because somehow they manage to make things worse than they really are. They cry over spilled milk instead of making the most out of what is still available. Being positive is facing the fact that what is lost is lost. Exactly because we recognize the loss that has already been incurred, we need to treasure what is still available to us even more. Suppose someone lost $2,000 to a pickpocket. Having reported the theft to the police and done what he can to seek help, the best strategy is to learn to be more careful and to get on with life as usual. If someone keeps thinking over the loss he would be piling a "mental good loss" *on top of* the loss of $2,000. Because we are human, most of us cannot easily leave the pain of the loss behind. In Chapter 11 we discussed mindfulness training in the form of a breathing and attention exercise, so instead of trying to suppress the troubling thought we can refocus our mind with a "mental anchor" that prevents our mind from being drifted away by these troubling memories.

Positive psychology will not accept that happiness is genetically determined. The evidence is that cases abound showing that when attitudes change, people's lives can change. Without dismissing the role of genes—a real constraint, at least for now—we must recognize that there is no immutable "set point" of happiness. The so-called set point of happiness is far from being set by our genes. It can be lifted up through accumulating mental capital or mental habits and getting rid of hurtful ones. For many unhappy people, a decision to acquire positive or helpful mental capital, relinquish hurtful mental capital, and develop the will to follow through is what it takes to start life afresh. Success in life is not about achieving any identified instrumental goal. It is about truthful, reflective living. Knowing that we are remaking ourselves each day and witnessing personal growth is most fulfiling and gives us a strong sense of self-worth.

Categorical imperative

Some people find Kant's categorical imperative in the form of answering one's call of duty objectionable because "duty" appears inconsistent with the exercise of free will. However, if the categorical imperative is doing one's best to realize one's life potential, it is consistent with free will. Given the huge potential that life has offered us, we owe it to ourselves to discover and realize it in a way that we choose. This is 'self-actualization' to the highest degree. We are happiest being ourselves when we follow our hearts and do what we truly believe in. Following our hearts means being truthful to our true selves by freeing ourselves from the bondage of the false, egoistic self, i.e., disallowing our false self from spoiling the true self's one-minded pursuit of self-actualization to the highest degree.

Some would disagree, saying that hedonistic people also follow their hearts as they chase after sensual pleasures, wealth, status, and power. They would ask if this is also self-actualization. In response to such a query, I would invite hedonistic people to be honest with themselves and ask themselves whether their way of life really makes them happy over the long term and really makes their lives worth living. Sensual pleasures and wealth come and go, but self-actualization in the sense of personal growth gives one enduring fulfilment, so one will not have any regrets at the end of one's life. Self-actualization in the sense of personal growth requires one to be reflective and open-minded. The way of life that we are used to reflects culture (Chapter 4). Following a way of life that we are used to without reflection is inertia. Inertia reflects a lower form of self-actualization that is constrained by our self-limited perspective. More importantly, chasing after sensual pleasures, wealth, status, and power is incompatible with sustainable development. Given the limited resources we have on earth and our huge population today, the materialistic culture will inevitably lead to a fight for limited resources. That means conflicts, clashes, and wars among humans. Humanity and the world will be doomed.

Humanity needs, therefore, to acquire a culture that is compatible with sustainable development. That means consuming what is necessary for a physically healthy life and acquiring our mental goods economically. We can build our self-esteem and self-worth while committed to ESG: care for our Environment and biodiversity, caring for our Society, and leading a life of responsibility and accountability (strong Governance). Governance is responsibility, truthfulness, and accountability.

To me, this is the highest Kantian call of duty: taking up the courage to be honest with ourselves and reflect honestly on our way of life, to learn to do better each day and be accountable to our true self. Adopting the growth mindset is both the highest call of duty and the happiest thing to do.

Is being selfish a form of following one's mind? Yes and no. Yes, because it is following one's mind. No, because it is NOT following the mind that is genuinely truthful. There is a distinction between the false, obsessive self and the true, enlightened self. The true self refers to the self that seeks enduring well-being. The false self refers to the obsessive self that seeks momentary gratification or relief of discomfort at the expense of the longer-term well-being. The true self has longer term goals and seeks personal development and growth. The false self, which is vulnerable to the seven deadly sins, is easily distracted by opportunities that offer momentary pleasures and material gains, but which often betray the interests of the true self. The true self has eyes beyond the narrow ego; the false self seeks nothing beyond gratifying sensory pleasures and an inflated ego.[2] The false self drags the feet of the true self. This is why it is often said that we are our worst enemy. It takes a strong will and strong discipline to tame the false self.

The LIFE formula

I have named Love, Insight, Fortitude and Engagement the formula for happiness. I have found, through statistical test after statistical test, that self-reported happiness is highly correlated with the mental habits that I call LIFE mental capitals. Yet, in truth, one would only need Love and Insight, otherwise called compassion and wisdom or loving others as much as ourselves and "loving God." This is taught by ancient spiritual teachers, including the Buddha and Jesus. We can interpret loving God broadly as humbly adhering to the laws of nature and the laws of life that govern our mental functions and mental states.[3] This is the essence of wisdom or Insight. Because Jesus is regarded as a prophet in Islam this is also an important teaching for Muslims. Insight or wisdom is respecting the laws of nature, both the laws that govern the physical world and the "laws of life." Love without understanding the laws of nature and the laws of life will not give us much mileage. With Love and Insight, Fortitude and Engagement will naturally accumulate over time. During the darkest moments in life, it is Love and Insight that enable us to tough it out. With Love and Insight, it would be silly not to live each day positively and actively. Insight and Fortitude are twin brothers. I prefer LIFE as the formula for happiness instead of naming the 24 character strengths purely for pedagogical reasons. It is not only much easier to remember, but also reminds us that LIFE is the true and ultimate value for humankind and resonates with the philosophy propounded and practiced by Albert Schweitzer. So, we should treasure life and do the best with it while we can.

We have called Love, Insight, Fortitude and Engagement "mental capital" for a good reason. "Capital" is a stock that can be accumulated. Mental capital is the accumulation of mental habits that have become so ingrained in our minds that they can be regarded as our second nature. While Love and Insight are the most fundamental, Fortitude does need to accumulate by going "through thick and thin." Without going through adversity, without reflecting and learning, Fortitude cannot build up. Similarly, Engagement requires maintaining a sense of purpose in everything we do every day, and that also requires an attitude that needs to be strengthened over time.

In separate studies in 2011, I tested the LIFE formula with businesses in Hong Kong and since 2011/2012 I have been doing annual surveys on schoolchildren from Primary 4 to Secondary 3. The evidence has confirmed that LIFE has a strong predictive power for both happiness at work and the happiness of schoolchildren.[4] The children study shows, however, that humans tend to become less loving, less wise and less happy as they grow into their teens. This appears to be associated with the rising pressures that come with adolescence. Adolescence is a big challenge both for children and for their parents. In line with earlier findings, we find that the relationship between one's parents is a key driver for the Love score of children and thus a key factor in explaining their happiness. The happiness at work study extended the LIFE formula and introduced the concepts of "Corporate Love," "Corporate Insight," "Corporate Fortitude," and "Corporate Engagement." Statistical analysis using a survey covering a total of 1,328 workers from over 600 firms shows that workers who find that their company is caring (Corporate Love), that can strike a good balance between centralization and decentralization (Corporate Insight), that can muster the will of staff to work together to meet challenges (Corporate Fortitude) and engages workers in purposive tasks (Corporate Engagement) are happier, and their companies also appear to be better performers in reducing staff turnover and absenteeism, and increasing profitability.

Spirituality and religion

A recent study of mine using World Value Survey data confirms that whether one has religion and which religion one adheres to does not really matter to Total Life Satisfaction. What matters is Love, Insight, Fortitude, and Engagement, which represent the main spiritual teachings of all worthy religions. Moreover, once the proxies for LIFE mental capital are included in the regression, the variable indicating people who think much about meaning and the purpose of life turns out to carry a negative and statistically significant coefficient, suggesting that those who have a lot of LIFE mental capital are already happy, while those who are low in LIFE mental capital and who are still searching for meaning are less happy! Without thinking much about meaning, people who have a lot of LIFE mental capital have already found meaning!

Table 13.1 shows the key findings in Ho (2024). Model 0 includes only socio-economic variables and religious affiliations as explanatory variables. The results indicate some variation in the coefficients of religion dummies, with Christians carrying a positive and statistically significant coefficient. Model 0a adds a single variable, which a scale variable (1 to 10) is indicating how important God is to the respondent. Interestingly, ALL major religious affiliations now carry a NEGATIVE coefficient. Model 1 now adds traditional religious/spiritual variables. Only *God_Important*, *Religious_Important*, and *Religious_Attendance* in the list added are significant and positive. Model 2 throws out all traditional religious/spiritual variables and adds LIFE mental capital variables. We found these LIFE mental variable proxies all carry positive and statistically significant coefficients. The constant term, which represents the variance in the dependent variable Total Life Satisfaction that is left unexplained, falls to a tiny fraction of what it was in Model 0 to Model 1. Finally, Model 3 includes both traditional and LIFE variables. The LIFE variables continue to carry very significant and positive coefficients. Spirituality_Meaning now carries a negative and statistically significant coefficient. The constant term shrinks further and is virtually zero. The fourth row shows the percentage of Total Life Satisfaction that is not explained by the model, which is constant term (third row divided by second row). **Table 13.2** presents the full results in a regression based on Model 3 but with religious denominations added (Model 3a). It clearly shows that one's religious affiliation has little to do with Total Life Satisfaction. What matters the most? LIFE mental capitals and humility[5] (*God_Important* is a good proxy for humility).

God_Important always carries a significant and positive coefficient for a good reason. First, those who hold God to be important in their lives will be humble and thus less likely to be arrogant. Second, they know that they have weaknesses and have a desire to improve themselves. Third, they believe that God is just and cherish the hope that despite all that appears unjust in the world, everything will finally be put right eventually. Interestingly, when this variable is put into the equation in Model 0, all major denominations carry a negative coefficient[6], suggesting that religious denominations generally do not matter to Total Life Satisfaction. *God_Important* is on a 1 to 10 scale. The coefficient has an important and continuous effect on TLS.

Many studies have shown that happiness is positively related to religiosity. But what is it in religiosity that makes people happy? Ho (2024) shows that it is mainly the teachings of religions about spirituality, about Love, Insight, Fortitude, and Engagement. Apparently, fellowship with members of the same faith, as indicated by religious attendance, and faith also play a part. But spirituality is not the monopoly of any particular religion. People not affiliated with any religion can also be spiritual. Religious affiliation is not important at all. Spiritual living is simply living with a deep respect for life and living with the realization that every human being is equally of value.

TABLE 13.1 Testing traditional versus LIFE variables in World Value Survey (Wave 5) in Regression Model

	Model 0	*Model 0a*	*Model 1*	*Model 2*	*Model 3*
	Only Socio-Economic Variables incl. Relig. Affiliation (52 countries)	*Add God Important Only (52 countries)*	*Traditional Religious/ Spiritual Variables only (46 countries)*	*LIFE Variables Only (45 countries)*	*Both Traditional and LIFE Variables Included (43 countries)*
Sample size**	62,415	61,551 (52)	52,125	50,591	45,220
Average of TLS in subsample	6.693	6.7007	6.7234	6.7404	6.7663
Constant term	1.766	1.503	1.304	0.149	-0.093
Unexplained TLS (%)	26.39	22.43	19.39	2.21	-1.37
Spirituality_Meaning			0.004		-0.01***
Spirituality_PrayMeditate			-0.016		-0.017
God_Important		0.04***	0.032***		0.032***
Religious_Important			0.021***		0.013***
Religious_Attendance			0.007**		0.008**
Love_Family				0.065***	0.064***
Love_Friend				0.025***	0.026***
Love_Help				0.03***	0.027***
Insight_Nature				0.012***	0.013***
Insight_Rich_Unimportant				0.012***	0.011***
Insight_Be_Myself				0.01**	0.009*
Fortitude_Hardwork				0.015***	0.012***
Fortitude_Faith				0.023***	0.024***
Engagement_Creative				0.029***	0.033***
Engagement_Lifegoal				0.017***	0.013***

Note: * indicates significance at 10% level; ** indicates significance at 5% level; *** indicates significance at 1% level. Socio-economic variables are included in all regressions but left out in this table for simplicity.

TABLE 13.2 Add back religious denominations to Model 3 (Model 3a)

Dependent Variable: Total Life Satisfaction		*Coef.*	*Std. Error*	*Beta*	*t*	*Sig.*
	(Constant)	-0.112	0.131		-0.85	0.395
LIFE Variables	*Love_Family*	0.066	0.009	0.029	7.455	<.001
	Love_Friend	0.025	0.004	0.024	5.912	<.001
	Love_Help	0.027	0.005	0.024	5.579	<.001
	Insight_Nature	0.013	0.004	0.012	2.944	0.003
	Insight_rich_unimportant	0.012	0.004	0.014	3.283	0.001
	Insight_be_me	0.008	0.005	0.007	1.707	0.088
	Fortitude_Hardwork	0.012	0.003	0.015	3.923	<.001
	Fortitude_Faith	0.024	0.003	0.031	7.367	<.001
	Engagement_Creative	0.034	0.004	0.036	8.571	<.001
	Engagement_Lifegoal	0.013	0.005	0.012	2.898	0.004
Religion Denomination	*Roman Catholic*	-0.019	0.034	-0.003	-0.547	0.584
	Protestant	0.023	0.036	0.004	0.635	0.526
	Eastern Orthodox	-0.159	0.059	-0.024	-2.718	0.007
	Buddhist	0.007	0.063	0.001	0.115	0.908
	Hindu	0.015	0.087	0.001	0.174	0.862
	Muslim	0.025	0.053	0.004	0.46	0.645
	Others	0.097	0.046	0.01	2.103	0.035
Religious and Spirituality variables	*Spirituality_Meaning*	-0.011	0.004	-0.012	-3.017	0.003
	Spirituality_Contemplate	-0.015	0.025	-0.003	-0.611	0.541
	God_Important	0.032	0.005	0.041	6.956	<.001
	Religious_Important	0.013	0.004	0.017	2.939	0.003
	Religious_Attendance	0.008	0.004	0.012	2.24	0.025

TABLE 13.3 Descriptive statistics of dummy variables

Domain	*Variable= 1 if*	*Frequency*	*Valid %*
Spirituality_Comtemplate (Moments of prayer, meditation)	*Yes*	34304	75.90
	No (excluded)	10916	24.10
Active_inCommunity(Active member of any mentioned organisation)	*Yes*	19107	42.30
	No (excluded)	26113	57.70
Religion Denomination	*None (excluded)*	6108	13.6
	Roman Catholic	10224	22.7
	Protestant	7863	17.5
	Eastern Orthodox	6057	13.5
	Buddhist	2429	5.4
	Hindu	1077	2.4
	Muslim	8583	19.1
	Others	2641	5.9
Marital Status	*Married or living together as married*	28608	63.30
	Divorced	1667	3.70
	Separated	844	1.90
	Widowed	2635	5.80
	Single/Never married (excluded)	11467	25.40
Employment Status	*Full time employee (30 hours a week or more) (excluded)*	16701	36.90
	Part time employee (less than 30 hours a week)	2931	6.50
	Self employed	5978	13.20
	Retired/ pensioned	5862	13.00
	Housewife not otherwise employed	6101	13.50
	Student	3173	7.00
	Unemployed	4474	9.90

(Continued)

TABLE 13.3 (Continued)

Domain	*Variable= 1 if*	*Frequency*	*Valid %*
Sex	*Male (excluded)*	22480	49.70
	Female	22740	50.30
Age Group	*age_under21 (excluded)*	3300	7.30
	age21_29	9700	21.50
	age30_49	18438	40.80
	age50_64	8936	19.80
	age65up	4846	10.70

Spirituality, however, is not just humanism and does require a degree of transcendence and self-forgetting. Having given up egotism, a spiritual person sees little distinction between himself and others, so he will never hurt others to advance his interests. His mind is free, so that he is always at ease, and able to avoid being biased by prejudices. The more spiritual the person, the more his has overcome his weaknesses and perfected his life.

No clash of civilizations

One of my earlier books carried the title *Human Spirituality and Happiness*. It is so titled because I firmly believe that the diversity of religious faiths in our world notwithstanding, there is only one spirituality, human spirituality, and that is the same spirituality that both the West and the East espoused more than two thousand years ago. If so, how can there be clash of irreconcilable civilizations? In particular, the ancient philosophy of stoicism from Europe extolls four virtues: courage, temperance, justice and wisdom. These align perfectly with the Confucian virtues of wisdom, benevolence, courage, and moderation. The fact that American author Ryan Holiday has sold 5 million copies of his books on the Stoic way of life shows that this is as cherished by Westerners today as during ancient times.[7]

I do not, therefore, agree with Samuel Huntington's notion that there is a clash of civilization between the East and the West that cannot be resolved. He first proposed this hypothesis in a *Foreign Affairs* article in 1993. Not long after, in 1996, he published a full-length book *The Clash of Civilizations and the Remaking of World Order*. Huntington (1993) warned that "the conflicts of the future will occur along the cultural fault lines separating civilizations." He proclaimed that such differences as "views on the relations between God and man, the individual and the group, the citizen and the state, parents and children, husband and wife, as well as differing views of the relative importance of rights and responsibility, liberty and authority, equality and hierarchy," being "the products of centuries," can hardly be reconciled (p.25). While arguing that with the decline in communism as a threat, Huntington (1996) sees cultural differences, rather than ideological differences, to be the main source of conflict between the West and the other civilisations. But given the universality of human nature, people from different "civilizations" all have similar ultimate needs and aspirations, as per Maslow's needs hierarchy. One key clash point is "Western political values such as human rights and democracy." However, why should there be clash since aspirations for human rights and democracy are not particular to the West at all. The problem is that most people in the West take electoral democracy as a value, but the ballot box is just one way of selecting leaders, and there are Western scholars, such as Jane Mansbridge (1980) and Jason Brennan (2012, 2016), who take issue with it. Which is the best way to select leaders to serve the interests of the people should be studied scientifically. It is too presumptuous to take electoral democracy as the best way to select leaders and a "Western value," when the true value in this context is an effective government that serves the people well.

To the extent that "different civilizations" share the same dreams in the pursuit of happiness and world peace, there cannot be any clash. Clashes occur when people mistake means for ends, or when people are disingenuous. If we are open-minded and engage ourselves in truthfully seeking better ways of governance, respecting one another as equals, the world will find peace. If we are open-minded and wise enough to understand that some ways of life are incompatible with sustainable development and go about addressing climate change and protecting the environment and biodiversity, the world will have enough for all of us. If we insist on unsustainable ways of life, clashes will be inevitable because we will always be fighting for resources, the world will continue to have wars, and humanity will come to its demise.

Hope for advancement in human civilization

To me, there is only one human civilization. While there are different cultures and different ethnicities, only when humans transcend cultural barriers and racial barriers and gender barriers, and genuinely respect one another as equal humans—i.e., when we have acquired a "transcendental culture,"—can we claim to be civilized humans. We know, deep inside ourselves, that people are not created equal. We have different genes; we are born into different families that vary greatly in wealth and in opportunities; different countries are in different stages of development; some appear to be in perpetual peace; others appear to be in perpetual wars. But we can and should respect one another as human beings equal in standing. We talk a lot about human rights, and that is because our true selves tell us that we should be equal in standing regardless of our cultural or ethnic backgrounds. But our false selves keep telling us that we should advance our egoistic interests without caring for sustainability. We say one thing and do another thing. Anyone who acts like that, regardless of their cultural or ethnic background, East or West, is uncivilized.

The paradoxical truth is that, as we act selfishly we are betraying our own longer-term well-being. Our world will become uninhabitable. We will all be doomed. Our spiritual mentors, from the West and from the East, have been telling us that we should love our neighbours as ourselves. Sadly, we are fighting and killing one another. Let me end this volume with the following prayer that I wrote back in 2002:

Peace—a tribute to those who have died in the Palestine-Israel conflict
(July 28, 2002, amended August 2, 2002)

We are apt
To mourn the death of our loved ones.

Have our lost ones found peace?
May they rest in peace!

Peace O Peace,
How the world cries out for Peace!

War O War,
How the world is at War!

Suicide bombs, crushing tanks,
Killing antagonism, killing sanctions!

To the loved ones who had lived in peace and died in peace,
Congratulations, not mournings, are due!

To the loved ones who had lived in war and died in war:
Let a prayer of love, hope, and peace—
A gentle flower from the heart
Bless them
Forever.

Notes

1 See: Christopher Peterson's (2008) 'What Is Positive Psychology, and What Is It Not?' *Psychology Today*, May 16. Downloadable from: www.psychologytoday.com/blog/the-good-life/200805/what-is-positive-psychology-and-what-is-itnot.

2 This use of the terms *false self* and *true self* is different from that used by British psychoanalyst Donald Winnicott (1896–1971), to whom the self that develops as a defense against impingements and in adaptation to the environment is the false self. The true self, in contrast, develops as one interacts with an environment that is friendly so the infant learns to discover and express true impulses without feeling alienated.

3 See John Marks Templeton's (1998) *Worldwide Laws of Life: 200 Eternal Spiritual Principles*, Templeton Press.

4 The study on happiness at work was commissioned by the HK Productivity Council in 2011. The study on happiness of children was originally commissioned by the Early Childhood Development Research Foundation and funded by Henderson Land Group. It was later largely funded by the Shih Wing Ching Foundation. More recently, it is jointly funded by the STEAM Education and Research Centre

of Lingnan University, the HK Pediatric Society, the Department of Pediatrics and Adolescence Sciences, and the Department of Pediatrics of the Chinese University of Hong Kong.

5 It is a pity that the World Value Survey does not include a question on humility.

6 See Table 5 in Ho (2024).

7 See "The Stoicism Secret: How Ryan Holiday became a Silicon Valley Guru," *The Guardian*, 2024 www.theguardian.com/books/2024/oct/28/the-stoicism-secret-how-ryan-holiday-became-a-silicon-valley-guru

Key points to note

- Life is the most precious resource that we have and whole personal development or growth is the categorical imperative for all of us humans. We owe it to ourselves to make the most out of our lives.
- As we set out to accumulate LIFE mental capitals, the false self would drag our feet. The false self is the self that is dominated by the seven deadly sins. It is the obsessive self. The true self is the enlightened self.
- Sustainable development and world peace can only be possible if the materialistic and egoistic culture gives way to the LIFE culture, which is predicated on taking the long view and a holistic view about life.
- Albert Schweitzer's philosophy of Reverence for Life, advising transcendence beyond national, ethnic, and cultural differences, offers hope for world peace and sustainable development.
- It is a lack of reverence for life that has led to a world facing crises and the so-called clash of civilisations. We need more efficient household production than that under the curse of the "keeping up with the Joneses" treadmill. This implies a transcendental culture.

Some questions to ponder

- Can religions iron out their differences? What are their differences?
- What constitutes freedom of religion? Should religions be regulated?
- Do we have enough resources for everybody to enjoy a good life?
- Are there fundamental differences in values between the West and the East?
- What is the origin of "American values" and "Asian values"?

BIBLIOGRAPHY

Abdel-Khalek, A. M. (2006). "Measuring happiness with a single-item scale," *Social Behavior and Personality, 34*(2), 139–150.

Achor, Shawn (2010) *The Happiness Advantage: The Seven Principles of Positive Psychology That Fuel Success and Performance at Work*, Crown Business.

Achor, Shawn (2012) "Is Happiness the Secret of Success?" March 19, CNN. Downloadable from: https://edition.cnn.com/2012/03/19/opinion/happiness-success-achor/index.html

Ainslie, George (1989) "Freud and picoeconomics," *Behaviorism*, 17:11–19.

Akoglu, H. (2018). User's guide to correlation coefficients. *Turkish Journal of Emergency Medicine, 18*(3), 91–93.

Andrade, C. (2020). "The limitations of online surveys," *Indian Journal of Psychological Medicine, 42*(6), 575–576.

Anusic, Ivana, Stevie C. Y. Yap, and Richard E. Lucas (2014) "Testing Set-Point Theory in a Swiss National Sample: Reaction and Adaptation to Major Life Events," *Soc Indic Res.* 119(3):1265-1288

Ariely, Dan (2008) *Predictably Irrational: The Hidden Forces That Shape Our Decisions*, HarperCollins.

Arnon S, Brunstein-Klomek, Visoki E, et al.(2022) "Association of Cyberbullying Experiences and Perpetration With Suicidality in Early Adolescence," *JAMA Netw Open*. 5(6):e2218746.

Banerjee, A. and E. Duflo (2012) *Poor Economics*, Penguin Books.

Banerjee, Abhijit V. and Esther Duflo (2011), "Poor Economics: A Radical Rethinking of the Way to Fight Global Poverty," Public Affairs.

Becker, Gary (1965) "A Theory of Allocation of Time," *Economic Journal*, 75(299): 493–517.

Becker, Gary (1998) *The Economics of Life: From Baseball to Affirmative Action to Immigration, How Real-World Issues Affect Our Everyday Life*, McGraw Hill.

Becker, G. S. and K. M. Murphy (1988) "A Theory of Rational Addiction," *Journal of Political Economy*, 96: 675–700.

Beier, Yosh (2017) "What Having A Self-Authoring Mind Means," *Forbes Coaches Council Post*. Updated Jan 27, 2017.

Benabou, Roland and Jean Tirole (2003) "Intrinsic and Extrinsic Motivation," *Review of Economic Studies*, 70: 489–520.

Blanchflower, David G. and Andrew Oswald (2007) "Is Well-Being U-shaped over the Life Cycle?" "National Bureau of Economic Research Working Paper 12935," Downloadable from: www.nber.org/papers/w12935

Bradberry, Travis and Jean Greaves (2009) *Emotional Intelligence 2.0*, TalentSmart.

Brennan, Jason (2012), *The Ethics of Voting*, Princeton University Press.

Brennan, Jason (2016) *Against Democracy*, Princeton University Press.

Brickman, Phillip, Dan Coates and Ronnie Janoff-Bulman (1978) "Lottery Winners and Accident Victims: Is Happiness Relative?" *Journal of Personality and Social Psychology*, 36: 917–927.

Buecker, Susanne, Marcus Mund, Sandy Chwastek, Melina Sostmann, and Maike Luhmann (2021) "Is Loneliness in Emerging Adults Increasing Over Time? A Preregistered Cross-Temporal Meta-Analysis and Systematic Review," *Psychological Bulletin*, Vol. 147, No. 8, 787–80

Byrne, B. M. (2016). *Structural equation modeling with AMOS*. Routledge.

Carlson, Daniel L., Miller, Amanda J & Rudd, Stephanie (2020). "Division of Housework, Communication, and Couples' Relationship Satisfaction," Sociological Research for a Dynamic World Volume 6: 1–17. Published. 06/01/2020.

Chan, S., Odetayo, A., Tsui, K. Y., Lam, S. C. (2024). "General happiness index from 2018 to 2024 in Hong Kong SAR: Dataset of repeated cross-sectional surveys," *Mendeley Data, V1*, https://doi.org/10.17632/czxznncsv2.3

Cheung, F., & Lucas, R. E. (2014). "Assessing the validity of single-item life satisfaction measures: results from three large samples," *Quality of Life Research*, *23*(10), 2809–2818. https://doi.org/10.1007/s11136-014-0726-4

Claiborn, James and Cherry Pedrick (2001) *The Habit Change Workbook: How to Break Bad Habits and Form Good Ones*, New Harbinger Publications

Cohen, J. (1988). *Statistical power analysis for the behavioral sciences* (2nd ed.). Lawrence Erlbaum Associates.

Cookerly, John R. (2001) *Recovering Love: Codependency to CoRecovery,* I Universe.

Cooper, Cary, Usha Goswami, Barbara J. Sahakian (2009) *Mental Capital and Wellbeing*, Wiley-Blackwell

Costello, A. B., & Osborne, J. (2005). "Best practices in exploratory factor analysis: Four recommendations for getting the most from your analysis," *Practical Assessment, Research, and Evaluation*, 10(1): 7.

Dambrun M. (2017) "Self-centeredness and selflessness: happiness correlates and mediating psychological processes," *PeerJ*. 2017 May 11;5:e3306. doi: 10.7717/peerj.3306. PMID: 28507820; PMCID: PMC5429736.

De Bono, Edward (1970). *Lateral Thinking: Creativity Step by Step,* Harper & Row.

Deci, Edward. (1975) *Intrinsic Motivation,* Plenum Press.

Deci, E. L., & Ryan, R. M. (2008). "Hedonia, Eudaimonia, and well-being: An introduction," *Journal of Happiness Studies*, *9*(1), 1–11.

de Graaf, John, David Wann and Thomas H. Naylor (2002) *Affluenza: The AllConsuming Epidemic*, Berrett-Koehler Publishers.

Deng, Xin and Yew-Kwang Ng (2004) "Optimal Taxation on Mixed Diamond Goods: Implications for Private Car Ownership in China," *Pacific Economic Review*, 9 (4): 293–306.

Diener, Ed and Robert Biswas-Diener (2011) *Unlocking the Mysteries of Psychological Wealth*, John Wiley.

Diener, E., & Seligman, M. E. P. (2002). "Very happy people," *Psychological Science, 13*(1), 81–84.

Dow, Gregory K. and F. Thomas Juster (1985) "Goods, Time, and Well-being: The Joint Dependence Problem," in F. Thomas Juster and Frank P. Stafford (eds.), *Time, Goods, and Well-Being*, Survey Research Center, Institute for Social Research, University of Michigan, Ann Arbor, pp. 397–413.

Duhigg, Charles (2012) *The Power of Habit: Why We Do What We Do in Life and Business*, Random House.

Easterlin, Richard A. (1974) "Does Economic Growth Improve the Human Lot?" in Paul A. David and Melvin W. Reder (eds.)(1974), *Nations and Households in Economic Growth: Essays in Honor of Moses Abramovitz*, Academic Press, Inc.

Easterlin, Richard A., Laura Angelescu McVey, Malgorzata Switek, Onnicha Sawangfa and Jacqueline Smith Zweig (2010) "The Happiness–income Paradox Revisited," *Proceedings of the National Academy of Sciences of the United States of America*, 107 (52): 22463–22468.

Eccles, Robert G., Vinay Shandal, David Young, and Benedicte Montgomery (2022) "Private Equity Should Take the Lead in Sustainability," *Harvard Business Review*, (July–August)

Finch, W. H. (2020). *Exploratory factor analysis*. SAGE Publications.

Fisher, J.W. (1998). *Spiritual health: Its nature, and place in the school curriculum.* Unpublished doctoral dissertation, The University of Melbourne, Melbourne, Victoria, Australia.

Ford, T, J Lipson and L Miller (2023). "Spiritually grounded character: A latent profile analysis," *Frontiers in Psychology*, 13, 1061416, doi: 10.3389/fpsyg.2022.1061416.

Frank, Robert (2008) *The Economic Naturalist: Why Economics Explains Almost Everything*, Basic Books.

Frijters, Paul and Tony Beatton (2012) "The Mystery of the U-shaped Relationship Between Happiness and Age," *Journal of Economic Behavior and Organization*, 82 (2–3), 525–542.

Fromm, Erich (1956) *The Art of Loving*, Harper & Row.

Fromm, Erich (1964) "The Heart of Man," Harper & Row.

Galbraith, John Kenneth (1958) *The Affluent Society*, Hamish Hamilton.

Gallop (2024), *State of the Global Workplace Report.*

Gino, Francesca and Lamar Pierce (2009) "The Abundance Effect: Unethical Behavior in the Presence of Wealth," *Organizational Behavior and Human Decision Processes*, 109: 142–155.

Goretzko, D., Siemund, K., & Sterner, P. (2023). "Evaluating model fit of measurement models in confirmatory factor analysis," *Educational and Psychological Measurement, 84*(1), 123–144.

Hair, J. F., Black, W. C., Babin, B. J., & Anderson, R. E. (2018). *Multivariate data analysis* (8th ed.). Cengage.

Harford, Tim (2005) *The Undercover Economist*, Little, Brown.

Harford, Tim (2009) *The Logic of Life: Uncovering the New Economics of Everything*, Abacus.

Hatfield, E., Cacioppo, J.T. and Rapson, R.L. (1993) Emotional contagion. *Current Directions in Psychological Science*, 2: 96–99.

Hawkley LC, Cacioppo JT.(2010) "Loneliness matters: A theoretical and empirical review of consequences and mechanisms," *Ann Behav Med.* 2010 Oct;40(2):218-27.

Hicks, J.R. (1939) *Value and Capital, An Inquiry into some Fundamental Principles of Economic Theory*, Clarendon Press.

Ho, L.S. (2001) *Principles of Public Policy Practice*, Kluwer.

Ho, L.S. (2011) "Hong Kong's Happiness Indices: What they Tell us About LIFE?" *Journal of Socio-Economics*, 40: 564–572.

Ho, L.S. (2012) *Public Policy and the Public Interest*, Routledge.

Ho, L. S. (2014). *The psychology and economics of happiness: Love, life and positive living*. Routledge.

Ho, L.S. (2018) "What Accounts for the Decline of Happiness of Children with Age: A Hong Kong Case Study, *Pacific Economic Review*. 23(2): 222-243, with Patrick Ip.

Ho, L.S. (2020) *Human Spirituality and Happiness*, 2nd edition. Independently published through Amazon

Ho, L.S. (2024) "Spirituality, Religiosity, and Happiness: Identifying the Nexus," *Singapore Economic Review*, 69(5) 1659–1684

Ho, L. S., Su, J. J., Chong, A. C. Y., Cheung, D. S. K., Ho, K. H. M., Siu, S. C. N., ... & Lam, S. C. (2025). "Validation of the Love, Insight, Fortitude, and Engagement (LIFE) Scale in measuring mental capital for happiness in the Chinese community," *Working Paper*.

Holder, M.D., Coleman, S. and Wallace, S. (2010). "Spirituality, religiousness, and happiness in children aged 8–12 years," *Journal of Happiness Studies*, 11, 131–150.

Holiday, Ryan (2016), *The Daily Stoic: 366 Meditations on Wisdom, Perseverance, and the Art of Living*, Profile Trade. ISBN-13978-1781257654

Huang, E. Y. Z., Cheung, J., Liu, J. Y. W., Kwan, R. Y. C., & Lam, S. C. (2022). "Groningen frailty indicator–Chinese (GFI-C) for pre-frailty and frailty assessment among older people living in communities: Psychometric properties and diagnostic accuracy," *BMC Geriatrics*, *22*(1), 788.

Huntington, S. (1993), "Clash of Civilizations," *Foreign Affairs*. Summer pp.22-49.

Huntington, S. (1993), Clash of Civilizations and the Remaking of World Order, NY: Simon & Schuster.

Jennifer E Stellar, Amie Gordon, Craig L Anderson, Paul K Piff, Galen D McNeil, Dacher Keltner (2018), "Awe and Humility," *Journal of Personality and Social Psychology*, 2018, Vol. 114, No. 2, 258–269

Joshanloo, Mohsen, et.al. (2014) "Cross-cultural validation of fear of happiness scale across 14 national groups", *Journal of Cross-cultural Psychology*, vol. 45, 2: pp. 246–264.

Jost, J. T., Glaser, J., Kruglanski, A. W., & Sulloway, F. J. (2003). "Political conservatism as motivated social cognition," *Psychological Bulletin*, 129(3), 339–375.

Jost, J. (2017). "Ideological Asymmetries and the Essence of Political Psychology," *Political Psychology*, 38(2), 167–208.

Juster, F. T., P. Courant and G. K. Dow. (1985) "A Conceptual Framework for the Analysis of Time Allocation Data," in: F. Thomas Juster and Frank P. Stafford (eds.), *Time Goods and Well-Being*. Survey Research Center, Institute for Social Research, University of Michigan, Ann Arbor.

Kahneman, Daniel and Angus Deaton (2010) "High Income Improves Evaluation of Life but not Emotional Well-Being," *Proceedings of the National Academy of Sciences of the United States of America,* 107(38): 16489–16493. Downloadable from: www.pnas.org/content/107/38/16489.full?sid=6699db95-04ed-45af-8450-074fe609aa6f.

Kant, Immanuel (1964) *Groundwork of the Metaphysics of Morals*, translated by H. J. Paton, Harper Torchbooks.

Kasser, T. (2003) *The High Price of Materialism*, MIT Press.

Kasser, T. (2009) "Can Buddhism and Consumerism Harmonize? A Review of the Psychological Evidence," *Journal of Religion and Culture*, 2: 167–193.

Kasser, T. and R. M. Ryan (1993) "A Dark Side of the American Dream: Correlates of Financial Success as a Central Life Aspiration," *Journal of Personality and Social Psychology*, 65: 410–422.

Kasser, T. and R. M. Ryan (1996) "Further Examining the American Dream: Differential Correlates of Intrinsic and Extrinsic Goals," *Personality and Social Psychology Bulletin*, 22: 280–287.

Kasser, T. and R. M. Ryan (2001) "Be Careful What you Wish For: Optimal Functioning and the Relative Attainment of Intrinsic and Extrinsic Goals," in P. Schmuck and K. M. Sheldon (eds.), *Life Goals and Well-being: Towards a Positive Psychology of Human Striving*, Hogrefe & Huber, pp. 116–131.

Kasser, T., R. M. Ryan, C. E. Couchman, and K. M. Sheldon (2004) "Materialistic Values: Their Causes and Consequences," in T. Kasser and A.D. Kenner (eds.), *Psychology and Consumer Culture: The Struggle for a Good Life in a Materialistic World*, American Psychological Association, pp. 11–28.

Keynes, John Maynard (1923) *A Tract on Monetary Reform*, Prometheus Books, Chapter 3.

Kruegar, Alan B. (ed.) (2009) *Measuring the Subjective Well-being of Nations: National Accounts of Time-use and Well-being*, National Bureau of Economic Research.

Krueger, Alan B., Daniel Kahneman, David Schkade, Norbert Schwarz, Arthur A. Stone (2009) "National Time Accounting: The Currency of Life, Chapter 1," in Alan B. Krueger (ed.) (2009) *Measuring the Subjective Wellbeing of Nations: National Accounts of Time Use and Well-Being*, University of Chicago Press. Downloadable from http://www.nber.org/chapters/c5053

Kwan, R. Y. C., Lam, S. C., Wang, S. L., Wong, A. K. C., Shi, L., & Wong, F. K. Y. (2022). "Perception of E-health Technology Scale in Chinese Brief (PETSC Brief): Translation, item reduction, and psychometric testing." *Digital Health, 8*, 1–12.

Lam, S. C., Chan, Z. S.-L., Chong, A. C.-Y., Wong, W. W.-C., & Ye, J. (2018). "Adaptation and validation of Richmond Compulsive Buying Scale in Chinese population," *Journal of Behavioral Addictions*, *7*(3), 760–769.

Lam, S. C., Chong, A. C. Y., Chung, J. Y. S., Lam, M. Y., Chan, L. M., Shum, C. Y., ... & Cheung, J. H. M. (2020). "Methodological study on the evaluation of face mask use scale among public adult: Cross-language and psychometric testing. *Korean Journal of Adult Nursing*, 32(1), 46–56.

Lam, S. C., Kwai, L., Huang, E. Y., Mi, E., Sze, D., & Yiu, R. (2023). "Sensitivity and specificity of conventional and new face validation in determining the incomprehensible items by older people: Empirical evidence of testing 106 quality-of-life items," *Aging Medicine*, *6*(3), 230–238.

Lam, S.C., Chan, S., Tsui, K. Y. & Odetayo, A. (2025a). "General happiness index of a repeated cross-sectional survey among the general population from 2018 to 2024 in Hong Kong: A data note," *BMC Research Note* (In press).

Lam, S. C., Odetayo, A., Chan, S., Tsui, K. Y. (2025b). "Family happiness index among general population: Dataset of repeated cross-sectional surveys from 2019 to 2024 in Hong Kong SAR," *Mendeley Data, V1*. https://doi.org/10.17632/wmh87245bj.1

Lancaster, Kelvin (1966) "A New Approach to Consumption Theory," *Journal of Political Economy,* 74 (2): 132–157.

Landsburg, Steven E. (2012) *The Armchair Economist: Economics and Everyday Life,* Free Press.

Levitt, Steven & Stephen J. Dubner (2005) *Freakonomics: A Rogue Economist Explores the Hidden Side of Everything,* William Morrow/HarperCollins.

Levitt, Steven and Stephen J. Dubner (2009) *Superfreakonomics: Global Cooling, Patriotic Prostitutes, and Why Suicide Bombers Should Buy Life Insurance,* HarperCollins.

Li, S., Kwok, S. W. H., Siu, S. C. N., Chung, J. Y. S., Lam, H. C. Y., Tsang, E. Y. M., ... & Lam, S. C. (2023). "Development of generic student engagement scale in higher education: An application on healthcare students," *Nursing Open, 10*(3), 1545–1555.

Lindqvist, Erik, Robert Östling, David Cesarini (2020) "Long-Run Effects of Lottery Wealth on Psychological Well-Being," *The Review of Economic Studies,* 87(6): 2703–2726, https://doi.org/10.1093/restud/rdaa006

Liu, T. W., Lam, S. C., Chung, M. H., & Ho, K. H. M. (2020). "Adaptation and psychometric testing of the hoarding rating scale (HRS): a self-administered screening scale for epidemiological study in Chinese population," *BMC Psychiatry, 20*(1), 159.

Lykken D & A.Tellegen (1996) "Happiness is a Stochastic Phenomenon," *Psychological Science.* 7:186–189.

Lykken D (2000) *Happiness: The Nature and Nurture of Joy and Contentment Golden Guides,* St. Martin's Press.

Luthans F. and C. M. Youssef (2004). "Human, Social, and now Positive Psychological Capital Management: Investing in People for Competitive Advantage," *Organizational Dynamics,* 33(2): 143–160.

Maese, Ellyn (2023), "Almost a Quarter of the World Feels Lonely," October 24 2023. https://news.gallup.com/opinion/gallup/512618/almost-quarter-world-feels-lonely.aspx

Mansbridge, Jane (1980) *Beyond Adversary Democracy,* Basic Books.

Maslow, A. H. (1943). "A Theory of Human Motivation," *Psychological Review,* 50(4), 370-96.

Maslow, Abraham (1954). *Motivation and Personality,* New York: Harper and Row.

Maurer, M. M., Maurer, J., Hoff, E., & Daukantaitė, D. (2023). "What is the process of personal growth? Introducing the personal growth process model," *New Ideas in Psychology,* 70, 1–11. https://doi.org/10.1016/j.newideapsych.2023.101024

McClelland, D. C. (1985). How motives, skills, and values determine what people do. *American Psychologist, 40*(7), 812–825. https://doi.org/10.1037/0003-066X.40.7.812

McClelland, D.C. (1987). *Human motivation.* New York: University of Cambridge.

Mogilner, Cassie, Sepandar D. Kamvar and Jennifer Aaker (2011) "The Shifting Meaning of Happiness," *Social Psychological and Personality Science,* 2: 395–402.

Morris LS, Grehl MM, Rutter SB, Mehta M, Westwater ML (2022). "On what motivates us: a detailed review of intrinsic v. extrinsic motivation," Psychological Medicine, 52(10), 1801–1816. https://doi.org/10.1017/ S0033291722001611

Moss, Jennifer (2023) "Creating a Happier Workplace Is Possible — and Worth It," *Harvard Business Review,* October.

Mui, Vai-lam (1995) "The Economics of Envy," *Journal of Economic Behavior & Organization,* 26 (3), 311-336.

Newcomb, M. D., L. M. Scheier, and P. M. Bentler (1993). "Effects of Adolescent Drug Use on Adult Mental Health: A Prospective Study of a Community Sample," *Experimental and Clinical Psychopharmacology*, 1(1–4): 215–241.

Ng, Yew-Kwang (1987) 'Diamonds Are a Government's Best Friend: Burden-free Taxes on Goods Valued for their Values,' *American Economic Review*, 77: 186–191.

Ng, Yew-kwang and Lok Sang Ho (eds.) (2006) *Happiness and Public Policy: Theory, Case Studies, and Implications*, Palgrave-Macmillan.

Ng, Yew-Kwang and Siang Ng (2000) *The Road to Happiness.* Downloadable from: www.utilitarianism.com/prof-ng/

Nie, Y.-Z., Zhang, X., Hong, N.-W., Zhou, C., Huang, Q.-Q., Cao, S.-Y., & Wang, C. (2024). "Psychometric validation of the PERMA-profiler for well-being in Chinese adults," *Acta Psychologica, 246*, 104248. https://doi.org/10.1016/j.actpsy.2024.104248

Odetayo, A., Shek, D. T. L., Ho, K. H. M., Cheung, D. S. K., Siu, S. C. N., Cheung, J., … & Lam, S. C. (2025, in press). "Predictors of family happiness in the COVID-19 pandemic: A cross-sectional study in Hong Kong," *Applied Research in Quality of Life*. https://doi.org/10.1007/s11482-025-10436-y

O.C.Tanner (published annually from 2019) *The Global Culture Report.*

Oswald, Andrew and Stephen Wu (2010) "Objective Confirmation of Subjective Measures of Human Well-Being: Evidence from the U.S.A.," *Science,* 327 (5965): 576–579.

Ototake, Hirotada (2003) *No One's Perfect,* translated by Gerry Harcourt, Kodansha.

Page, Liam F. and Ross Donohue (2004), *Positive Psychological Capital: A Preliminary Exploration of the Construct*, Department of Management Working Paper 51/04, Monash University.

Pathak, D (1985). *George Bernard Shaw: His Religion and Values.* Delhi: Mittal Publications.

Pausch, Randy and Jeffrey Zaslow (2008) *The Last Lecture*, Hyperion.

Peel, M.J., Goode, M.M.H. and Moutinho, L.A. (1998), "Estimating consumer satisfaction: OLS versus ordered probability models", *International Journal of Commerce and Management*, 8(2), pp. 75-93. https://doi.org/10.1108/eb047369

Peterson, C and M.Seligman (2004). *Character Strengths and Virtues: A Handbook and Classification.* Oxford University Press; American Psychological Association

Peterson, C., Park, N., & Seligman, M. E. P. (2005). "Orientations to happiness and life satisfaction: the full life versus the empty life," *Journal of Happiness Studies, 6*, 25–41.

Portney, L. G. (2020). *Foundations of clinical research: Applications to practice* (4th ed.). F.A. Davis Company.

Piff, Paul K., Daniel M. Stancato, Stéphane Côté, Rodolfo Mendoza-Denton and Dacher Keltner (2012) "Higher Social Class Predicts Increased Unethical Behavior," *Proceedings of the National Academy of Sciences*, 109 (11): 4086–4091.

Rao, Srikumar S.(2010) *Happiness at Work: Be Resilient, Motivated, and Successful - No Matter What*, McGraw Hill.

Raudenská, P. (2023). "Single-item measures of happiness and life satisfaction: The issue of cross-country invariance of popular general well-being measures," *Humanities and Social Sciences Communications, 10*(1), 1–18.

Redding, Richard E. (2002) "The Impossibility of Parental Licensure" *American Psychologist* · 57(11): 987-991.

Richard, A. and Rudnyckyj, D. (2009) "Economies of Affect," *Journal of the Royal Anthropological Society,* 15 (1): 55–77.

Room, R. J., Rehm, R. T. Trotter, II, A. Paglia,and T. B. Ustun (2001) "Cross-cultural Views on Stigma, Valuation, Parity and Societal Values Towards Disability," in Ustun, T. B Bedirhan, Jurgen T. Rehm, Robert T. Trotter, Jerome E. Bickenbach, Robin Room (eds.), *Disability and Culture: Universalism and Diversity*, & Huber, pp. 247–291.

Rubin, Zick (1970) "Measurement of Romantic Love," *Journal of Personality and Social Psychology*, 16(2): 265–273.

Russell, Bertrand (1968) *The Conquest of Happiness*, Unwin.(first published 1930)

Ryan, Richard M. and Edward L. Deci (2000). "Self-Determination Theory and the Facilitation of Intrinsic Motivation, Social Development, and Well-Being," *American Psychologist*, 55(1), 68-78.

Samuelson, Paul A. (February 1938). "A note on the pure theory of consumers' behaviour," *Economica*. New Series. **5** (17): 61–71.

Sandel, Michael (2012) *What Money Can't Buy*, Farrar, Straus and Giroux.

Schmuck, P. (2001) "Intrinsic and Extrinsic Life Goal Preferences as Measured via Inventories and via Priming Methodologies: Mean Differences and Relations with Well-being," in P. Schmuck and K. M. Sheldon (eds.), *Life Goals and Well-being: Towards a Positive Psychology of Human Striving*, Hogrefe & Huber, pp. 11–28.

Schmuck, Peter, Tim Kasser and Richard M. Ryan (2000) "Intrinsic and Extrinsic Goals: Their Structure and Relationship to Well-Being in German and U.S. College Students," So*cial Indicators Research* 50 (2): 225–241.

Schumacher E. F. (1973) *Small is Beautiful: Economics as if People Mattered,* Harper Perennial (2nd edn, 27 September 1989).

Schwartz, Barry (2004) *The Paradox of Choice – Why More Is Less*. Harper Perennial.

Seligman, Martin (2002) *Authentic Happiness*, New York: Free Press.

Seligman, Martin (2011) Flourish: A Visionary New Understanding of Happiness and Well-being, New York: Free Press.

Seligman, M. (2018). "PERMA and the building blocks of well-being," *The Journal of Positive Psychology*, *13*(4), 333–335.

Sherman, Carl; Patrick Griffith; Laura Reynolds (2017), *Successful Aging and Your Brain*, https://www.mcgill.ca/infoneuro/files/infoneuro/successful-aging-book let.pdf.

Skidelsky, Robert and Edward Skidelsky (2012) *How Much is Enough: Money and the Good Life*, Other Press.

Smith, Adam (1759) *The Theory of Moral Sentiments,* Clarendon Press, 1759/1976.

Smith, Vernon L. (1998). "The Two Faces of Adam Smith," *Southern Economic Journal*, 65(1), p. 3 (pp. 1–19.

Soper, B., Milford, G. E., & Rosenthal, G. T. (1995). "Belief when evidence does not support theory," *Psychology & Marketing*, 12(5), 415–422.

Sissons, Beth and Zawn Villines (2023) "What is Obsessive Love Disorder," *Medical News Today*, https://www.medicalnewstoday.com/articles/327098

Stevenson, Betsey and Justin Wolfers (2009) "The Paradox of Declining Female Happiness," *American Economic Journal: Economic Policy* 1(2): 190–225.

Stone, Arthur A., Joseph E. Schwartz, Joan E. Broderick and Angus Deaton (2010) "A Snapshot of the Age Distribution of Psychological Well-being in the United States," *Proceedings of the National Academy of Science*, 107 (22): 9985–9990.

Streiner, D. L., & Kottner, J. (2014). "Recommendations for reporting the results of studies of instrument and scale development and testing," *Journal of Advanced Nursing, 70*(9), 1970–1979. https://doi.org/10.1111/jan.12402

Strong, Rebecca (2022) "Why self-worth and self-esteem are both important, plus 5 expert-approved tips to build them up," *Business Insider*, Nov 12, 2022

Szuchman, Paula and Jenny Anderson (2011) *Spousonomics: Using Economics to Master Love, Marriage, and Dirty Dishes*, Random House.

Tabachnick, B. G., & Fidell, L. S. (2019). *Using multivariate statistics* (7th ed.). Pearson.

Templeton, John Marks (2008) *Worldwide Laws of Life: 200 Eternal Spiritual Principles*, Templeton Press.

Thaler, R. (1980) "Toward a Positive Theory of Consumer Choice," *Journal of Economic Behavior and Organization*, 1: 39–60.

Throsby, David (2001) *Economics and Culture*, Cambridge University Press.

Tversky, A. and Daniel Kahneman (1991) "Loss Aversion in Riskless Choice: A Reference Dependent Model," *Quarterly Journal of Economics*, 1039–1061.

U.S. Surgeon General (2023) *Our epidemic of loneliness and isolation*. https://www.hhs.gov/sites/default/files/surgeon-general-social-connection-advisory.pdf

Vittersø, J. (2013). 'Feelings, meanings, and optimal functioning: Some distinctionsbetween hedonic and eudaimonic well-being," In A. S. Waterman (Ed.), *The best within us: Positive psychology perspectives on eudaimonia* (pp. 39–55).

White, M. (2022). "Sample size in quantitative instrument validation studies: A systematic review of articles published in Scopus, 2021" *Heliyon*, *8*(12), e12223.

Whitley, E., & Ball, J. (2002). Statistics review 3: Hypothesis testing and P values. *Critical Care*, *6*(3), 222.

Wallace, Mike and Paul Gates (2005) *Between You and Me: A Memoir*, Hyperion.

Warren, H. C. and L. Carmichael (1930) *Elements of Human Psychology* (revised edition),Houghton Mifflin, p. 333.

Weber C. (2019). *Ideology and values in political decision making*. Oxford research encyclopedia of politics. https://doi.org/10.1093/acrefore/9780190228637.013.998

Wike, Victoria S. (1994) *Kant on Happiness in Ethics*, State University of New York Press.

Wong, P. T. P. (2023). "Pioneer in research in existential positive psychology of suffering and global flourishing." Applied Research in Quality of Life, 18(4), 2153–2157. https://doi.org/10.1007/s11482-023-10207-7

Wong, Paul T.P. et al. (2023) "Editorial: A new science of suffering, the wisdom of the soul, and the new behavioral economics of happiness: towards a general theory of well-being," Frontiers in Psychology, Sec. Positive Psychology Volume 14 https://doi.org/10.3389/fpsyg.2023.1280613

Wood, Wendy and David T. Neal (2007) "A New Look at Habits and the Habit– Goal Interface," *Psychological Review*, 114(4): 843–863.

INDEX

FSC
www.fsc.org
MIX
Papier | Fördert gute Waldnutzung
FSC® C083411

Kolibri 360 GmbH
Ferdinand-Jühlke-Straße 7
99095 Erfurt, Deutschland
produktsicherheit@kolibri360.de